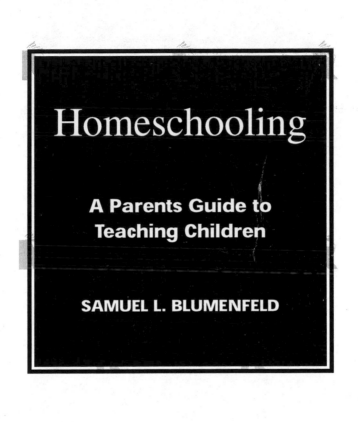

Homeschooling

A Parents Guide to Teaching Children

SAMUEL L. BLUMENFELD

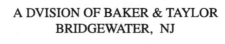

REPLICA BOOKS

A DVISION OF BAKER & TAYLOR
BRIDGEWATER, NJ

FIRST REPLICA BOOKS EDITION, FEBRUARY 1999

Published by Replica Books, a division of Baker & Taylor,
1200 Route 22 East, Bridgewater, NJ 08807

Replica Books is a trademark of Baker & Taylor

Biographical Note

This Replica books edition, first published in 1999, is an
unabridged republication of the work first published by
Citadel Press, Carol Publishing Group, New Jersey in 1998

Baker & Taylor Cataloging-in-Publication Data

Blumenfeld, Samuel L.
Homeschooling: a parents guide to teaching children /
Samuel L. Blumenfeld. —1st Replica Books ed.
p. cm.
ISBN 073510087X
Originally published: Secaucus, N.J. : Carol Pub. Group, c1997.
Includes bibliographical references and index.
1. Home schooling - United States - Handbooks, manuals, etc.
I. Title. II. Title: Home schooling.
LC40.B58 1999
371.04'2—dc 21

Manufactured in the United States of America

HOMESCHOOLING
A Parents Guide
to Teaching Children

Also by Samuel L. Blumenfeld

How to Start Your Own Private School and Why You Need One
The New Illiterates
How to Tutor
The Retreat from Motherhood
Is Public Education Necessary?
Alpha-Phonics: A Primer for Beginning Readers
NEA: Trojan Horse in American Education
The Whole Language/OBE Fraud

HOMESCHOOLING

A Parents Guide
to Teaching Children

Samuel L. Blumenfeld

A Citadel Press Book
Published by Carol Publishing Group

For Rush and Dorothy
With Affection

Contents

Acknowledgments

O ver the last fifteen years or so, I have spent much time in the homes of many homeschooling families, lectured at many homeschool conferences and conventions, and gotten to know some of the most active members of the homeschool movement. Thus, much of the information in this book is the result of direct involvement in the movement as an observer and participant. Some of the home-schoolers who have been especially helpful to me over the years are Guy and Maggie Wickwire, Gary and Bev Somogie, Sarah and Lynn Leslie, Ed and Kathy Green, Eugene and Robin Newman, Alan and Gail Stang, Andrea and Ford Schwartz, Claire Aumonier, Carolee Adams, Virginia Birt Baker, Susan and Robert Blount, Larry and Sarah Bailey, David and Ann Drye, Sharon and Ed Pangelinan, Aaron and Theresa Rivera, and Dave and Janelle Hickerson.

Among the leaders of the homeschool movement whom I have gotten to know over the years are Michael Farris of the Home School Legal Defense Association, Brian Ray of the National Home Education Research Institute, Mary Pride of *Practical Homeschooling,* Paul Lindstrom of Christian Liberty Academy, Pat Montgomery of Clonlara, Pat Farenga of John Holt Associates, and Gregg Harris of Christian Life Workshops, to name a few. I have gleaned much from their writings and conversations.

Others who have contributed to my knowledge and understanding of the education issues involved are Polly Anglin, Anna Lee Bear, Jane Boswell, Michael Brunner, Brian Camenker, William Coulson, Dennis Cuddy, Cathy Duffy, Bev Eakman, John Eidsmoe, Dave Exley, Kathy Finnegan, Marshall Fritz, John Taylor Gatto, Dean Gotcher, Rosalind Kress Haley, Shelley Hall, Tracy Hayes, Donna Hearne, Jane and Arnold Hoffman, Ian Hodge, Anita Hoge, Charlotte Iserbyt, Karen Iacovelli,

William Jasper, William Kilpatrick, Berit Kjos, Steven Kossor, Mary Larkin, Geoff Leo, Peg Luksik, Joanna and Bob Manesajian, Bob Marlowe, Sandi Martinez, Ed Miller, Barbara Morris, Chuck Morse, Debby Nalepa, David Noebel, Tom Parent, Jack Phelps, Roslyn and David Phillips, Ming Roberson, R. J. Rushdoony, Mark and Darlene Rushdoony, Andrew Sandlin, Douglas and Beverly Schmitt, Arnold and Barbara Simkus, Jeanne and Martin Sussman, Robert Sweet, Marianna Thomas, Robert Unger, and Paul Zylstra. Their friendships have greatly enriched my life.

Grateful acknowledgment is made for permission to quote from *Homeschooling: A Patchwork of Days* by Nancy Lande With 30 Families, copyright © 1996 by Nancy Lande. WindyCreek Press, 706 Sussex Road, Wynnewood, PA 19096-2414.

I am grateful to Grace Llewellyn for permission to quote from *Freedom Challenge: African-American Homeschoolers,* edited by Grace Llewellyn, copyright © 1996 by Grace Llewellyn. Lowry House Publishers, P.O. Box 1014, Eugene, OR 97440.

Finally, warm thanks must go to my agent, Gareth Esersky of the Carol Mann Agency, for her lively interest in education and sympathetic encouragement, and I am much indebted to my astute editor, Jim Ellison, for his wise suggestions.

Introduction

The purpose of this book is to introduce the reader—parent, educator, or innocent bystander—to the ever-broadening world of the homeschool movement. What first started as a negative reaction against government monopoly education and all of its shortcomings, has now become a positive attempt by thousands of parents to create and enjoy a new family lifestyle built around the nurturing and teaching of children. The new family lifestyle could not be known until thousands of families had homeschooled long enough so that the results of their efforts could actually be measured in terms of family happiness and well-educated and adjusted children.

And so, as experience has taught us, homeschooling offers more than just an escape from bad schools. It offers a new view of family life and its possibilities. In a culture that seems to be starved for values, young parents have found an ever-growing minority of families that are experiencing family life to its fullest. And this includes the fathers who have rediscovered the crucial and fulfilling role they can play in the upbringing of their children. And it is homeschooling that has made the difference.

The homeschool movement also offers a new view of education. It does not replicate a school where bells and rules regulate the behavior and thinking of hundreds of students. It broadens the parent-child relationship by including education and all of the intellectual and spiritual activities and growth that go with it. Thus, it enriches family life in a way that only thirty years ago would have seemed impossible.

In this book I have tried to convey the sense of discovery and newness that the homeschool movement is bringing to American cultural life at a time of profound change, when many people seem to have lost their bearings. While many people in our society seem to be searching for a way to escape our civilization, homeschoolers have an amazing sense of reality and responsibility when it comes to raising children and imparting to them an inherited body of knowledge, wisdom, and values. Undoubtedly, their strongest motivation is their love for their children and their desire to have their children inherit all that is good and affirmative in life.

And so, if you have picked up this book in order to find out what homeschooling is all about, I hope that you will find in it the answers to many of your questions. In the Appendix you will find more sources of information about homeschooling than any one book could supply. In the meanwhile, I hope to meet you at a homeschool convention sometime in the future!

Samuel L. Blumenfeld
Waltham, Massachusetts
March 1997

Whom, then do I call educated? First, those who control circumstances instead of being mastered by them, those who meet all occasions manfully and act in accordance with intelligent thinking, those who are honorable in all their dealings, who treat good-naturedly persons and things that are disagreeable; and furthermore, those who hold their pleasures under control and are not overcome by misfortune; finally, those who are not spoiled by success.

—SOCRATES (469-399 B.C.)

School is a twelve-year jail sentence where bad habits are the only curriculum truly learned. I teach school and win awards doing it. I should know.

—JOHN TAYLOR GATTO, *Dumbing Us Down*

No area of the life of any nation is of greater importance to its future than that of education of the young.

—WILLIAM BENTLEY BALL, *Mere Creatures of the State?*

-1-

Why Homeschool?

Homeschooling is now the fastest growing educational phenomenon in the United States. It is also becoming increasingly popular in Canada, Australia, New Zealand, and England. And with good reason. More and more parents have become convinced that the public schools—that is, schools owned and operated by the government—are incapable of the kinds of reforms that parents want.

Ironically, government education is in the process of massive restructuring and reform under such titles as Outcome-Based Education, Performance-Based Education, School-to-Work, or by some other descriptive designation, but it is not the kind of reform parents have clamored for. It is reform imposed from above by a cadre of change agents who are carrying out their own agenda which has nothing to do with traditional concepts of academic excellence and individual intellectual growth. In fact, what they are imposing is in direct conflict with traditional educational philosophy. Therefore, many parents have simply given up on the system, opted out, and decided to do it themselves. And do it they can, for what they have wanted and asked for is simply a return to the teaching of basic academic skills, which the schools no longer want to do, but which thousands of parents have now learned they can do quite effectively.

Also, there are those parents who are not interested in returning to a traditional educational philosophy at all, but are convinced that schooling itself, and particularly the public school, has become too constrictive and controlling and is nonconducive to the development of a free, independent spirit. These parents call themselves unschoolers, and follow the philosophy of John Holt, the legendary father of the unschooling movement.

1

How big is the homeschool movement? No one knows for sure. Estimates are that in 1996 about a half-million to a million children were being home educated, or about 2 percent of the school-age population. But it may be lots more. A *New York Times Magazine* article (2/2/97) suggested that the number may be as high as 2.5 million. When I first started lecturing and doing workshops at homeschool conventions back in the early 1980s, attendance figures were usually around 300. In 1996, this writer lectured to homeschool audiences in the thousands at huge convention centers with hundreds of vendor exhibits! And at least half the attendees were young parents with babes in arms determined to home educate their youngsters. Why? Not only because of what has happened to public education but because the new wholesome family lifestyle that comes with homeschooling has become increasingly attractive to young parents eager to experience the best that family life has to offer.

THE RISKS IN PUBLIC EDUCATION

As for public education, its shortcomings have become more and more apparent to those Americans who read newspapers. Today, children in the public schools are at risk in four major areas: academically, spiritually, morally, and physically. The academic risk is very real: 40 to 60 percent of schoolchildren emerge from the process seriously handicapped and intellectually crippled because of the educational philosophy and teaching methods used in the primary grades. These methods can cause reading disabilities which are later diagnosed as dyslexia or attention deficit disorder. In other words, some of the teaching methods widely used in the public schools can and do cause cognitive dysfunction among millions of perfectly normal children.

Almost everyone today knows someone with a reading problem. The pain, frustration, and misery these problems cause cannot be understated. But we do know that they can be avoided with the proper teaching methods. And home education provides parents with the opportunity to use the best and most rational methods of teaching reading, writing, and arithmetic. When children master the basic academic skills, they can learn just about anything else. The satisfaction that parents get in imparting these skills to their children is what makes homeschooling so enjoyable and worthwhile for both parents and children.

In addition, there is the growing problem of ADD—attention deficit disorder—which now afflicts millions of schoolchildren. Four million children are now being given the drug Ritalin every day so that they can sit in class and do their schoolwork. There is something wrong with a school system that must drug four million children in order to be able to "educate" them. Is it possible that ADD is caused by chaotic, irrational education in the classroom? One hardly hears about ADD among homeschoolers. Maybe homeschooling will produce a miraculous cure for the ADD-diagnosed child!

Children are also at risk spiritually in the public schools because what is being taught often contradicts the teachings of traditional religion. Programs such as values clarification, sensitivity training, and situational ethics are viewed by many parents as tending to undermine the child's belief in traditional religion and moral absolutes. This risk has motivated thousands of Christians and other adherents of traditional Biblical religion to remove their children from the public schools.

But even nonreligious, humanist parents realize that their children do not get the necessary spiritual nourishment in school that would enhance their sense of being. The result is that many children, who get no religious reinforcement at home, emerge from public schools not as rational humanists, but as amoral nihilists.

THE MORAL RISK

Then there is the moral risk. Many suspect that sex education programs lead to premature sexual activity among children, which in turn leads to unwanted pregnancies, unwed motherhood, abortions, venereal disease, and emotional traumas. Many parents are convinced that the distribution of condoms to schoolchildren sends the wrong message to children who should be persuaded to abstain from sex until marriage. The schools have also become the chief marketplace for drugs. Most children get started on drugs through peer pressure from fellow students. Much touted drug programs, such as DARE and Quest, have failed to make a real dent in student drug experimentation and trafficking. In fact, recent years have shown a dramatic increase in drug use, alcohol consumption, and smoking among schoolchildren. Homeschooling removes children from the drug culture that now permeates our public schools.

There is also a very intelligent movement among homeschoolers to encourage courtship rather than dating. Dating implies many premature romantic relationships which often involve premarital sex. Such relationships inevitably lead to breakups, jealousy, and partner switching, all of which can lead to physical abuse and severe emotional breakdowns. Add to this what young people ingest from television and movies, popular music, rock concerts, etc., and many parents have come to the inescapable conclusion that their children need all the protection they can get while growing up.

Last, but hardly least, is the physical risk. More and more children are assaulted, robbed, and murdered in school than ever before. More and more children come to school with guns and knives. Some children carry these weapons for self-protection against other students. A culture of violence, abetted by rap music, drug trafficking, movies, television, and racial tension, has engulfed teenagers. And there seems to be no improvement on the horizon. Also, the bus rides to and from school entail numerous risks. In other words, parents can greatly reduce the physical risks of going to school by educating their kids at home.

In addition to these risks, there are other reasons why home education is preferable to the schoolroom. In a class, the child is constantly forced to measure himself or herself against others. The learning experience is constantly undercut by the comparisons made by grading students on their performance. This is particularly harmful when the class is organized according to the educator's own view of intelligence and ability. Feelings of inferiority and inadequacy easily develop among many students in this kind of atmosphere. At home, there is no classroom hierarchy of intelligence that sets up a constant comparison with others. The child learns and explores on his or her own, guided by loving parents, developing interests that satisfy youthful curiosity about the world instead of being constrained by the need to do better than others in teacher-directed study.

These are the reasons why parents should consider removing their children from the public schools and putting them in a private school they can trust or educating them at home. While the private school may be an attractive option for working parents, it still involves enough risks to make it a nonstarter for those parents who are attracted to the homeschool lifestyle. In addition, the private school still subjects the child to that comparative environment in which he or she is constantly measured against others. If you are a single parent who must work, however, then the private school is undoubtedly the only option available. But private schools charge tuition and in many sections of the country there aren't that many good ones to choose from. Some single working parents have found homeschoolers willing to take their children into their homes. A single parent may be able to find such an accommodating homeschool family by contacting a local homeschool support group.

As for working parents, one parent may have to give up a full-time job in order to homeschool. This decision may require economic adjustments for the family as a whole, but there are desirable and beneficial trade-offs. Also, sometimes a parent can earn money by doing work at home, thereby contributing to the family budget and home educating at the same time.

In other words, there are a number of ways of adapting the family to the needs of home education. If freedom from the risks of government education is the goal, then the family must be prepared to make whatever sacrifices are necessary to achieve that goal. Once that goal is achieved and the benefits of home education become more and more apparent, the sacrifices will seem all the more worthwhile.

-2-

It All Starts With Parenting

*Schools stifle family originality by appropriating the critical time
needed for any sound idea of family to develop—then they blame the
family for its failure to be a family.*

—JOHN TAYLOR GATTO

It goes without saying that homeschooling starts with parents who enjoy parenting. Love of one's children is the key to the concern over their education. That is not to say that parents who put their children in public schools don't love them; they are simply doing what their parents did and what generations did before them. And many of them actually get to know their children's teachers and are pleased with what they find in their classrooms.

But when problems arise, they usually assume that these are natural phenomena over which no one has control. For example, if the child is having trouble learning to read, the first reaction is that the child must have some sort of learning problem. There is never any suspicion that the teacher may have a teaching problem because of a faulty instruction method being used. In such cases, the child is then core evaluated by a battery of counselors and psychologists, diagnosed dyslexic and placed in special education.

Another phenomenon that parents readily accept as natural and inevitable is teenage rebellion. But if teenage rebellion is so natural and inevitable, why is there so little of it among homeschoolers? Perhaps teenage rebellion is more the result of values acquired by the child in public school that conflict with the values of the child's parents.

Homeschooled children tend to adopt the values of their parents, and therefore rebellion rarely occurs among them.

There was a study done some years ago by a popular women's magazine to find out what children wanted most. It was discovered that what they wanted most was more time with their parents! The separation of children from parents can be one of the most traumatic experiences in children's lives. The tearful separations of children from mothers on that first day of school is familiar to all. Some children adapt themselves to the new school experience very nicely; others are not happy with the separation at all. These are the children who grow to hate school and rejoice when their parents decide to home educate.

As for mothers putting their children in school for the first time, their feelings vary. Some may feel relieved that their children are going to be taken care of during the next three or six hours by someone else, freeing them to use their time as they wish, doing whatever it is they want to do. Other mothers experience a depressing sense of loss as they deliver their child up to a group of strangers who will "educate" him, thus depriving the parent of the wonderful experience of educating one's own child. Isn't transferring one's most cherished values to one's own child the greatest pleasure a parent can have?

A parent who wants to educate his or her children must have a strong sense of values. These are the kinds of parents who pioneered in the homeschool movement. They were the earliest to homeschool, because they had the strongest desire to bond with their children culturally and intellectually as well as emotionally. The idea of strangers bonding with their children and inculcating values the parents opposed was a strong enough incentive to homeschool.

For Christian parents, the imperative to pass on spiritual values to their children is quite strong. Before there were schools, the Bible commanded parents to educate their children in the knowledge and love of God. Thus, it is not difficult to understand why Christians have been the strongest and earliest advocates and practitioners of homeschooling.

But the notion of bonding with one's children intellectually and culturally is by no means limited to religionists. It is one of the reasons why private schools exist in America. Parents generally seek private schools that reflect their own values, but the fact that most children are still in the public schools despite the well-publicized failures of government education, indicates that most parents are either satisfied with their public schools—and this is generally the case in affluent suburban communities—or are willing to comply with societal norms, since they have neither the desire nor the will to contest them. They may complain about the schools, but their general lack of knowledge about the system inhibits them from doing anything about them.

In addition, many parents have been so poorly educated by the system that they themselves can barely read or write and must depend on the schools to educate their children. Parents like these must rely on television for their knowledge of what is going on in today's classrooms. And, as we know, television provides the most superficial and often misleading information about our educational problems. But, believe it or not, more and more of these parents are beginning to shake off their educational dependency and are showing up at homeschool conventions to find out what is going on. The word is getting out!

DISTRUST OF THE CULTURE

Clearly, what is bringing more and more parents to the homeschool movement is not only a dissatisfaction with public miseducation but also a distrust of the popular culture that has such a strong hold on today's youth. Many parents now realize that protecting one's child from this negative cultural onslaught means turning off the TV set and turning on to literacy and good books.

It is not surprising that most homeschooling families live in small towns where the negative cultural influences are less apparent in the rural lifestyle. Urban dwellers, for the most part, have been so thoroughly influenced by the culture they live in, that the idea of trying to escape it never occurs to them. Some live in it but remain apart from it.

Thus, the homeschooling family, thinking of maintaining a wholesome and healthy lifestyle for its members, feels obliged not only to withdraw from public education but also to withdraw from the general popular culture. But that isn't all. The homeschooling family also finds itself in the peculiar position of defying the state. Even though homeschooling is legal throughout the United States, the existence of compulsory school attendance laws has given superintendents and other educational bureaucrats the idea that they can and should control what homeschoolers do. The result has been an ongoing battle between homeschoolers and the government over who has the right to do what.

From the very beginning, parents have asserted their right to educate their children as they see fit. In the first place, families existed long before governments were formed, and therefore families are quite capable of managing their affairs, including education, without the help of the government. Since for many parents the transfer of values from them to their children is their most important parental duty, they are quite adamant in keeping the government out of their family life.

Since education is nowhere mentioned in the U. S. Constitution, Americans in general tend to believe that the government does not have a right to dictate to parents how their children should be educated. Some parents even contend that the compulsory school attendance laws, in and of themselves, are unconstitutional because they constitute a form of involuntary servitude which is outlawed by the Thirteenth Amendment.

So far, homeschoolers have been quite successful in keeping the government at bay. The Home School Legal Defense Association has been quite successful in defending parents' rights to educate their children at home with a minimum of government interference. Thus, if you wish to homeschool your children, be aware that you will be taking part in a quiet but assertive revolution by parents who are rebelling against government education.

By becoming a homeschooler you will also become part of that revolution to restore educational freedom and parents' rights to America. If we wish our nation to survive as a bastion of individual freedom with a government kept in check by a vigilant citizenry, then homeschoolers must take part in the political life of their country. They have no choice if they wish to leave to their children and their grandchildren a legacy of freedom and of hope for the future.

-3-

Devising Your Own Philosophy
of Education

Most parents, when they first think of homeschooling, have the idea that homeschooling is merely doing at home what is done in school. If they proceed on this assumption, they usually wind up frustrated, overworked, confused, and in time burned out. The simple fact is that homeschooling is a totally different kettle of fish. It is not a replication of the public school in the home, it is something else.

Homeschooling is an opportunity to think about education, to think about what it is you want your children to learn and how best to accomplish this in your home. What it really requires is devising a philosophy of education—a set of principles that enables you to conduct education in a manner that helps you achieve your goal. An interesting example of how a philosophy of education can be summed up to provide a guide to the educator was given by Father John A. Hardon, S.J., at a conference of the Separation of School and State Alliance, in 1996. He said: "The true purpose of education is to teach people of the purpose of their life on earth, to know why they exist, and why the rest of the world exists." Such a profound yet succinct statement will definitely set you to think of a curriculum that will enable you to instill such understanding in a child.

Because there are so many different homeschool programs available these days, many beginners often buy programs that may not serve their purpose very well, or even defeat the purpose of homeschooling. Thus, it is imperative to know the source of the program you are buying and the educational philosophy behind it. By speaking to a user of a particular program, you may be able to ascertain whether or not it suits your purpose.

Most homeschoolers, however, accept the philosophy of education implicit in the home-education program they have purchased, and most of these programs are based on pretty traditional views on education. They put a heavy emphasis on the teaching of the basic academic skills and the kinds of subject matter associated with a good general education. Thus, if one is not inclined to think of devising one's own philosophy of education, one can easily accept what is being offered by the major suppliers and be satisfied that their programs are based on sound, traditional ideas about education.

The point I am making is that homeschooling provides the parent with the opportunity, the freedom, to think all of this over and do something other than what is standard practice. Once you have thought this out and actually come up with a philosophy of education, you will have established guidelines that will help you choose the program that best reflects your views of how you want your children to be educated, and what kind of adults you want them to be when you have completed your child-rearing mission.

Most parents would say: "I want my child to become independent, be able to earn a good living, develop a career or profession, be able to make his or her way in this competitive world, find a good mate, find happiness, become a good human being. I don't want my child to be ignorant, apathetic, lazy, forever dependent on his parents, afraid to venture out in the world, mediocre, a potential couch potato."

So, in a sense, most parents have had a kind of unspoken and undefined philosophy of education which they expected others to articulate in the form of a school curriculum. But now they realize that the school is not giving them what they want. It is too often giving them what they don't want: ignorant, apathetic, rebellious, drug-addicted, semiliterate kids.

Devising a philosophy of education will enable the parent not only to choose a course of study for the child but determine what the parent's role will be in the actual education process. Sometimes that philosophy can be summed up in pretty simple terms. For example, Mary Foley, a homeschooling mother on Cape Cod, Massachusetts, when required by the local superintendent to submit for approval her education plan for her nine-year-old son Christian, wrote:

"The priorities of our curriculum are daydreaming, natural and social sciences, self-discipline, respect of self and others, and making mistakes.

I encourage an acceptance of failure so that he will be comfortable taking risks. By the time he is ten he will be competent in life, if I have done my job, and if he chooses he can spend his life in school. But, for now, he is not ready to make that decision and I must do what I believe is best. My curriculum was best expressed by Blake: 'To see a world in a grain of sand, And Heaven in a wild flower, To hold infinity in the palm of your hand, And eternity in an hour.'"

This mother's other homeschooled children had all achieved honors in academics, and her daughter had received a full scholarship to the University of Massachusetts at Amherst. The superintendent took Mary Foley to court, but the judge decided in favor of this homeschooling mother. The beauty of homeschooling is that you can apply your own philosophy of education to your own children and need not accept someone else's or the state's. Mary Foley's philosophy has helped her choose the kind of learning she intends to impart to her son. She wants her son to be "competent in life," and she believes that daydreaming is an important part of that learning process.

My own view is that the purpose of education is to transfer to the younger generation the skills, knowledge, wisdom, and moral and spiritual values of the previous generation. And that transfer can be made lovingly, patiently, and enthusiastically. I also believe that the purpose of education is to enable an individual to control his or her own life and not become the victim of prevailing forces. We live at a time when survival requires an astute intelligence that enables us not only to read books and magazines, but also the handwriting on the wall. There is more misinformation and disinformation being diffused throughout the world today than ever before, and a well-educated person should be able to dig out the truth under a mountain of lies. One might even say that the ultimate aim of education should be not only to enable an individual to discern the truth but to make the individual *want* to know the truth and dig for it when necessary.

-4-

How to Teach and What to Teach

Once we've established our educational goal, we must start thinking about what to teach and how to teach it. A good first step is to look at how children learn. As we all know, children are great self-teachers. They teach themselves to speak their own language with amazing mental agility and effectiveness. Sometimes, if a family is bilingual, children will learn to speak both languages pretty well. This is because all normal children are born with an innate language faculty, the power of speech, and the ability to develop speech logically. That is why children quickly learn to speak with great grammatical accuracy without any formal lessons in grammar. Children are programmed to think logically, because that's what grammar is: logic applied to the structure of language.

So we begin with the premise that children are very effective self-teachers who use logic and trial and error in learning language and making sense of the world around them. This makes children feel very intelligent. Why? Because at that early age their brains are growing in cognitive power at an incredible pace, much faster than any adult brain, and anyone interested in good education will understand and take advantage of this marvelous period of rapid growth. That is why some children as early as three and four can learn to read. But as every parent knows, each child is different. Little Elizabeth at three may be able to learn to read while her brother Willy won't hack it until he is six or seven. Should that alarm a parent? No. It simply means that each child is different, and that this has to be taken into consideration. It doesn't imply inferiority or superiority, for as we all know some child prodigies, as adults, do not live up to their early promise, while many so-called average children develop into productive, inventive, creative adults.

But if you keep in mind what your ultimate goal is in educating your children, you will recognize that the differences among them will sometimes require different timing or approaches. The beauty of homeschooling is that you have the flexibility and the time to do whatever it is that has to be done and you don't have to measure your child against a roomful of other kids. Schools pay much lip service to the idea that children have different learning styles, but the school is rarely able to act effectively on that idea. The flexibility and time and one-on-one interaction that parents have is something the school, public or private, cannot duplicate.

Any sound educational program should begin with teaching the three basic academic skills which we all know as the three Rs—reading, writing, and 'rithmetic. The very word education implies teaching children these basic skills. Since children are dynamos of language learning in these early years, they usually can learn the three Rs without any great difficulty, provided that the teaching is logical and adapted to the child's own idiosyncracies. Today's public schools use such illogical and irrational teaching methods that perfectly normal, intelligent children have their brains severely damaged in the first two years of schooling. As we noted, the child is born with an innate language-based logic which, when confronted with the illogic of classroom teaching, results in the same kind of damage that occurs when gears don't mesh. Sometimes this damage can be undone if caught early enough, but the tragedy is that most children who suffer such damage must live with it throughout the rest of their lives.

DYSLEXIA

One of the most prevalent results of such damage is the condition known as dyslexia. Most parents have been led to believe that dyslexia is the result of some genetic defect in their child which can be cured only by prolonged, expensive remediation. Actually, true dyslexia is limited to a very small number of retarded individuals with serious language learning problems easily detected in preschool years, or persons who have suffered brain injuries through strokes, accidents, or oxygen deprivation. However, the kind of dyslexia that afflicts perfectly normal children is the result of faulty teaching in the classroom. It is a fact that the present whole-word method of teaching reading does cause the symptoms of dyslexia among many children and we shall explain how this happens. (By the way, this artificial cause of dyslexia has been known since 1929 when Dr. Samuel T. Orton wrote about it in the *Journal of Educational Psychology* under the title "The 'Sight Reading' Method of Teaching Reading as a Source of Reading Disability.")

Dyslexia is caused when the teaching method requires that the child develop a holistic reflex when looking at our printed words. A holistic reflex is developed when the child is taught to look at each printed word as a whole configuration, like a Chinese character. The child is expected to look at the word and see a picture. This is done in the classroom before the child has been taught any phonics. Children are taught to read by using such strategies as looking at pictures on the page, guessing the word on the basis of its configuration or context, skipping the word, and substituting words. For example, if the word says "horse" and the child reads it as "pony" the teacher will be quite satisfied. Unbelievable, you say? Then here's a quote from a book about teaching reading in the whole-language style. The book, by Jane Baskwill and Paulette Whitman, *Evaluation: Whole Language, Whole Child* (New York: Scholastic, Inc., 1988), states on page 19:

> The way you interpret what the child does will reflect what you understand reading to be. For instance, if she reads the word *feather* for *father,* a phonics-oriented teacher might be pleased because she's come close to sounding the word out. However, if you believe that reading is a meaning-seeking process, you may be concerned that she's overly dependent on phonics at the expense of meaning. You'd be happier with a miscue such as *daddy,* even though it doesn't look or sound anything like the word in the text. At least the meaning would be intact.

Does anyone in his right mind believe that a child who reads the word "father" as "daddy" knows how to read? The child who reads "daddy" for "father" is looking at a picture, not a sequence of letters that stands for a specific sequence of speech sounds. This child is being taught to develop a holistic reflex, that is, a habit of automatically looking at all words as whole configurations. Once the child has developed this holistic reflex, he or she has also acquired a block against seeing the phonetic structure of our alphabetically written words. This *block* is what causes "dyslexia."

In other words, the kind of dyslexia which afflicts millions of perfectly normal children is induced by the whole-word teaching method, and the only way to avoid creating this form of dyslexia is to make sure that your child develops a phonetic reflex, that is, an automatic ability to associate letters with speech sounds. How does one accomplish this? First, by teaching the child to recognize the letters of the alphabet, which is not difficult to do, and second, by drilling the child in the sounds the letters stand for. For hundreds of years this was done by drilling the child in consonant-vowel combinations, such as *ba, be, bi, bo, bu, ma, me, mi, mo, mu*, etc. The purpose of the drill was to enable the child to develop a phonetic reflex—the ability to automatically associate letters with sounds. When that was achieved, the child was given words to read, short sentences, and then little stories. Once a child develops this phonetic reflex, he or she cannot become dyslexic.

TEACHING READING AND THE ALPHABETIC PRINCIPLE

In my own reading program, *Alpha-Phonics*, I basically repeat this ancient but highly effective methodology, with some variation. The English alphabetic system has a number of anomalies or irregularities that create some teaching problems. Much of this has to do with the fact that the English language has forty-four irreducible speech sounds while our alphabet has only twenty-six letters. A little historical background is necessary if one is to understand what all of this means.

The alphabet was invented some 2,500 years before the birth of Christ. Prior to that invention, the earliest form of writing was pictorial—that is, the earliest scribes drew pictures on the walls of their caves or on other surfaces. We call that form of writing pictography. In pictography, the symbols look like the things they represent. The symbol for a human being looks pretty much like a human being, the symbol for an animal looks pretty much like an animal, etc. But as civilization became more complex the scribes had to begin drawing things that did not lend themselves to depiction. For example, how do you draw pictures of such ideas or words as good and evil, now and eternity, success and failure? You can't. So what the scribes did was create symbols—we call them ideographs or logographs—which stood for these ideas or words but which had no pictorial resemblance to them. Whereas with pictographs, nobody had to teach you what the symbols stood for, with ideographs, somebody did. And the scribes created thousands of such symbols, which were very difficult to learn and easy to forget. In fact, learning them became the lifelong profession of scribes and scholars and priests, and the governing rulers were completely dependent on this literate class for their information. All in all, literacy was restricted to a small literate elite that had enormous power and influence in the culture.

But things changed radically when, about 4,500 years ago, someone invented the alphabet, someone who lived in the area today known as southern Lebanon or northern Israel. By then, some scribes had begun to use some of the logographs, or characters, as sound indicators as an aid to memorization. But the inventor of the alphabet decided to discard the enormously complex ideographic-logographic system in its entirety, and replace it with a very simple set of symbols to stand for the irreducible speech sounds of the language. Obviously he had made a remarkable discovery: that all of human language is composed of a small number of irreducible speech sounds and that by creating a set of symbols to stand for those speech sounds, all of human language could be transcribed as a permanent record on some sort of surface.

The use of the alphabet spread throughout the ancient Western world. It did for the ancient world what the computer is doing for the modern world. With the alphabet you could do so much more with so much less. The Israelites wrote the holy Scriptures in alphabetic writing, the Greeks wrote philosophy, history, and drama in alphabetic writing, and the Romans devised their own alphabet based originally on the Greek. Here's where we come to our modern-day problem with the English alphabet.

When the Romans conquered the British islands, they imposed their own Latin alphabet on the people who lived there. English is composed of forty-four sounds whereas the Latin alphabet has only twenty-six letters, hardly enough to go around. So what did the Brits do? They adapted the Latin alphabet to their language, and they did this by having some letters stand for more than one sound and having some sounds represented by more than one letter. For example, the letter *a* stands for the long *a* as in *apron* and *April*, it stands for the short *a* as in *cat* or *fan*, it stands for the *a* as in *father* or *car*, and it stands for the *a* as in *all* and *ball*. So how does a child learn which sound to articulate when he or she sees the letter *a?* If you teach the letter sounds in their spelling families, children learn them very well. That is the way we teach them in *Alpha-Phonics*.

As for some of our sounds being represented by more than one letter, our typically English "th" is represented by t-h, the "sh" is represented by s-h, and "ch" is represented by c-h. And of course we have many irregularities in our spellings. Such simple words as *to, do, who, have, any, eye* are either at variance with the other words in their spelling families or are one of a kind. But children seem to learn the exceptions to the rules with no great difficulty since these words, if pronounced as they are spelled, would make no sense.

MAKING LEARNING TO READ EASY

In developing my *Alpha-Phonics* program I took all of these problems into consideration. Inasmuch as I wanted to make learning to read as easy and enjoyable as possible, I decided to start with the simplest and most regular aspects of our alphabetic system, introducing the irregular words as they came up in the context of regular spellings and pronunciations. I found that this system works quite effectively.

Thus, in seeking a reading program, I highly recommend my own. This doesn't mean that there aren't other good programs on the market. There are, and you can look them over at any homeschool convention or book fair. However, the most important thing to remember is that the child must develop a phonetic reflex in order to become a reader who enjoys reading and can read easily, accurately, and fluently. At what age should you begin to teach a child to read? As we said earlier, each child is different. However, if your child has developed a decent speaking vocabulary and expresses a desire to learn to read, then you can start very simply by first teaching the child the alphabet letters and then teaching the letter sounds and letter combinations in as simple and direct a manner as possible.

Patience is the most important ingredient in home education. Patience and the ability to try something else if what one is doing is not working very well. If the child is having difficulty remembering a particular sound or can't seem to catch on to the idea that letters represent sounds, do not get impatient. You may be dealing with the matter of intellectual growth and understanding. Our alphabetic system is an abstract system dealing with abstract graphic symbols. Spoken words in and of themselves are abstractions. For example, the word *table* is an utterance that represents a concrete object. Children learn such speech abstractions quite naturally. But the idea that letters stand for irreducible speech sounds may be difficult for a preschool child to grasp, since he or she would tend to look at the printed word as a total configuration, like a Chinese character. And that often happens when preschool children are "reading" preschool books by memorizing the words in the stories.

THE DR. SEUSS TRAP

That is a danger that parents of preschoolers must be aware of when they give their children little readers like the Dr. Seuss books before the child has been taught the alphabet or the letter sounds. In fact, the Dr. Seuss books were written to enable the preschool child to develop a sight vocabulary as a prelude to being taught to read in the whole-word method. This was confirmed by Seuss himself in an interview in *Arizona* magazine in 1981. Because his books were so simple, many people assumed that they were easy to write. He said:

> They think I did it in twenty minutes. That damned *Cat in the Hat* took nine months until I was satisfied. I did it for a textbook house and they sent me a word list. That was due to the Dewey revolt in the Twenties, in which they threw out phonic reading and. went to word recognition, as if you're reading a Chinese pictograph instead of blending sounds of different letters. I think killing phonics was one of the greatest causes of illiteracy in the country. Anyway, they had it all worked out that a healthy child at the age of four can learn so many words in a week and that's all. So there were two hundred and twenty-three words to use in this book. I read the list three times and I almost went out of my head. I said, I'll read it once more and if I can find two words that rhyme that'll be the title of my book. (That's genius at work.) I found "cat" and "hat" and I said, "The title will be *The Cat in the Hat*."

The lesson to be learned is that when a parent reads to a child a Dr. Seuss book, or any other preschool reader, and points to each word as it is being read, the child may indeed develop a holistic reflex by simply memorizing the several hundred words in these books. And if the book comes with an audiocassette tape which the child can listen to while "reading" the words, that too may lead to the development of a holistic reflex. Converting that child into a phonetic reader will not be easy if the habit of looking at each word as a total configuration is strongly established.

Thus, if you are going to read to your preschool child, explain that the words are made up of letters that stand for sounds, and demonstrate that concept by sounding out the words in the story. In that way, the child will anticipate being taught to read in the proper phonetic way. However, if the child is too young for that, simply read the story and have the child look at the pictures instead of the words. If the child wants to know a word, then explain the phonetic structure of the word. Most preschool children will understand you when you say that the letter *d* in dog stands for "duh," etc. In that way you will prevent future problems, problems that will be costly to remediate.

There are special, very expensive, private schools that deal with dyslexic children. They are filled with children from professional homes. Simply because a father or mother is a professor or a lawyer or a chemist doesn't mean that he or she understands how children should be taught to read and how they develop reading problems. Professionals in other fields assume that the professional educators know what they are doing and that they would not be using teaching methods that cause learning problems. But the facts speak for themselves.

It was Rudolf Flesch who in 1955 revealed the cause of reading disability in his famous book, *Why Johnny Can't Read.* In that book Flesch made it quite clear that the cause of reading disability was the whole-word teaching method. Yet, over forty years later the problem persists because the educators have their own progressive agenda and refuse to return to the tried and true methods of the past. I strongly recommend that parents read Dr. Flesch's book, which is still in print in paperback. It will give them an insight into the ongoing war between advocates of whole language and advocates of intensive, systematic phonics.

After reading Dr. Flesch's book, then read my book on the same subject, *The Whole Language/OBE Fraud.* It will round out your education on the matter of teaching reading and make you an expert on the subject, which is good to be as you embark on a homeschooling program and have to confront the professional educators and district superintendents. It's good to be able to question them with the confidence that you have a knowledge and understanding of the problem which many of *them* don't even have. The most ignorant are usually the directors of reading instruction in your school district. Half of them probably never heard of Rudolf Flesch, let alone Sam Blumenfeld. But if you do your homework you will be able to let them know that they can't deceive you, and that you actually know more than they do. In fact, it is not at all difficult to know more than the professional educators for the simple reason that they will have been kept away from knowledge of the truth by their own biased professors of education.

On the other hand, you have the freedom to read the books that the educators shun, and that puts you at an advantage. Being able to tell the educators what's wrong with what they teach and how they teach it will stand you in good stead should you have to contend with an arrogant, condescending superintendent who thinks he knows it all. Nothing will bring such a superintendent down to size more effectively than an awareness that you know more than he does. And it doesn't take much to become an expert in reading pedagogy. All you have to do is read the two books already mentioned. But don't be surprised if the knowledge you supply the superintendent doesn't result in any change in policy. He may decide, however, to avoid any further contact with you and thereby leave you alone.

REMEDIATING A POOR READER

Meanwhile, if you are going to homeschool a youngster who has already been victimized by whole language, you will have a tough remedial job to do. First, listen to your child read aloud. You will notice that he or she leaves out words that are there, puts in words that aren't there, misreads words, substitutes words, mutilates words, guesses at words, and truncates words. For example, if the word says "newspaper" the child may read it as "paper," or if the word says "telephone" he or she may read it as "phone." To remediate this kind of sight reader, the first thing you must do is teach the youngster our entire English alphabetic system. That can easily be done with *Alpha-Phonics*. Even though the older child may already know many of the letter sounds, you will want to make sure that the student knows all the sounds and spelling forms in the system so that he or she can begin to develop a phonetic reflex.

Then you must show the learner how to apply this phonetic

knowledge to his or her reading. The way you do that is to have the learner read some text aloud—it could be an article in the *Reader's Digest*—and you must stop the reader every time he or she makes an error. Ask the student to reread the sentence until he or she becomes aware of the error that was made. The problem with sight readers is that they are not aware of the errors they make since they were taught that it is okay to guess at words, substitute words, leave out words, put in words, etc. Thus, to be told that these are errors will be news to the sight reader. But explain to the sight reader that in order to become a phonetic reader, accuracy is more important than speed.

Also, keep a lined notebook at hand so that any new words the reader comes across can be written down, divided into syllables, and reread from time to time as the list of new words grows longer. Going over several pages of these words will help the reader recognize them quickly when seeing them later in print. Also, for purposes of comprehension, have the reader look up these words in the dictionary and write their definitions. Don't even assume that the child knows the meaning of all the words he or she can read. Words that often seem simple to adults may be totally unknown to the learner.

Expanding vocabulary requires real work. It requires a lot of reading and writing, a lot of looking up of definitions. The stunted vocabularies of so many young people today is due to the fact that they don't read enough challenging material; they don't hear enough good vocabulary spoken in their everyday conversations. But you can help your child develop a good vocabulary by having him or her read stories and novels by Edgar Allan Poe and Charles Dickens and other nineteenth-century writers. In fact, the more nineteenth-century literature your child reads, the more extensive his or her vocabulary will become. And it is generally recognized that the better your vocabulary, the better your chances of becoming a leader. This insight was gleaned from an interview of John Gaston, head of the Human Engineering Laboratory in Fort Worth, Texas, published in the *Dallas Morning News* of August 26, 1971. Mr. Gaston said:

> The one thing successful people have in common isn't high aptitudes—it's high vocabulary, and it's within everybody's reach. Success actually correlates more with vocabulary than with the gifts we're born with.

Who do you think ranks at the top in vocabulary? It's executives. They beat everybody. A man of little education might own or head an enterprise or a well-educated man might head a big corporation, but both of them will know the hard words that stump other people. It's vocabulary that makes the boss the boss.

In other words, the smaller the vocabulary of your child, the lower the chances are that he or she will be able to attain the kind of position in life that he or she would like to have. And the best way to expand vocabulary early in life is to have your child read books written in the nineteenth century, with their more extensive vocabularies and complex sentences. Each new word your child learns increases his or her knowledge, for each word represents additional knowledge.

Anthony Robbins, the well-known peak-performance coach and consultant, had these wise words to say about developing a good vocabulary:

> People with impoverished vocabularies lead emotionally impoverished lives. People with rich vocabularies have a multi-hued palette of colors with which to paint their life's experience, not only for others, but for themselves as well.

Need more be said?

-5-

Teaching Writing

Teaching your child to write should be a very important part of your homeschooling program. The public schools have done such a terrible job in teaching students to write that we've seen an incredible decline not only in handwriting but also in the ability of young Americans to write intelligent, grammatically correct sentences. Since children acquire a grammatic sense early in life as they learn to speak their mother tongue, how is it that they lose this grammatical sense as they mature into young adults? The answer is quite simple. Schools no longer emphasize or even teach grammar, and the teaching of penmanship is a thing of the past. The result has been a national handwriting disaster.

In the previous chapter we emphasized the need to teach a child to read in the proper phonetic way, and we emphasized the need for your child to develop a good vocabulary. We feel equally strongly about the need to teach a child to write well. In the first place, writing is the opposite side of the literacy coin. As Francis Bacon wrote many centuries ago: "Reading maketh a full man . . . and writing an exact man." In other words, the ability to express your thoughts on paper requires that you think out clearly what it is you want to say, and what it is you want to communicate to others.

The first step in helping your child develop a decent handwriting is to teach the physical and mechanical aspects of writing. In the last ten years or so, schools have been encouraging children to write even before they know how to read. They call this method "invented spelling," in which the child is told to write before he even knows how to hold the writing instrument or form the letters. It is alleged that this kind of writing exercise encourages spontaneity and creativity. What it actually does, however, is produce poor spellers and poor handwriting. The idea that a child no longer has to be taught how to hold a writing instrument correctly has led to some of the worst writing habits that now afflict Americans.

All of that can be avoided by teaching your child how to hold the pen or pencil correctly and how to write in the correct traditional manner. First of all, as a homeschooling parent, it is assumed that you want your child to learn to write well. That assumption is based on my questioning of parents at my seminars on handwriting. I pose the question thus: "Educators now tell us that children no longer need to be taught handwriting because they now have typewriters, computers, word processors, and laptops to do the writing for them. How many parents believe that the educators are correct and that we should therefore stop teaching children how to write?" The answer I invariably get is that parents still think that children should be taught how to write. Why? Because it is a skill that will be used by the child for the rest of his or her life, and no one can know or predict what needs the future adult will have for good handwriting twenty years down the line. Also, you can't carry a laptop or a word processor everywhere you go.

The question then becomes: "How should we teach children to write? Should we start with ball-and-stick and then in the third year switch over to cursive, or should we start with cursive first?" My answer is quite clear: teach your child to write a standard cursive script from the very beginning. Do not, I repeat, do not teach ball-and-stick! If you teach ball-and-stick first, your child may never develop a good cursive script. However, if you teach cursive first, your child will always be able to learn to print well later on and in a style much more pleasing than ball-and-stick.

The reason for this is simple. If you teach ball-and-stick first, the child develops habits of holding the writing instrument and forming the letters in ways that make a transition to cursive difficult if not impossible. That is why so many people keep printing for the rest of their lives. Some learners develop a kind of hybrid script—part print, part cursive. The only children who manage to develop a good cursive script are those who have been practicing it secretly on their own or those willing to take the time and make the effort to develop a good cursive script. And, as we know, the latter are in the minority.

Another reason why the transition from ball-and-stick to cursive produces such poor results is that many children resent having to learn an entirely new way of writing after having spent two years perfecting their printing. Why should they change? they ask. Also, in the third grade, teachers do not have the time to supervise the development of good cursive penmanship and the students, already doing a lot of writing in class, are often unwilling to take the time and do the practice required to develop a good cursive script.

But apparently all of those schools that introduce cursive in the second and third grades must believe that it has some value, otherwise why would schools even bother to teach it at all? One good reason to teach cursive, of course, is that if you can't write cursive you may not be able to read it when others write it. However, the problem is that by requiring the students to learn ball-and-stick first, the schools create obstacles to the development of a good cursive handwriting.

The usual reason given for teaching ball-and-stick first in school is that first graders do not have the fine motor skills or muscular dexterity in their fingers to be able to write cursive at that age. But that, of course, is utter nonsense, since this author was taught cursive writing in the first grade back in the days when everyone was taught cursive in the first grade. At that time it was established practice to do so. We were all trained in penmanship and did the various exercises—the ovals, the rainbows, the ups and downs—that helped us develop good hand and arm movements that contributed to good handwriting. What most parents or teachers do not know is that cursive writing was taught in the first grade in all schools until about the late 1930s when the changeover to ball-and-stick took place.

That changeover had a lot to do with the implementation of the progressive agenda which downplayed the development of the academic and intellectual skills in favor of developing the social skills and the affective domain, which deals with values, beliefs, and feelings. But homeschooling permits a parent to reinstate the primacy of developing the academic and intellectual skills, and the best time to start that process is in the first grade.

Many parents start that process in the preschool and kindergarten years when children are learning language so rapidly. They enjoy reading to their children, teaching them the alphabet and numbers. But as we have pointed out, each child is different and parents should not be disappointed if Johnny and Susie do not show signs of being child prodigies. A prodigy by definition is someone with extraordinary talent or genius, and thus prodigies are rare.

However, when it comes to writing, you must start by teaching your child how to hold the writing instrument: cradled between thumb and forefinger (also known as the index finger), which is next to the thumb, with the tip of the instrument resting on the long finger next to the forefinger, in a relaxed position, enabling a writer to write for hours without tiring. In other words, the instrument is held lightly and comfortably by the three extended slightly bent fingers so that these fingers do all the work. I've seen some individuals holding a pen with the three fingers folded under, forming a fist. This is a very uncomfortable way of holding a pen and requires movement of the entire fist to form the letters. In the correctly held position, the three fingers meet and the pen pokes out from the small triangle formed by the fingertips. When the child is ready to write, the paper (for those who are right-handed) is tilted counterclockwise so that the proper slant of the cursive letters can be made.

On the other hand, when children are taught to print first, the writing instrument is held straight up with three or four fingers in a tight grip with much pressure being applied downward on the paper placed in a straight position. When these children are then taught cursive in the second or third grade they do not change the way they hold the writing instrument because a muscular habit has been established that is not easy to alter. That is why so many children develop poor cursive handwriting—because of the way they hold their pens.

Children do not easily unlearn bad habits. That is why it is so important to teach the basics in the right manner from the very beginning, and why I advise parents that there are two very important no-no's in primary education: Do not teach anything that later has to be unlearned, and do not let a child develop a bad habit. Instruct the learner to do it right from the start. It will require close supervision and diligence on the part of the parent, but it will all pay off in the future.

HOW CURSIVE WRITING HELPS READING

A question most often asked by parents when the assertion is made that cursive should be taught first is: Won't learning cursive interfere with learning to read words in print? The emphatic answer is: Not at all. Those of us who learned cursive first had no problem learning to read print. In fact, it helped us. How? Well, one of the biggest problems children have when learning to read primary-school print and write in ball-and-stick is that so many of the letters look alike—such as b's and d's; f's and t's; g's, q's, and p's. This causes many children to become confused and make many errors. In cursive, however, there is a big difference between a b and a d. In writing cursive, a b starts like an l while a d begins like writing the letter a. In other words, in cursive, children do not confuse b's and d's because the movements of the hand— the muscular reflexes—make it impossible to confuse the two letters. And this knowledge is transferred to the reading process. Thus, by teaching children the distinctive differences between letters, learning to write cursive helps learning to read print.

Another aid to reading is that cursive requires children to write from left to right so that the letters will join with one another in proper sequence. The blending of the sounds is made more apparent by the joining of the letters. In ball-and-stick, some children write the letters backwards, and often the spacing is so erratic that you can't tell where one word ends and another begins. Cursive writing teaches spatial discipline and gives the writer greater control over the formation of letters and the spacing between words.

Another important benefit of cursive is that it helps the child learn to spell correctly since the hand acquires knowledge of spelling patterns through repeated hand movements. This is the same phenomenon that occurs when pianists or typists learn patterns of hand movements through continued repetition. These patterns of hand movement become so well learned, that a typist or pianist knows when he or she has made an error merely by an irregular hand movement, one that just doesn't feel right. Of course, the pianist also has the sound of the music to go by, but hand movement and sound go together. The typist, on the other hand, feels the error before he or she actually sees it on the paper in the machine or on the computer screen. And one is annoyed when an error slips by without being detected. But errors can be reduced to a minimum when hand and eye, cursive writing and printed text, work in harmony.

Another question often asked by parents of six-year-olds is: What will their children do when asked on a job application to "please print." My answer is that I don't advocate not teaching a child to print. I simply say teach cursive first, teach print later. Besides, that child will have plenty of time to learn to print between the first grade and applying for a job as a teenager.

The question is often asked: "Isn't cursive harder to learn than print?" No. It's just the opposite. It is difficult, if not unnatural, for children to draw straight lines and perfect circles, which is required in ball-and-stick, when they would much rather be doing curves and curls. In fact, all of cursive consists of only three movements: the undercurve, the overcurve, and the up and down. That's all there is to it. In addition, in cursive the child writes a whole word before lifting the pen, while with ball-and-stick printing each separate letter can become a slow and laborious production.

Another important point is that it takes time and supervision to help a child develop a good cursive script, and one has the time in the first grade, not the third grade. That's why it seems like such a waste of time to have the child develop competency in ball-and-stick when all of that is going to be replaced by cursive. The time would be much better spent working on cursive to begin with. The first-grade child may start out writing in a large scrawl, but in only a matter of months, that scrawl will be controlled by those little fingers and become a very nice manageable script. Practice makes perfect, and children should be given plenty of practice writing cursive.

And so, if you've wondered why your grandparents usually had better handwriting than you do, well, now you know the answer. They were taught cursive first at a time when penmanship was considered important since people in those days did much more writing than they do today. But even with our laptops and word processors, the need to write by hand will always be with us. As long as people want to jot down poetry in a notebook, keep private diaries, write love letters, send postcards, take notes at a meeting or seminar or press conference, compile shopping lists, send Christmas and birthday cards, sign autograph albums, write names and addresses in a date book, write a story or an article without a typewriter or computer, writing by hand will be one of the most useful skills anyone can have. As an author, I get many handwritten letters from readers who obviously don't have writing machines at their disposal. But if you *can't* write, you won't write.

Thus, if you concentrate on helping your child develop a good cursive handwriting, you eliminate the nonsense of first starting with ball-and-stick, then moving to slant ball-and-stick, or some other transitional script, finally ending up with a horrible-looking cursive, or having your child print for the rest of his or her life. Children will only make the effort to learn one primary way of writing which they will use for the rest of their lives. They don't need to be taught three ways, two of which will be discarded.

Incidentally, one should not object to children drawing letters on their own when learning the alphabet. But once they start learning to read, then formal instruction in cursive should begin so that they can do the writing exercises that go with the reading.

TEACHING THE LEFT-HANDED

Can left-handed children also be taught cursive first? Yes. In fact, left-handed children gain special benefits from that method. When left-handed children start with ball-and-stick, their tendency is to use the hook position in writing since the writing instrument is held straight up and the paper is also positioned straight. This means that as the child proceeds printing from left to right, the child's arm will cover what has already been written. This can be avoided if the left-handed child learns to write from the bottom up, the way right-handed children write. But this is difficult, if not impossible, to do when printing ball-and-stick.

However, if a left-handed child is taught to write cursive first, he or she must then tilt the paper clockwise and must write from the bottom up, since it is impossible to use the hook position if the paper is turned clockwise. Right-handers, of course, turn the paper counter-clockwise. But left-handers are quite capable of developing as good a cursive handwriting as any right-hander by writing from the bottom up, provided they learn to hold the writing instrument in the same relaxed manner as the right-handed cursive writer. It is even possible that the secret of good handwriting may be in the way the pen is held and the proper tilt of the paper.

All of this must lead to one simple conclusion: teach cursive first and print later. There are few things that help enchance a child's academic self-esteem more than the development of good handwriting. It helps reading, it helps spelling, and because writing is made easy, accurate, and esthetically pleasant, it helps thinking.

However, as in teaching anything, be patient with your child as he or she learns to write. There are some children for whom writing, no matter which style you teach, is a difficult art to master. Just as some children are physically inept but otherwise perfectly normal, one simply has to accept the idiosyncracies a child is born with. Aim for good performance, but if you see that your child is having inordinate difficulty in learning to write, relax and let the child work out the problem for himself. But give him plenty of opportunity to practice using the correct forms and encourage him to do the best he can.

I've been asked by some parents about the desirability of teaching a child to write D'Nealian or italic rather than cursive. There is no doubt that italic is esthetically nice to look at, but I believe that it is more a form of calligraphy than a standard cursive handwriting. The child may want to learn this form of writing later on when making greeting cards or posters. As for D'Nealian, it is too close to a print script to be considered as a desirable form of handwriting. It is mostly used as a transition script from ball-and-stick to cursive. As for teaching a basic handwriting that will be used for a lifetime, I recommend sticking to our standard, practical cursive script. Children are always free in later life to learn calligraphy, printing, or any other form of writing that pleases them.

-6-

Teaching Spelling

There is a movement among educators to denigrate the teaching of spelling as an unnecessary waste of time. In this day and age of computers, we are told that we no longer have to learn to spell but can now rely on "Spellcheck" to do the spelling for us. When a vice president can be ridiculed into political oblivion for having misspelled "potato," however, it is obvious that the ability to spell still remains something of importance in the minds of average Americans. Poor Dan Quayle, no matter what else he does in life, he will be remembered for his spelling gaffe. He will be the butt of comedians' jokes for as long as he lives and, because of that, many people will never take him seriously. Even those who consider him to be a competent politician will tend to regard him as damaged goods. So no matter what the educators say about wasting time learning to spell, Americans, particularly employers, now and forever, will rightly or wrongly judge the intelligence and education of individuals by their ability to spell correctly. All of which means that homeschoolers have no choice but to teach their children the importance of learning to spell correctly.

Learning to spell, like learning anything else, requires diligence, repetitive work, and above all, an interest in, if not a love of, learning language. And learning to spell English requires particular effort because we have so many irregular spellings—that is, spellings that do not conform to a regularly phonetic system of writing. The reasons for this are quite compelling. First of all, as we explained in an earlier chapter, we have an alphabet of twenty-six letters to stand for forty-four language sounds. Some of our letters, particularly the vowels, stand for more than one sound, and some sounds are represented by more than one letter. So learning to spell requires a thorough knowledge of our alphabetic system with its many spelling forms. In addition, we have many archaic spellings in English that go back to the way these words were pronounced centuries ago. The pronunciations may have changed, but not the spellings.

Also, English has incorporated many foreign words with their foreign spellings, such as *bureau, façade, lieutenant,* and *rendezvous*. Another problem is that English is pronounced differently in different English-speaking countries and often in different parts of the same country. But the spellings remain essentially the same except for such words as *honor-honour, center-centre, theater-theatre*—the first version being American, the second British. Otherwise, anyone who can read English will be able to read an English-language newspaper or magazine published in the United States, England, South Africa, Australia, Hong Kong, India, Israel, New Zealand, or elsewhere.

Once we've decided that spelling is important, how do we go about teaching it? First, we teach a child to read phonetically; that is, we teach the child our English alphabetic system. Then we teach the child how to spell all of the single-syllable words that conform to that system. We also teach all of those frequently used single-syllable words that have irregular spellings, such as: *to, do, two, who, the, are, eye, were, there, their, four,* etc. These spellings are best learned by writing them in simple sentences. Then we learn to spell those words with archaic spellings and silent letters, such as: *should, would, ought, caught, cough, eight, light, high, write, hour, ghost, know,* etc.

We then teach the spelling of two-syllable words. We start with the simplest combinations of two regular short-vowel syllables, such as: *hotdog, boxtop, hatbox, jacket, rocket, napkin, picnic, cabin, topic, traffic,* etc. Then we teach two-syllable words with short vowels and consonant blends, such as: *chopstick, plastic, strictness, Franklin, bashful, singing, craftsman, draftsman,* etc. Next, we teach two-syllable words with short, long, and other vowel spellings with and without consonant blends, such as: *carport, viewpoint, eyeful, triumph, phantom, earful, telltale, goodbye, thinker, welcome, token, report, contact,* etc.

When you teach the spelling of a word like *contact*, you can also teach the spelling of *contract, attract, subtract, tractor, retract, distract,* etc. Likewise, with a word like *strict*, you can also teach the spelling of *district, restrict, strictly, strictness, constrict,* etc. In other words, we teach spelling in word families, so that the child can learn to spell a whole group of words rather than one word at a time. In fact, this was the methodology used by Noah Webster in his famous spelling books that sold millions of copies to the parents and teachers of the young scholars of early America.

From two-syllable words, we go to three-, four-, and five-syllable words. Again, wherever possible, teach groups of words, such as: *emphasis, emphasize, emphasizing, emphatic, emphatically; temper, temperate, temperance, temperament, temperamental, temperamentally.* Of course, there are many one-of-a-kind words that must be learned individually, such as: *chocolate, vertigo, licorice, Mississippi,* etc.

One of the most frequent questions asked by parents of older children who can't spell is, how can such a youngster be taught to improve his or her spelling? The problem with such children is that they were obviously not taught our English alphabetic system in primary school and therefore tend to spell everything as they hear it or say it. Thus, *write* or *right* is spelled *rite, honest* is spelled *onist, rough* is spelled *ruff, have to* is spelled *hafta, going to* is spelled *gonna,* etc.

The only way to correct this kind of situation is to first teach the youngster our English alphabetic system with all of its idiosyncrasies. Then have the student copy good text into a notebook. By correctly copying interesting text, the student will become accustomed to spelling the words correctly, for when the muscles of the hand repeatedly perform the same sequence of movements, the hand gains the same kind of knowledge that the hands of a touch typist or a pianist acquire. Professional skaters and dancers apply the same principle in training their muscles to perform certain movements in a specifically desired sequence. In other words, the student must write the words frequently in order to acquire that muscular knowledge. Therefore, the more copying of good text the student does, the better he or she will learn to spell.

Let the student choose the texts to be copied, so that he or she will be interested in the content of the text. An article from an encyclopedia, a short piece from a magazine, a column from a newspaper, a poem, the Declaration of Independence, Lincoln's Gettysburg Address—all of these would provide suitable copy material. To see how well the student is improving in spelling, test her, using words from the texts that she has copied. If the student complains, just remind her of what happened to Dan Quayle when he misspelled a simple word like *potato.*

Also, learning to spell will give the student many opportunities to use the dictionary, the greatest language source book at the student's command. And, inasmuch as the student will be learning to spell words with meanings that he or she may not have yet learned, this will be an excellent occasion to expand vocabulary by defining the words being spelled. Reading the dictionary itself can be entertaining as well as educational. Also, games such as Scrabble can be useful in helping a child develop an interest in language. Remember, language was what the child learned first because he had a compelling interest in being able to understand the words of others and being able to communicate with others by using words. Therefore, new words should be as intrinsically interesting as the first words learned as an infant.

Concerning vocabulary, Mark Twain once said: "A powerful agent is the right word. Whenever we come upon one of those intensely right words...the resulting effect is physical as well as spiritual, and electrically prompt." This is the kind of experience with words that a child should be taught to enjoy. As we pointed out in the previous chapter, mastery of one's language and its expansive vocabulary is the key to success. Learning to spell can be an adventurous challenge on the high road to success.

-7-

Teaching Arithmetic

Civilization advances by extending the number of important operations which we can perform without thinking about them.

—ALFRED NORTH WHITEHEAD

Anyone looking over a primary school curriculum these days will notice that the word arithmetic is no longer used. Everything having to do with numbers is now called math. But by doing away with the word arithmetic, the educators have also managed to erase the substantial difference that exists between arithmetic and mathematics. Indeed, the difference between arithmetic and mathematics is so substantial that not knowing the nature of this difference can greatly handicap a student.

First, it is important to know that arithmetic is a counting system, pure and simple. It basically answers the question of "how many" or "how much." It deals with quantity in four ways or four functions. In *addition* we count forward. In *subtraction* we count backward. In *multiplication* we count forward in multiples. In *division* we count backward in multiples. Mathematics, on the other hand, deals with relationships. It uses arithmetic calculations as well as a host of other symbols in carrying out its various functions. But before anyone can become proficient in mathematics, he or she must first master arithmetic.

Whenever I give a seminar on arithmetic to homeschooling parents, I ask the audience how many of them use algebra frequently. Maybe a hand or two go up. There are always a couple of engineers in the audience. I then ask how many of them use geometry frequently. Again maybe a hand or two go up. Then I ask how many use trigonometry frequently. Again, a hand or two go up. I then ask how many use calculus frequently, and I get the same sparse response. Finally I ask how many in the audience use arithmetic frequently, and every hand goes up. "So why don't they teach arithmetic anymore?" I ask.

The point is that everyone uses arithmetic every day: buying groceries, making change, balancing checkbooks, calculating income tax, measuring floor space, calculating mortgage interest, etc. In other words, while learning math may lead to good technical careers in science and industry, you need arithmetic for common everyday use. Indeed, you need arithmetic in order to survive! So why don't the schools teach arithmetic anymore? Most educators would reply that they do teach arithmetic, but not in the way that it used to be taught. Now they teach "problem solving," and they don't mind if the students work together in cooperative groups, or count on their fingers. It's the new new math that we're in!

But the homeschooler need not be bound by the dysfunctional theories of educators. Any parent knows why his or her child should be taught arithmetic. This does not mean that the child should not, at some later date, be introduced to higher math. In fact, a good grounding in basic arithmetic provides the student with an essential introduction to mathematics. But it is obvious that most people will never make use of higher math even though they will have been taught some of its basic elements in high school or college. But they will, of necessity, be using arithmetic every day for the rest of their lives.

The challenge then becomes how do we go about teaching arithmetic most effectively in the primary grades. When I was writing my book, *How to Tutor*, back in the 1970s, I became fascinated with the subject of arithmetic. What were its origins? Who invented it? How has it been taught over the centuries? Like so many Americans, I had been taught arithmetic in public school in simple rote fashion with no understanding whatever of what arithmetic was. The teacher taught the arithmetic functions in a perfunctory way, and we all learned them — some better than others. But we were never given any insight into the marvels of the system itself.

We all learn to count pretty early in life and we take for granted the symbols that stand for numbers and functions. But where did these symbols come from? Who invented them and when were they invented? According to an article in *The World of Mathematics* (Vol. 1, p. 453):

> [A]lthough our European and American numerals are often spoken of as Arabic, they have never been used by the Arabs. They came to us by means of a book on arithmetic which apparently was written in India about twelve hundred years ago, and was translated into Arabic soon afterward. By chance this book was carried by merchants to Europe and there was translated from the Arabic into Latin. This was hundreds of years before books were first printed in Europe, and this arithmetic book was known only in manuscript form. Since it had been translated from Arabic, the numerals were supposed to be those used by the Arabs, but this was not the case. They might be called Hindu-Arabic, but since they took their present shapes in Europe they may better be called European or Modern numerals.

Prior to the invention of our modern number symbols, the earliest forms of number notation were simple unit lines, which later gave way to alphabet letters. The Roman numerals were a combination of unit lines and letters. Homeschoolers can help their children understand the nature of modern arithmetic by studying the number notation systems of the ancient world, including Roman numerals which are still used today. This should be done well after the student has memorized the arithmetic facts.

Most children begin learning to count soon after they have begun learning to speak the language. As they learn the letters of the alphabet, they should also be learning the number symbols. Since a number is merely a symbol for a specific quantity, you can use any kind of convenient concrete units to first demonstrate this. Pennies are an excellent way to introduce counting and the number symbols which represent specific quantities. Rather than using pictures of monkeys or candy canes to represent concrete units, pennies are far more appropriate since much of what we use arithmetic for has to do with money. When the child has firmly understood the meaning of the symbols in terms of the quantities they stand for, then the use of these symbols will be well understood. They save time and make life easier. The number symbols are also used to designate age, time, days in the calendar, baseball innings, etc.

The transition from the use of ancient quantity notations to modern numerals provided mankind with a new, highly efficient way of mental calculation. Man no longer needed concrete units such as beads, or sticks, or abacuses with which to do calculations. He could now use his brain and paper and pencil. But in order to do this he had to memorize the basic arithmetic facts.

At age five and six children can learn the arithmetic facts by rote. But before having the child memorize an arithmetic fact, first demonstrate it with concretes. For example, to demonstrate that 3 plus 4 equals 7, line up three pennies and four pennies and have the child count them to get the total. Then write the fact in numerals, $3 + 4 = 7$, and tell the child that this is what he must memorize in order to be able to use this fact in the most convenient way. After you've demonstrated all of the addition and subtraction facts, then demonstrate the multiplication facts. You can demonstrate 8 times 9 by setting eight rows of nine pennies each. Have the child count them out until he gets the total of 72. After this laborious task, he will realize that the symbolic representation of $8 \times 9 = 72$ is a much easier and faster way to state this fact which he must now commit to memory by rote. Also show how nine rows of eight pennies each produce the same total with the symbolic representation of $9 \times 8 = 72$

Rote learning is the easiest form of learning. All it requires is repetition. The best way to teach anyone to learn anything by rote is to have the learner see the fact over and over again until it is indelibly imprinted on the mind. Flash cards and tables can be used most effectively. But if a learner can't remember a particular fact, do not ask him or her to "figure it out," because the learner will then start counting by ones or by using fingers. Once that becomes habitual, the learner will not bother to memorize the fact, and this will become a handicap to effective mental calculation. Flash the correct answer to the learner until he or she learns it cold and no longer has to "figure it out."

When the youngster has mastered the arithmetic facts, he or she should be taught about another important feature of our modern arithmetic system: the idea of place value. Place value is derived from a device used by the Hindus in India to organize counting. The device was a counting board divided into columns. The column to the farthest right was for units, the next column to the left was for tens, the next column to the left was for hundreds, the next to the left for thousands, etc. Concrete indicators, such as pebbles or beads, were placed in each column. The ten number symbols—0 1 2 3 4 5 6 7 8 9—were used to designate totals at the bottom of each column. The zero was invented to designate an empty column. Thus, the number 4,506 meant that there were, from right to left, six units, no tens, five hundreds, and four thousands. The invention of zero, by the way, is considered one of the great inventions of mankind even though the inventor is unknown. The idea that you can have a symbol for nothing sort of boggles the imagination.

Thus it was the combining of the Hindu counting board and the ten number symbols that gave us our magnificent base-ten, place-value counting system. It is a system that relies on memorization of the basic arithmetic facts for its most effective use. That is why it is so ridiculous for modern educators to denigrate rote learning when our arithmetic system requires it. That is why children must be taught the arithmetic facts by rote memorization. Rote memorization can be fun if taught in the proper way. It need not be tedious or tiresome or boring if the teacher or parent comes to the subject with as much excitement and wonder as it deserves. Memorizing the arithmetic facts will give the child a power virtually as great as his or her power to use language.

The alphabet and the base-ten, place-value arithmetic system are mankind's two greatest intellectual inventions. They represent the basic intellectual technology without which the computer age could never have come into existence. And they remain the basic intellectual technology that every child must master if he or she is not only to survive but to thrive in the new information age. When you come to that realization, you understand why it is so important for your child to acquire this intellectual technology, and you are inclined to teach it with genuine reverence and excitement.

Believe it or not, our arithmetic system is less than five hundred years old. First, our number symbols, including the symbol for zero, had to evolve from their ancient notations to their present forms and be universally accepted. Second, our place-value system, derived from the counting board, had to be perfected and standardized. All of this took hundreds of years. But it required the invention of the printing press, in the fifteenth century, and the development of paper before standardization could take place. The multiplication table itself was not invented until the late fifteenth century, and the present method of long division first appeared in an arithmetic book published in Italy in 1491, a year before Columbus discovered America.

All of the standardized methods used to carry out a variety of arithmetic calculations, called algorithms, also took years of development. But once these calculating tools are learned by a student, they will be used for the rest of one's life. It is usually after the mastery of our arithmetic system that a student can become interested in the mysterious, baffling, and wonderful world of numbers and number patterns that has fascinated mathematicians for centuries. But most of us will be content to be able to use arithmetic for the practical, mundane, everyday purposes for which it was devised.

Which arithmetic curriculum should you use in your home education? There are many on the market, and they can be inspected at any book fair held at any homeschool convention. The Saxon math books have achieved a rather good reputation among homeschoolers. Better still, talk to other homeschoolers and ask them how they taught their children arithmetic and whether or not they were pleased with the curriculum they used. You might as well take advantage of the experiences of other homeschoolers. Also, consult the various publications that now evaluate homeschool products and curricula. Incidentally, my own book, *How to Tutor*, has a complete section on arithmetic with a history of how the system was developed.

Also, since you will want your child to understand the practical uses to which arithmetic can be applied, open a savings account for your child and teach him or her how to calculate the interest earned. Have your child purchase shares in a mutual fund or stock in a company whose products he or she likes. That will introduce the student to the stock market and the ups and downs of which are reported daily in the newspaper. A child who gets into the habit of saving and investing early in life will have a considerable nest egg for retirement.

Now you know how interesting arithmetic can be, not only for the child but for the parents as well. Best of all, you have the freedom at home to teach the subject in the manner that makes sense to you and your child. Also, your child will be spared the damage that is being done to millions of children in public schools by educators who lack the appreciation of our wonderful arithmetic system and are required to teach the latest version of the new math. Recently, I watched one of our esteemed nightly news programs do a story on the new new math as practiced in a public school classroom. The children were diligently at work problem solving, and as the camera zoomed in on one child at work, one could see that she was counting on her fingers. That's the way counting was done before the invention of the abacus! And people wonder why so many children can't make change or do simple calculations in their heads these days. Clearly, it is not the children's fault, but the fault of an education system that refuses to teach what children have to learn.

-8-

Choosing a Curriculum

Now that you've taught your child to read phonetically, write in a good cursive script, spell words correctly, and perform the four basic arithmetic functions with ease, what do you do next? Here, you have a great deal of flexibility. You can purchase one of the very well prepared curricula available to homeschoolers or you can devise your own curriculum and choose your own books.

But first, it's best to reexamine your philosophy of education, which should guide you in your choices. What do you want your child to know? What do you want your child to be able to do? What kind of a person would you like your child to be when he or she is twenty years old? So much of what is learned and experienced in those early years can have an impact on what we later become as adults. For example, when I was in the third grade in public school in New York City, we had a very simple weekly lesson in class called Music Appreciation. Our teacher placed a crank-operated portable phonograph on her desk and played a number of short classical pieces of music some of which I remember to this day, sixty years later. The selections included "Marche Slav" by Tchaikovsky and "The Swan" by Saint-Saens. We all listened quietly and attentively to the music and were required to remember the names of the selections and their composers. I believe it was this simple introduction to classical music that opened an entire world of beauty to me and, in the years that followed, provided so much pleasure and enjoyment.

That's the sort of thing parents can easily provide for their own children. Today, the resources available are so much more plentiful and the technical equipment so much better than anything we had in the 1930s. Thus, if you want your child to develop an appreciation of classical music, you can get the cassettes and the tape player and do the job at your convenience. In this day and age of trying to find ways to reduce stress, classical music can provide an excellent source of serene, soothing, emotionally beautiful, and uplifting musical sound.

What do you want your child to know? An awful lot! But you have a good many years in which to accomplish this task. The first two years of education are devoted to learning the academic skills, but in the process of teaching reading you can use books with interesting content. In teaching writing, you can have your child copy text that is worth reading. And in teaching arithmetic you can also teach about money, coinage, and savings, which will be useful for the rest of the child's life.

By the third year you will want your child to begin knowing something about the history and geography of the country he or she lives in. American history is an exciting story that teaches us who we are and why we are a country which so many people want to become part of. Start first with local history, visiting local historical sites, reading about the first settlers, the local Indian tribes, the first form of government, etc. Then teach local geography, the cities and towns you live in, their location on the map, the rivers, the mountains, the harbors, the local climate, etc. The child will be doing a lot of reading, and learning many new words.

The child will also be learning grammar—how our language is put together so that one develops good speech and can write coherent sentences and paragraphs. This is also a good time to introduce poetry at an elementary level and some of the children's classics. Trips to the library should become a regular part of your weekly or monthly schedule.

In arithmetic, the child will learn about fractions, decimals, and percentages, and be able to expand his or her knowledge of banking and storekeeping. Trips to the supermarket can provide plenty of opportunities to practice what one has learned in terms of prices, weights, measures, change-making, etc. In other words, learning takes place everywhere, all of the time. One can practice reading in the supermarket by reading labels, signs, circulars, coupons, advertisements. The written word is all around us wherever we go, providing lots of opportunities to practice sounding out.

Then there are the housekeeping chores that children should become involved with. I know a homeschooling family in which the young daughter has become the family's chief cookie maker. Children should also be taught how to organize their own books and materials and to try to be as neat as possible. But don't worry if your homeschool becomes a little messy. Just don't let it become *too* messy.

Should you purchase a prepared curriculum and, if so, which one? The advantage of using a prepared curriculum is that it will make the job of homeschooling easier and provide the assurance that you and your child are covering the subjects you want to cover and are not wasting valuable time. For example, a workbook on grammar will ensure that your child covers the entire subject in an organized way over a specified period of time. Although one is free to be as flexible as possible in using any workbook, the curriculum specifications will provide helpful guidelines. Also, if you have several children, it will free you to devote attention to the younger child who still needs one-on-one instruction in the three Rs, while the older child can be left to concentrate on his or her workbook. Prepared curricula usually come with children's workbooks and parents' guides so that the parent can check the child's work.

Many parents have found the prepared curricula to be much more intensive and demanding than one would like. The reason why these programs are indeed as thorough and demanding as they are is because the program makers want homeschoolers to perform better and know more than their public school counterparts. Then homeschoolers cannot be accused of not educating their children above and beyond what is theoretically required by the state.

I once accompanied a homeschooling mom and dad to a meeting with local school officials who wanted to make sure that the children were being adequately educated at home. The parents brought with them several boxes of books plus the children's workbooks as evidence that education was indeed taking place at the home. Not only were the school officials impressed, but they seemed speechless as they went through the children's workbooks, realizing that the pupils in their own public schools were getting a far less thorough and demanding education. Apparently, parents have far more leeway than schoolteachers in prescribing how their children are to be educated. Precocious children with a great deal of native curiosity about the world may want to devote a great deal of time to a particular project, and a parent is free to encourage that kind of endeavor. While individual education plans are difficult to implement in a classroom of thirty kids, they are easy to implement at home.

An interesting case comes to mind. Some years ago at a homeschool conference, I was approached by a father who wanted my advice about his son who couldn't buckle down to the strict curriculum the father wanted to impose on the lad. He had already gone to a guidance counselor, who advised putting the boy on Ritalin. He wanted to know if that was the only recourse available. The father strongly believed that discipline and obedience were most important in education, and the child's rambunctious behavior had be to curtailed. I asked the father if his son had any interests that could command his attention and concentration. The father replied affirmatively. I then suggested that he loosen his demand for discipline and obedience and try a regimen of freedom for the lad. Maybe that's what he needs, I said. The father was somewhat taken aback. Freedom? Let the boy do what he wanted? It never occurred to him that that was a possible alternative. I asked, what would the boy do if he were given the freedom to do what he wanted? Would he just play all day in a sandpile or run amuck? No, the father replied. He was a serious boy. He'd probably work on whatever it was that interested him. Obviously, he needs freedom, I said.

The father thanked me for my advice. He was probably relieved to know that he didn't have to beat the boy into submission. That's the kind of advice he might have gotten from someone else. Incidentally, the father had a second younger son who very much wanted structure and was thriving under his father's strict supervision. But the older boy was clearly different. At the time it never occurred to me to get the man's address and follow up on the story, but I felt intuitively that I had given the man the right advice. The idea of drugging a child with Ritalin so that he would buckle down to a homeschool regimen just seemed to negate what homeschooling was truly all about. Homeschooling is about freedom! Freedom from the state, freedom from miseducation, freedom from ridiculous rules and regulations, and above all, freedom to educate your children in a manner that conforms with your values and how your children learn best.

Another important freedom that homeschooling provides is the freedom to use time for the benefit of the entire family. No more time is wasted on long bus rides to and from school. No more time is wasted in study halls and recess periods and waiting for others to catch up. Usually, homeschoolers can complete their academic work by noon, after which they are free to pursue whatever extracurricular activity they wish. Time can now be spent visiting museums, the state legislature, the city council, historical sites, zoos, county courthouses, local industries, radio and television stations, the local newspaper, university libraries, conventions and exhibitions, taking long walks, exercising by skating, cycling, sledding, swimming at the local Y, shopping for educational supplies, making videos, visiting retirement homes and meeting interesting people, taking one's pets to the vet, visiting farms, attending concerts, going to the theater, the ballet, the opera, and visiting other homeschoolers.

When do public schoolers have time for such things? They come home so exhausted that all they want to do is play computer games or watch TV. And before they know it, it's time for dinner, some homework, more TV, maybe an argument with mom or dad or sister or brother, and then to bed so that they can get up at the crack of dawn in order to stand out in the cold and wait for the yellow bus.

The homeschooling family makes much better use of the best hours of the day. The hours are theirs to fill with whatever they enjoy doing. Add up those hours over a twelve-year period and what one has is a richness of family life that the public schooler can never experience. Of course, there are many families in which both parents work, therefore making homeschooling just about impossible. But there are also many families in which at least one parent is at home and can homeschool if he or she wants to. Those are the families that are missing out on the great homeschooling experience. And if the homeschool movement continues to grow, it's because more and more of those parents are beginning to see the light.

Back to the matter of purchasing a curriculum. There are prepared programs for just about every kind of family, religious and secular. Christian-oriented programs rely heavily on biblical principles in their approach to any subject. Thus, while explanations of what the theory of evolution is all about will be found in Christian-oriented science programs, a strong case for creationism will also be made in the same text. If a parent wants a more secular approach, books can be found at bookstores and libraries to fill that need. In the appendix, we list the best-known curricula and programs available, with a note about their orientation.

However, the best way to become acquainted with the variety and quality of what is available is to attend a homeschool convention with its hall of vendor exhibits. One will be amazed at what is now available to homeschoolers. Most of the large homeschool conventions cover two days.

Many parents spend the first day looking over the various competing programs, inspecting, browsing, gathering brochures and literature, listening to salesmen, attending vendors' workshops, asking advice of other homeschoolers, and finally deciding what to buy on the second day. Also, most homeschool conventions now feature a hall with used books that homeschoolers no longer need and now want to sell. Great bargains are available at such book fairs.

The beauty of such conventions is that they prove that there are lots of parents who are truly interested in the education of their children and are willing to spend the time and money to get the right materials. Such intense parental interest can only accrue to the benefit of our country.

-9-

Subject Matter

At this point, we might as well discuss what it is we want to teach and why we ought to teach it. Mary Foley, in our chapter on developing a philosophy of education, spoke of her curriculum as including "natural and social sciences." I'm not sure exactly what subject matter would be included under those rubrics. I prefer to use the terms that were used when I was going to school: history, geography, English, French, Spanish, Russian, composition, algebra, geometry, trigonometry, biology, chemistry, physics, science, touch typing, drawing, etc. At least you knew what you were studying. There was a body of knowledge arranged in a rational, chronological way, so that you could learn basic principles and facts that helped you develop a pretty good view of the world, how it worked in the past, how it works now, and how it may work in the future.

The fact that knowledge has come down to us arranged in these particular categories is a revelation of man's need to organize knowledge so that it can be retained and passed on to future generations in an orderly, integrated manner. This manner of organization not only permits one to understand what is already known, but permits us to gather additional knowledge in each field of endeavor. And then it permits us to continue the process of passing it on to future generations. In other words, this wise and highly efficient organization of knowledge, which uses the alphabet as one of its organizing tools, is a kind of bridge, a marvelous intellectual continuum, between generations. It permits us to effectively use the accumulated power of the greatest brains that have come before us. The results of all their labors, experiments, and cogitations are at our disposal. What an incredible treasure they have bequeathed us, and what a sin it is for an education system to deny American children the benefits of this priceless heritage.

What has happened is that our progressive educators, discarding several thousand years of useful educational experience, decided early in this century to reorganize knowledge to serve their own social purposes. So instead of history, geography, psychology, anthropology, and sociology, we get "social science" or "social studies," so that knowledge which is rationally organized and makes sense, is reorganized or disorganized so that it doesn't make sense but feeds a prejudice or a perversion or an aberration or an agenda which has nothing to do with the pursuit of true knowledge.

Therefore, if you are going to homeschool your children, teach them a subject so that it will enhance their understanding of the world rather than serve the interests of a group with an agenda. There are many such groups: Marxists, socialists, communists, deconstructionists, etc., all of whom have social and political agendas and use bits and pieces of knowledge and information to enhance their drive to gain power over society.

It is not easy in this day and age of rampant disinformation to pursue knowledge and truth for their own sake, for the simple reason that there are not enough people in the education establishment interested in knowledge and truth for their own sake. If you, as a parent, belong to one of these groups, then obviously you will have the power to indoctrinate your children in any way you wish. But then you must grant other parents, not interested in your agenda, the right to educate their children in the love and pursuit of knowledge and understanding, because such a pursuit brings us closer to what reality is. The closer one is to reality, the saner one is.

Let us consider the subjects we may want to teach and why we may want to teach them. A good subject to start with is history, the story of mankind. Why should anyone study history? Because history has many lessons to teach us. History, which includes biographies and autobiographies, teaches us about the lives of nations and the lives of individuals. It teaches us about the lives of whole civilizations. It permits us to review the completed lives of others so that we can compare the productive and virtuous against the destructive and criminal and we can learn from them what we ought and ought not to do. It gives us insight into how men succeed and how they fail.

History is no doubt the greatest depository of wisdom available to us. And it should be taught chronologically, so that we can see how the accumulated wisdom and disasters of the past have affected succeeding generations. The philosopher George Santayana wrote that those who cannot remember the past are condemned to repeat it. It has also been said that the one thing we have learned from history is that we do not learn from history, that each generation seems determined to learn everything the hard way, by experience.

How can we teach our children to learn from history? The only way to do that is to first teach history and hope that exposure to it will develop in the child a fascination with the past and a philosophical attitude toward life. I was first introduced to history in the third grade where I learned about the Dutch origins of New York City. It was fascinating to read about Henry Hudson, who discovered the Hudson River, Peter Minuet, who bought Manhattan Island from the Indians for twenty-four dollars' worth of trinkets, and Peter Stuyvesant, the autocratic Dutch governor with a wooden leg who was forced to surrender New Netherland to the English in 1664. New Amsterdam then became New York. Knowing that history enabled me to understand why so many of the geographical names in the region were Dutch. It was a wonderful way to introduce history to a child so that I could see that history in the names and places all around me.

The Bible is the oldest history book we have, giving us a chronological history of man since Genesis and the Garden of Eden. Whether you believe in the Bible or not, history is organized in the same chronological manner so that we can see cause and effect, discovery and growth, progress and destruction. The order in which things happen is very important in establishing truth, and the more detail we have the closer we can get to the truth. Truth, as Noah Webster defined it in his dictionary, is "conformity to fact or reality; exact accordance with that which is, or has been, or shall be. The truth of history constitutes its whole value."

So a study of history inculcates an understanding of what truth is and why it is so valuable. The history of America is an incredibly inspiring story of men and women trying to create a society based on individual freedom and responsibility, a society based on moral principles derived from religious belief. Despite its past failings and some ominous trends as to its future, America still remains the only country where the full possibilities of a truly free society exist. Preserving this society should be the business of every American who loves what America stands for.

Homeschooling parents will find a plethora of materials which teach children our history from the early settlements to our present age. What a story it is! Begin at the beginning and methodically work your way to the present. It will take years, but you have as many years as you want to do the job. Biographies and autobiographies are a wonderful source of historical knowledge. They make fascinating reading for young people. G. A. Henty's wonderful historical novels for young readers remain a vastly entertaining way to get to know world history. One need not rely merely on dry textbooks. Great storytellers have found history to be a tremendous source of materials for their books. Also, visits to historical sights can enhance the study of history.

Study our wars, what caused them, how they started, and how they ended. Study the history of American economic development, the freedom of inventors to invent, the transformation of an agricultural society into an industrial society and then into a high-tech society of computers, jumbo jets, satellite communications, etc. Is there a more fascinating story to be told than the history of America? What a great opportunity to teach it in as exciting a way as it can be taught—as it ought to be taught.

There are also wonderful books available for teaching the history of the ancient world written at an elementary level. The Bible, of course, provides a wonderful entry into the ancient world of Canaan, Egypt, Israel, Babylonia, Persia, Rome, etc. There are all sorts of books and materials available that make the history of many nations come alive and excite the young mind.

Geography. Here, history and exploration can combine to teach us about oceans and continents and the courageous men and women who built settlements and cities so that modern civilization could thrive. Start with one's immediate region, then expand to the state, the nation, the continent, other continents, other nations, the world.

So few young people today can tell you the capitals of other nations, let alone the capitals of our states. I tutored a teenager for a short time who could not name a single country on the continent of Africa. I was astonished at such basic ignorance. So I assigned the youngster the task of listing alphabetically every country in Africa, its capital, its population, its language, its form of government, its major exports, etc. He started the project quite diligently, even drawing a picture of the country's flag in full color. But after I left, I was told by his parents that he gradually lost interest in the project. Unfortunately, his parents were not that much interested in geography themselves and therefore did not see to it that the youngster completed the assignment. Apparently, they could not see the value of expanding the youngster's geographical knowledge of a part of the world in which they had little interest. And so they did not put pressure on the youngster to complete the project.

I doubt that I would have bothered to study much of chemistry, or physics, or trigonometry if I had not been forced to do so by the schools I attended. And I suspect that that is why so many homeschooling parents rely on prepared curricula. They dare not rely on their own interests alone as the spur to get their children to study subjects that require real mental effort.

The advantage of homeschooling is that you need not use dry textbooks to do the instructing. For example, I learned more about atomic physics from a popular book by a journalist on the history of the atomic bomb, than from any textbook. Seek out these books about pioneers in science whose work is better explained by writers who want to reach millions of readers than by textbook writers who are compelled to write in the dullest style possible. Make use of the computerized catalogs in your libraries to find the best written and most popular books on the subjects you want to cover. These will be the kinds of books your children will eagerly devour. You'll find such books covering virtually every subject: economics, mathematics, psychology, chemistry, physics, art history, astronomy, invention, anthropology, geology, botany, zoology, biology, etc. There are also various organizations and associations that publish magazines on particular subject areas which may be helpful to the homeschooler. And then there is the Internet! We shall talk more about that in our chapter on homeschooling and technology.

If your child is having difficulty finding a subject that really interests her, provide an academic smorgasbord so that she can get a good taste of each subject matter. It is hard to know offhand what a youngster will become interested in. Sometimes a book about a particular area of activity will awaken an interest. I remember listening to a popular TV interviewer describe how he became interested in getting into radio. When he was about thirteen he read a book in which the hero was a radio announcer, and that's when he decided that that was what he wanted to be. He was willing to accept the most menial position available as long as it got him his first job in radio, and he succeeded. Homeschooling will permit your child to discover his own interests because he will be free to pursue what he finds to be fascinating and absorbing in what he is learning. Thus, his choice of career will most likely reflect a strong natural aptitude for the kind of work the career will require.

-10-

Homeschooling High Schoolers

Can one homeschool a high schooler? Yes, of course. Thousands of parents are doing it every day quite successfully, and there are excellent materials for high school homeschooling. Many homeschooling families consider middle and high schools to be dangerous places for their children. The public school curriculum puts great emphasis on the affective domain in middle and high schools. The affective domain is that part of the curriculum dealing with beliefs, values, attitudes, emotions, sexuality, etc. It's also a time when peer pressure to do drugs and engage in sexual experimentation is greatest, and it's a time when teenage rebellion begins to emerge as the most serious threat to family harmony. And so, many homeschooling parents decide to educate their high schoolers at home right through the twelfth grade.

However, some parents, usually at the insistence of their children, will permit them to attend a public or private high school, particularly if the youngster is very sportsminded and wants to play on the football team or is musically inclined and wants to play in the school orchestra. Some school districts permit part-time attendance for homeschoolers. Sometimes the kids enjoy the novelty and social life of the school. But then there are kids who don't find the experience as enjoyable as they thought and opt to return to schooling at home.

Then, there are parents who become concerned with what their kids are being exposed to in the middle or high school and hear the alarm signals. They then decide to get their kids out and start homeschooling. Sometimes the teenagers object. At other times, the kids are delighted at the prospect of not having to go back to the "zoo," as they call it. These are the teenagers who can't stand school and would like to get out in the worst way. In the case of those kids who resist being homeschooled, there is always a difficult period of transition and adjustment. But in many cases, after six months to a year, the children begin to understand and appreciate the wisdom of their parents' action and discover in home-schooling a whole new dimension to learning. It can be quite an experience for a teenager to find himself free from the regulations and routines of the school where bells determine when to switch from one subject to another. I remember a story a homeschooling mom told me about her son. They were driving by the school her son had attended, and she asked him if he missed it. He replied that he did miss some of his friends. When she asked if he would like to return to the school, he replied, "I don't miss them that much!"

How does one take a son or daughter out of high school and educate the child at home? It depends on the educational state the youngster is in. If he or she was badly damaged by educational malpractice and is dyslexic or functionally illiterate or can't spell or has a math phobia or attention deficit disorder, you'll have to deal with these problems before you can do anything else. You may also have to deal with an attitudinal or motivational problem that older children with a history of academic failure often acquire. They may really think they're stupid or that they have something physically wrong with their brain. In order to disabuse them of such attitudes, you must start from the beginning and teach them what they were never taught: our phonetic alphabet system, basic spelling, basic arithmetic, etc. Many kids get through high school without ever having been taught these basics, and the result is that their education is a mess.

Colleges are now supposed to take care of these deficits in the freshman year. But more and more colleges are balking at the idea of having to do in the freshman year what should have been done in the primary, middle, and high school years. For the homeschooler, that first year at home will have to be one of intensive remediation and reeducation. Parents embarking on such a difficult course should consult with remedial experts among homeschoolers. They can be found by talking with other homeschoolers who have had similar problems. A home-schooling network will include all kinds of experts who may be able to help you or refer you to someone who can help you. Homeschoolers, you will find, are usually more than happy to share their knowledge or experiences with other homeschoolers, for there is a kind of collegial feeling among homeschoolers that they must help each other succeed, for the success of others is a reflection on the movement as a whole.

My own method of remediation consists of the following: first test the student on his or her ability to read. This can be done by having the youngster read some appropriate text to you aloud. If the reader leaves out words that are there, puts in words that aren't there, mutilates or truncates words, substitutes words, and stops cold because he or she cannot sound out a new word, then you know the reader is a victim of the whole-word teaching method. You can also administer a very simple reading test I've devised which tells you at what grade level your child is reading and where the problems are. It is called the *Blumenfeld Oral Reading Assessment Test* and consists of thirty-eight columns of words, ten words to each column, proceeding from the simplest single-syllable words to complex multisyllabic words. The purpose of the test is, first, to see if the reader knows our phonetic system, second, how he or she handles multisyllabic words, and third, at what grade level the learner is reading. The test takes about ten minutes.

I devised the test because, as a tutor, I wanted a simple and quick way of finding out what the student's reading problem was. I discovered that students who lack basic phonetic knowledge will make errors reading some of the simplest words. I also discovered that students who knew their phonics would often have trouble reading the multisyllabic words, indicating that they were basically phonetic readers but had had very little vocabulary development.

When a student is deficient in basic phonics, I will first teach him or her our alphabetic system using the *Alpha-Phonics* program. I start at the beginning and go through the entire program to make sure that nothing is missed and that the student grasps the entire system. When that is done then the job becomes one of seeing to it that the youngster knows how to apply this new phonetic knowledge to his reading. This is done by having the student read aloud some appropriate text and being made aware of his bad reading habits. For example, if the student has left out a word that is in the sentence, you have him reread the sentence until he notices that a word has been left out. When the student reads a word that isn't there, you have him reread the sentence until he sees that he has put in a word that isn't there. In other words, you stress the need for accuracy over speed in reading. When the student comes across a new multisyllabic word, you get him to break it up into syllables and sound it out. You also keep a notebook in which all the new words are written and gone over every so often. Eventually, the student will become a phonetic reader.

Thus, if you have a high schooler who needs such remediation, you can probably do the remediating yourself. It can be very expensive to hire someone else to do it for you. You may be able to find a good tutor through the homeschool network. But make sure that the tutor understands the difference between a sight reader and a phonetic reader and knows how to turn a bumbling sight reader into an accurate phonetic reader.

I tutored one senior high schooler who was entering college but was a nonreader. He was your typical sight reader making all of the errors that sight readers make. He had never read a book outside of what he had to read in school, and in general he disliked reading because it was so difficult for him. I used the remediation program outlined above, and after many months of tutoring him twice a week he finally became a phonetic reader. What was especially important was his high motivation to succeed. He was ambitious, and so I gave him some of Napoleon Hill's popular books to read on how to succeed in business and get rich. Learning that there was extremely valuable and inspirational information in books, he made excellent progress. When finally the tutoring ended he had become hooked on books. But even though he had become a good phonetic reader, he would occasionally make a sight reader's error, which meant that the sight-reading habits he acquired in the first and second grades could not be completely eradicated. But as long as the reader has the means to see his or her errors, such errors will be minimal.

Assuming that your child is now ready to do high school work, the question becomes: what kind of subjects should the child study? It is in the high-school years that young people generally begin to know what they are really interested in, what kind of career they would like to pursue, what they want to do with their lives. It is also the time to prepare for college, which means that the student must also prepare to take the Scholastic Aptitude Test (SAT) and the American College Testing (ACT) Program Assessment. Check with the college of your son's or daughter's choice since some colleges rely less on the results of these tests. The SAT is divided into Verbal and Mathematical parts. The ACT includes four tests: English, Mathematics, Reading, and Science Reasoning. If the homeschooler intends to apply for a scholarship of some kind, taking one or both tests may be necessary.

Of course, not all homeschoolers intend to go to college. For them, high school should provide the skills and knowledge needed to succeed in the working world. For example, the skill of touch typing should be taught much earlier than in the past since today's youngsters will be using computer keyboards in the elementary grades. (We shall deal with the matter of computers and technology in a later chapter.)

Since many homeschoolers will be starting their own businesses and services, it is obvious that they will keep on learning and gaining in experience as they advance in their chosen endeavors. The homeschooler has been so well imbued with the spirit of self-teaching that he will want to continue to learn as he enters the work world. In fact, advances in technology and the increasing costs of tuition now strongly suggest that homeschooling can continue into the college years. Indeed, technology will make it possible to bring the best of professors and their courses into the homes of thousands of students.

Since high school is a time when students can discover their true interests, the curriculum should offer a wide range of courses. Since we live in a country where the basic principles of government and economy determine the kinds of lives we live, knowledge of these basic principles is absolutely essential if we are to defend and maintain our inalienable rights to life, liberty, and the pursuit of happiness. Therefore, an intensive course in the history and structure of our governmental and political system should be included in the curriculum.

And so, what kind of courses would help us fulfill this basic American ideal of individual freedom? We must start, of course, with what has already been learned in grades one through eight. We assume that the basic skills of reading, writing, spelling, grammar, arithmetic, touch typing, and computer technology have been mastered in varying degrees, and that such subjects as American history, geography, science, economics, and a foreign language have been studied to the extent that a fourteen-year-old can handle them.

We assume also that the youngster has been engaged in a variety of hobbies, sports, and activities such as drawing, acting, singing, swimming, skiing, tennis, soccer, softball, and other sports; stamp or coin collecting, caring for pets, horseback riding, learning a musical instrument, hunting and target practice, running a small business, cooking, baking, helping parents, etc. We also assume that if the child is being reared in a religious home that he or she will have acquired a solid foundation in spiritual values—values that help to guide his or her family's life. The enhancement of the family's spiritual life has become part and parcel of the new lifestyle created by homeschooling, where the family is free to make religious values and religious teaching part of the curriculum.

High school simply continues to build on what has already been learned in the earlier years. It continues growth in such subjects as English, composition, mathematics, history, geography, science, economics, and foreign languages. It should particularly emphasize the expansion of vocabulary and the ability to write clearly and logically. The student must also study those subjects required for college entrance; college catalogs generally list these requirements. However, before settling on a definite curriculum, the homeschooler should write to the colleges and even speak to admissions officers for their advice and to find out if they require taking the SAT and/or ACT test. Many colleges now seek out homeschoolers as potential students and are more than willing to help them prepare for entry.

-11-

Learning Languages

The learning of a foreign language has always been accepted as an important part of becoming educated. Of course, the word educated means different things to different people. To some "educated" means "cultured," to others it means the gaining of practical knowledge with which to build a career. But virtually all agree that the most important part of education is, for obvious reasons, the mastery of one's own language. The ability to think is a direct outgrowth of language facility, and the ability to express oneself clearly, persuasively, and forcefully is a direct consequence of our ability to use language.

It is obvious why we would want to study another language. First of all, it permits us to communicate with people from other nations. It permits us to conduct business and diplomacy with other peoples. It creates a bridge between different cultures. It enhances our understanding of language in general as we compare our language to other languages and learn to translate from one language to another by learning how different thought patterns emerge from the sentence structure and grammar of another language. So there are many benefits to be obtained from the study of a foreign language, not the least of which is having entry to the literature and culture of an entirely different group of people.

In my own case, I was introduced to French in junior high school by a lovely middle-aged woman of impeccable taste. To me, learning French was the epitome of becoming cultured, even though I lived in a tenement in the Bronx and my parents spoke Yiddish, the German dialect spoken by the Jews of Eastern Europe. I loved the sound of French and was determined to learn to speak it. And so, with great effort I did in time learn to speak French as my second language. As a result I can make my way easily in France, Belgium, Switzerland, Quebec, and other places in which French is spoken. Knowing French opened a whole new world and permitted me to learn all of the French words in the English language and how to spell them correctly. And so I have always felt that it was one of the best things I learned in school.

In my opinion, I do not believe that you can be truly literate unless you have mastered a second language. I also studied Latin in college, which was a very great help in understanding so many of our multi-syllabic words which are derived from Latin. Incidentally, knowing French and Latin can be very useful in doing crossword puzzles!

If I were a student today, I do not know if I would take up French or some other language like Chinese, Japanese, Russian, or Spanish. Today's world is quite different from the world of fifty years ago. With a growing Latino population in the United States, it might make sense to study Spanish, which is spoken in Puerto Rico and throughout Central and South America, with the exception of Brazil, where Portuguese is the dominant language. And we have large Spanish-speaking populations not only in the American Southwest but in all of the large cities of the North. French may have more cultural prestige, but Spanish clearly has more practical uses for Americans.

Make your decision on a foreign language early so that you can begin teaching your homeschooler at an age when language learning seems to be easier. You can start by teaching a simple vocabulary, simple sentences, and simple grammatical rules. The best way to have your child develop a good accent is to have him or her listen to the language on cassette tapes and repeat the words as they are spoken. At that early age, the vocal cords are still flexible enough to be able to articulate the sounds of another language. If we haven't developed the ability to articulate a wide range of language sounds in those early years, we will probably not be able to do so later, after the vocal cords have stopped their growth and solidified their limited range.

Children who come from bilingual families are usually able to speak other languages with less of a foreign accent because of the wider range of their vocal cords. Perhaps this phenomenon can be compared with the ability of individuals to sing within a range of tones. But probably the vocal cords are much more flexible in the earlier years. We certainly know that singers are limited in their ranges. Sopranos cannot sing like baritones, and some people cannot sing at all. However, when it comes to developing a good accent in learning a foreign language, it may be that some people are born with a wider range of vocalizations. But we do know that a child learns to speak his own language with the local accent without any difficulty. Which means that a child is capable of learning to speak in any accent, provided that it is his first language. In fact, he is even capable of speaking more than one language without a foreign accent if they are all learned at the same time and the child's vocal cords are required to articulate all of the sounds of the several languages.

If you would like to stretch your child's vocal cords, you might use simple songs in the foreign language which would give him or her practice in articulating the sounds of that language. Audio and video cassettes are now available to help you acquaint your child with the language being learned. And there are books, magazines, and newspapers available in the foreign language. But as you progress, teach your child to speak the foreign language as grammatically correct as possible. We all know what pidgin English sounds like!

Some languages use different alphabets which have to be learned at the outset. Russian, Arabic, Hebrew, Greek, Hindi, and Armenian all use their own alphabets. The Chinese use characters, or logographs, to stand for their words. Some of these logographs are also used as phonetic indicators. The Japanese use Chinese characters (called *kanji*) as well as two sets of phonetic syllabaries or *kana* (known as *hiragana* and *katakana*). Spanish and French will seem like a lark, compared to Russian, Chinese, or Japanese.

There is also the option of learning Latin and Greek as ancient languages which have become the sources of so many of our modern words that incorporate their spellings. Latin, of course, is the favorite of classicists who truly believe in the development of expertise in the ancient classics and a knowledge of vocabulary development. Choosing the foreign language to learn can be difficult because of the many options available. If you have Japanese friends who can help, or if you yourself learned French or Russian when you were in school, or if you are of an ethnic background which you would like your child to learn more about by learning the language, then any of these factors may help you make your choice.

Back in the days when I was in school, you learned French because that was the foreign language taught to everybody; the public schools were limited in what they could offer the students. But in homeschooling, the world is your oyster. You can make your decision on the basis of a number of factors: the availability of a good program, the existence of a group of homeschoolers all learning the same language, the preferences of your child, your own knowledge of a foreign language, or your desire to acquaint your child with an ethnic heritage.

Some of the best aids to teaching your child a foreign language are knowledge of friends, neighbors, or relatives who speak that language, trips to countries where the language is spoken, foreign films in that language, student exchanges, visits to cultural centers or departments at universities that specialize in the language, foreign language bookstores and libraries, cassettes and computer software programs, local restaurants associated with that language group, ethnic fairs, etc.

Knowing a foreign language will greatly impress the admissions officers of colleges and universities, and it will certainly be a plus in looking for a job or developing a career that includes foreign travel or communication with foreigners. Journalism, diplomacy, publishing, advertising, criminal justice, intelligence work, teaching, multinational corporations—all of these require individuals who can read and speak foreign languages. We've been told until we're numb that we live in a global economy and that we must be competitive if we are to survive. What better way to meet the challenges of that global economy than by the homeschooler learning a foreign language that will give him or her an edge in the job market?

-12-

Homeschooling and the New Technology

Nothing has been a greater boon to homeschooling than the development of computer technology. In fact, it is being said that the new technology is making the schoolhouse obsolete. Lewis J. Perelman, in his landmark book *School's Out*, writes:

> This book... is not about education. It is about an economic transformation that is being driven by an implacable technological revolution. It is not about saving schools, or improving schools, or reforming schools, or even reinventing schools—it's about removing altogether the increasingly costly barrier that schooling poses to economic and social progress....
>
> Learning was an activity thought to be confined to the box of a school classroom. Now learning permeates every form of social activity—work, entertainment, home life—outside of school. For what piano lessons would cost, you now can buy an electronic piano that will teach you to play it.... Of the more than sixty million Americans who learned how to use personal computers since 1980, most learned from vendors, books, other users, and the computers themselves, not in schools....
>
> The very power of modern technology to liberate learning leaves no role for the sprawling empire of academic bureaucracy but self-serving protectionism.

And so, according to Perelman, the schoolhouse is going to go the way of the horse and buggy, but it doesn't know it yet. Homeschoolers, though, seem to know it as they fill their homes with computers, camcorders, cellular phones, VCRs, fax machines, copiers, tape recorders, CD-ROMs, printers, modems, word processors, laptops, video and audio cassettes, calculators, electronic musical instruments, and other new gadgets of the technological revolution.

But homeschoolers must never lose sight of the basic technology of alphabetic reading, cursive writing, and arithmetic, all of which must be mastered before one can make maximum use of the new technology. The purpose of the new technology is to enhance life, not distort it. It may make the school obsolete but it doesn't make learning obsolete. The basics must still be mastered.

How should the new technology be used? In the beginning, it should not be used at all by young children. They should be learning to read and getting to know books and writing by hand, not machine. They should be learning their arithmetic facts by memorization and practicing them with paper and pencil, not calculators.

Thus, the first three years of homeschooling should find minimal use of the new technology. Some good video and audio cassette tapes can be used in instruction where it makes sense. But when it comes to learning reading, writing, and arithmetic skills, there is no substitute for direct practice. The book is still the most ingenious way to pack the greatest amount of information in a portable format. And the ability to accurately and easily decode the words in that book is still the most important skill to be mastered by an individual. In other words, high literacy is a prerequisite to being able to make the greatest use of the new technology.

Most children are introduced to the computer through playing video games. Whether or not you want your children to indulge in this kind of activity is up to you. Ask yourself, What skills are my children learning by playing such games? Are some games just an exciting way of killing time? Couldn't that time be better spent reading a good book? Games, of course, are a part of a child's life. There are all sorts of board games to choose, from checkers to Monopoly. Games, including some computer games, which require thought and strategy are good exercises for the mind. And games like Monopoly can be played by the entire family.

Before using CD-ROMs, first show your child where that same information can be obtained in an encyclopedia or world atlas. Make your child feel at home in the world of books before showing how the contents of books have been put onto CDs. There are now encyclopedias on CD-ROMs; all sorts of reference books are being put onto CD-ROMs. In fact, an entire law library has been put on a few CD-ROMs, thus permitting a lawyer to carry his entire library on a plane and to have access to it with a laptop. But these are the conveniences the new technology affords adults. Children still have to go through the process of learning the basics before they can make use of this marvelous new technology.

As we pointed out in an earlier chapter, teach your child touch typing before letting him or her loose on a word processor; otherwise, your child will be hobbled by hunting and pecking for the rest of his or her life. Before learning to touch type, the child can use the keyboard to find information on the computer, if all he or she has to do is press the "enter" key or some other instructional key, or move and click a mouse.

Surfing the Internet is something parents should learn to do first before setting their children loose. The Internet permits immediate worldwide access to incredible amounts of information on just about any subject one can think of. However, the various moral dangers of the Net have been well publicized by the media, and so it is up to parents to decide whether or not to make the Internet available to their children. My view is that neither computers nor Internet access are desirable or necessary in the primary years of homeschooling. Professional parents who already have computers in their home may want to make use of them for their children. But it is better to get the child hooked on books before letting him get hooked on the computer. Most of the homeschoolers I know do not rely much on the new technology in teaching their children the traditional subjects. Some homeschoolers have even eliminated the television set from their lives.

TV OR NOT TV, THAT'S THE QUESTION

Back in 1993, the *Boston Globe* reported the story of a Maine family with two elementary school kids that decided to eliminate television in their home for a year. Pretty soon they were all reading books for entertainment, and at dinner they had lively family discussions that extended well beyond the meal's end. The transition from TV to no TV was not as difficult as they thought it would be. They all adjusted nicely to their new way of life. To make the situation more palatable, the parents decided to pay their children one dollar for every day they stayed away from the tube. According to the parents, the expense was well worth it. They saw wonderful changes in their kids' behavior. There was a decrease in aggression, a deeper friendship between the two children, more leisure time spent in imaginative play, an increase in book reading from almost zero to three or four books a week, and an increase in family time.

Prior to the experiment, one of the children, who had been a good reader until the third grade, was spending many hours a week watching TV and only five or ten minutes a day reading. But once the TV was turned off, things began to change. The kids began to play together, to seek out each other's company. They played card games, Legos, and read lots of books. In fact, the parents had to ban book reading at the dinner table.

The TV ban was for only a year. But the parents noticed that the children did not OD on TV when it was restored. They became more discriminating watchers. Parents can learn much from this experiment. One thing, however, is certain. Homeschooling parents are in a much better position to control what goes on in the home and how their kids are to be brought up than those parents who send their kids to school to be "educated."

Getting back to the new technology and its uses, it is the homeschooled high schooler who stands to benefit most from having all of the new high-tech equipment at home, simply because he has more time to use it. In school, the computer is not always available when one wants it. It must be shared with many other students, and after school hours it is locked away. The homeschooler, on the other hand, has the computer available whenever she wants to use it. She may have to share the equipment with other members of the family, but because the computer is at home, it is much more readily available. Thus, home-schoolers can spend many more hours learning how to use the computer and developing overall computer competency. The student may also want to develop his or her own Web page and start communicating via e-mail with others around the world.

If, as a parent, you don't know much about computers, you will find many excellent articles in homeschool magazines about computers and how to make the best use of them. Also, you will find that many homeschooling dads are programmers and, by now, many teenage homeschoolers have become computer experts. They will help you choose a good computer and show you how to use it. For example, many libraries now have their card catalogs on computers which are "on line" and therefore accessible through a modem. A modem is simply a gadget that hooks up your computer to the phone system so that you can have access to other computers on line. That's how one gets onto the Internet or gets into the computerized card catalog of a library. Check with your local library to see if its catalog is on line. If it is, it can save you the bother of going to the library to get a book that is out on loan and it can help your children find the books that are of interest to them.

Another great instrument of the new technology is the camcorder. Playing with a camcorder will introduce the homeschooler to the art of moviemaking. The student may produce a documentary video about the history of his or her hometown, or produce a video of how a parent prepares his or her famous recipe. Why not video the parent as a homegrown Julia Child or Galloping Gourmet and get it shown on your local public access television? Also, a good video about one's grandparents may serve not only to preserve some family history for future generations but may also provide needed practice in making good videos, thus preparing the child for a possible career in television production.

After the student has learned to write compositions by hand and has also learned how to touch type, you can introduce him to the word processor. Here the child will find the most convenient way to write letters, compositions, articles, and stories. With word processing, it is as easy as pie to correct a wrong spelling, to revise the text, to insert or delete a word, to capitalize, italicize, use different fonts, different type sizes, etc. The student can create his own letterhead, and publish a family newsletter which can be sent out at Christmastime to far-off relatives and friends.

There is also computer software that permits one to do artwork on the computer. New ways of using the computer are being invented daily by ingenious programmers and software engineers. Any perusal of the many magazines now devoted to computer technology will tend to overwhelm the average individual with advances in the field. Like the invention of the alphabet, the computer is permitting us to do so much more with so much less. While we of the older generation got along pretty well without computers, the younger generation will have little choice but to make computers an integral part of their lives. The self-employed will find computers providing them with a power hitherto unavailable to those who worked at home or in their own small companies. And homeschooling will encourage more and more young people to become entrepreneurs, using computers to give them as much economic freedom and power as possible.

All in all, the new technology is not only making the school obsolete, it is providing the homeschooler with a variety of ingenious learning tools that can best be used in the home. In other words, in the new information age, the home has become the most convenient place in which to learn and communicate with the world. And with parents sharing in the learning experience with their children, everyone is getting educated.

-13-

What About Socialization?

Yes, what about socialization? That's the question most frequently asked by people skeptical of homeschooling. When the litany of public school failures and risks is recited as reasons why parents choose to homeschool, the skeptics will ignore all of that and ask what is supposed to be the stumping question of all questions: what about socialization? The answer, believe it or not, is that homeschoolers are far better socialized than public schoolers.

Several highly sophisticated research studies confirm that home-schooled kids are better socially adjusted than their public school counterparts. Two such studies were published in 1992 in the *Home School Researcher*, edited by Dr. Brian D. Ray of the National Home Education Research Institute. The studies followed the guidelines in the *Publication Manual of the American Psychological Association* and are therefore considered highly professional and reliable in their methodology.

Perhaps the most interesting study done thus far on socialization is one by Dr. Larry E. Shyers in central Florida with seventy homeschooled kids and seventy traditionally schooled kids aged eight, nine, and ten. The seventy kids from each group—thirty-five boys and thirty-five girls—were of the same socioeconomic group, were also involved in the same outside activities and, in general, were as similar as possible. The only significant difference was that one group was being homeschooled while the other group was in school outside the home.

When Dr. Shyers started the study in 1981, he believed that the social adjustment of the homeschoolers would be far worse than that of the traditionally schooled, and he expected that his research would confirm that. But the results proved him wrong. From every standpoint the homeschoolers proved to be much better socially adjusted than the traditionally schooled kids. Even Dr. Shyers was surprised at the degree of difference in social adjustment he found between the two groups.

How does one go about measuring socialization? Social scientists do it by first defining social skills and then providing a framework for classifying social skills difficulties. Dr. Shyers writes:

> Their definition of social skills includes peer acceptance, socially acceptable behavior, and validation of behavior by significant people in the child's life. . . . For a child to be socially well adjusted, therefore, he or she must meet several conditions. First, he or she must possess a knowledge of the skill to be performed. Second, he or she must feel comfortable enough to both learn and perform the skill acceptably. And thirdly, he or she must be able to perform the skill appropriately at levels deemed acceptable by others.

Dr. Shyers used three assessment instruments to measure the children's socialization skills: the *Children's Assertive Behavior Scale (CABS)*, the *Piers-Harris Children's Self Concept Scale (PHCSCS)*, and the *Direct Observation Form (DOF)* of the *Child Behavior Checklist*. In other words, the study was about as scientific as one could make it. The results, according to Dr. Shyers, were as follows:

> The results of the data analysis indicated that both groups of children received scores on the *PHCSCS* that were above the national average. This suggests that how children view themselves may be independent of where they obtain their academic training. . . .
>
> Both groups of children received raw scores on the *CABS* that were indications that they choose slightly passive responses to social situations. This indicates that the children in this study were not aggressive, but rather somewhat passive in their understanding of social situations. . . .
>
> The most significant results of this study were found in actual observed behaviors. The *DOF* records problem behaviors by type and frequency. Home schooled students received significantly lower problem behavior scores than did their agemates from traditional programs. . . .
>
> Bandura (1977) suggested that children learn to behave from observing and imitating others. It is reasonable to expect that children will imitate the behaviors that they observe most often.

Traditionally schooled children spend an average of seven hours per weekday over a nine-month period in the presence of other children and few adults. It would seem then, that their behaviors would most often reflect those of the majority of the children with whom they associate. In the case of this study, it was observed that traditionally schooled children tended to be considerably more aggressive, loud, and competitive than were the home schooled children of the same age.

In the case of the home schooled children, most of their day is spent with their parents and very few children. The primary models for behavior, therefore, are adults. Based on the social learning theory that children learn by imitating the behaviors of people whom they observe, home schooled children would thus most likely imitate the behaviors of their parents. The home schooled children in this study tended to be quiet, nonaggressive, and noncompetitive. Each child appeared to make up his or her own mind on how to behave.

The results of this study, therefore, draw into question the conclusions made by many educators and courts that traditionally educated children are more socially well adjusted than are those who are home schooled. . . . Although the traditionally educated children participating in this study achieved high mean self-concept and acceptable assertiveness scores, their mean problem behavior scores were well above the normal range . . . indicating a lack of appropriate social behaviors. This finding supports many parents', educators', and researchers' suggestions that traditionally schooled children may not be socially well adjusted.

In contrast, the home schooled children in this study received mean problem behaviors scores well within the normal range on the *DOF.* This finding supports the belief held by home school proponents that home schooled children are socially well adjusted.

What could be plainer than that? Traditionally schooled kids tend to be socially maladjusted because they learn their social skills from other kids. All you have to do is observe students emerging from a public school. The noise, rowdiness, and foul language are widespread. A good number of the kids light up cigarettes as soon as they get out of the school building. They behave badly on buses and subways, rattling the nerves of adults who must travel with them. The schools themselves have become violent places. John Holt, the pioneer founder of *Growing Without Schooling*, observed in letters to a friend written in 1980:

> Since I last wrote a man in Boston called me up. . . . What he has to say was that one of his boys was in the second grade at school in Roxbury, which is known for being one of the best elementary schools in the city, and that there was so much racially organized group violence in the second grade... that his son couldn't think about anything but whether he would be beaten up that day. Finally the father decided that he had no choice but to take him out of school.
>
> This may not be a bad place to say that, from the reports I get, which means hundreds of letters from all parts of the country, children in schools are noticeably more violent, among each other, than they were ten or fifteen years ago. This is equally true in small towns and big cities, and in all parts of the country, and among all income classes. . . .
>
> I see that in my previous letter I referred to the many letters I get about the brutal treatment of children in our elementary schools. These letters continue. I don't print them in *GWS* {*Growing Without Schooling*}, for many reasons: we don't have enough space, most of our readers already know that schools are bad, we are more interested in how to get out and what to do instead. But these letters, about stupid, brutal, and cruel treatment of even very young children in schools, continue to come in, from all parts of the country.

And so, if you are asked, "What about socialization?" Just reply: "Yes, I am concerned about socialization, and that's why I'm getting my kids out of the public school and have decided to homeschool." The only kind of socialization the schools can provide these days is the negative kind. Even in the good old days socialization was a problem. I was beaten up by a fellow classmate in kindergarten. I was terrorized by a group of kids in junior high school. But that was nothing compared to what students must put up with today. Kids now bring weapons to school to protect themselves from assault and even murder. Many kids won't even go into a school bathroom because of fear of being robbed or beaten up.

There is also another kind of negative socialization that Lewis Perelman talks about in *School's Out*. He calls it social polarization. He writes:

Penelope Eckert, an anthropologist at the Institute for Research on Learning, has found in her studies that a major social impact produced by the normal schooling context, culminating in high school, is to divide youth into lifelong cultures of winners and losers. "While curricular tracking has come and gone in the American public schools, adolescent social categories remain as an enduring and uncontrolled social tracking system," Eckert observes. "It is largely as a result of the polarization between the Jocks and the Burnouts that people are thrown into a choice between two set patterns of behavior on the basis of a variety of unrelated interests and needs...."

Moreover, this pernicious form of socialization is the result not of school quality or administration or location but of the inherent structure of the institution itself. In particular, Eckert finds that "the segregation of adolescents in an age-graded institution, isolated from the surrounding community, focuses their attention on the population, the activities and the roles that are available within the school," instead of those of what we commonly call *the real world.*

In homeschooling there is no social polarization. There are no losers; there are only winners. Another pernicious form of negative socialization is that suffered by girls who must compete with boys in coed schools. According to Perelman, there is "a growing body of research showing that girls in all-female schools maintain high levels of self-esteem and accomplishment in all fields including math and science, while the confidence and performance of girls in coed schools take a steep and steady nosedive after about grade seven or eight." Why does this happen? Perelman explains:

Detailed analyses of video records of classroom behavior show that teachers or professors, both male and female, persistently call on, praise, and encourage males several times more frequently than they do females. The teachers rarely realize they are being biased; they are reflexively acting out rituals deeply embedded in the culture of schooling.

No such bias would be found in a homeschooling mom or dad who would want all of their kids to do the best, regardless of gender. Homeschooling eliminates school-manufactured failure, social polarization, and gender bias. Perelman writes (p. 163):

These are just a few facets of the dark side of the force that school passes off as socialization. "[B]y the time students reach high school," Eckert observes, "the Jocks and the Burnouts are all too generally perceived as representing good and bad, cooperation and rebelliousness, success and failure, intelligence and stupidity." For the losers, the lessons of socialization become articles of surrender—Eckert finds that "[r]ather than asking themselves how they can succeed in spite of the school, Burnouts discard goals along with the means to achieve them."

The myth of the decline of schooling is that our students are failing to learn. The real outrage of schooling is that our students are learning to fail.

Another fascinating study on socialization was conducted by Thomas C. Smedley and published in the *Home School Researcher* in 1992 (vol. 8, no. 3). Mr. Smedley writes:

> The insights and tools of communication study enable us to operationalize and test the variable "socialization." This paper borrows from the concepts of the "interactional" school of thought, which holds that communication is the means by which people create social reality. Socialization and communication are seen as inseparable components of life experience. A well-socialized child, from this perspective, can ably navigate the social and communications environment.

The survey instrument used to measure socialization was the *Vineland Adaptive Behavior Scales (VABS)*. The data were collated and processed using the *Statistical Program for the Social Sciences (SPSS)*. The children studied in this project consisted of thirty-three homeschooled children of white, middle class, Protestant families, sixteen females, seventeen males, recruited mainly from a homeschool support group in Virginia, the Greater Roanoke Home Educator's Association (GRHEA). An equal number of public schoolers from similar white, middle class, Protestant families were chosen for the control group. All in all, only thirty-three forms were adequately completed by parents under field conditions. Twenty of the cases were homeschoolers; thirteen were public schoolers. The results were quite dramatic. Mr. Smedley writes:

> The findings of this study indicate that children kept home are more mature and better socialized than those who are sent to

school. . . . The public school students surveyed attend well-funded and well-staffed middle-class schools. The public school students even share the religious values of the home school children. Yet, the socialization difference is there.

What, then, is the best mechanism for socializing children? . . . If good socialization is synonymous with communication excellence, is the classroom an enriched or impoverished *communication* environment?

The classroom is mostly one-way communication, along stereotyped and rote channels. Information flows at the pace dictated by the teacher. Given the size of classes, few meaningful interchanges are possible on a given day between teacher and individual student.

This contrasts to the home education communication environment. Ten children is small for a class, but large for a family. Each child at home has immediate access to the attention of a significant adult. Home educators stress the initiative and responsibility of the individual student, and build community through voluntary cooperation rooted in a common faith, a common perception of duties. . . .

An unnatural aspect of the public school environment is the age segregation. Learning to get along with peers does not necessarily prepare the student for interactions with older and younger people in real life.

In the home school family, on the other hand, people of various ages and generations mix easily together in a variety that more accurately mirrors the outside society. . . . Younger siblings are best friends, not embarrassments. When 100+ home school kids roller skate together, it is often reported that the crowd is noteworthy for its orderliness and pleasantness. . . .

[P]arental availability means that, during the course of an average day, home school adults and children likely have hundreds of interactions.

And that's the key to the better social adjustment of homeschooled kids: the availability of parents. How often do we hear adults lamenting the lack of parental interest and availability they experienced as children? It's a constant theme in the lives of drug addicts or delinquents or alcoholics. It's the "where-were-you-when-I-needed-you?" syndrome.

Finally, when I was in Australia in 1991, I visited James Cook

University in Townsville, Queensland, where I was able to spend a couple of hours reading the Ph.D. dissertation of Brian Cambourne, head of the Centre for Studies in Literacy at Wollongong University. Dr. Cambourne is one of Australia's leading advocates of Whole Language instruction, not a particular friend of homeschooling. The aim of his thesis was to determine in which environmental setting first-grade children learned language best: in school, on the playground, or at home. His findings were quite startling. He wrote:

> [O]f the three settings in which spontaneous speech was recorded, it would appear that the home setting is the most nurturant and the classroom setting is the least nurturant in terms of the development of the skills of sentence-combining. The results obtained in this study would suggest that the agents and conditions experienced by the child in the home setting interact in such a way as to predispose him to a more extensive application of embedding transformations than either of the other two settings. In terms of the way in which Moffett (1968) conceptualises the relationship between language and thinking, the home environments sampled in this study appear to be ones in which the child is most constrained to "specify" and "relate," which in turn helps move him toward mature thought and speech. . . .
>
> On the basis of sociolinguistic theory, it is reasonable to generalise these findings to other aspects of language-use. That is, from the point of view of, say, arguing, giving directions, explaining, defining, describing and even increasing vocabulary skills, the same relationship ought to hold—i.e. one-to-one dialogue with older, more skillful users of the language, is a basic requirement. It is also interesting to note that, from the point of view of spontaneously produced speech, the home setting appeared to be the one in which the higher levels of sentence-combining occurred. This suggests that a secure, warm, parental-like relationship between interlocutors is one of the factors which is conducive to higher levels of performance.

I think that Professor Cambourne just about makes the case for homeschooling. As far as socialization is concerned, for many parents the public school variety all too often means violence, drugs, sex, alcohol, foul language and a dumbed-down, impaired intellect.

-14-

Homeschooling and Spiritual Values

For the first twenty years of the homeschool movement, religion has clearly been the strongest motive for parents to remove their children from the public schools. The increasingly hostile attitude of the schools toward biblical religion apparently has disturbed Christian parents more than any other school deficiency. The result is that today the homeschool movement is largely Christian in character with strong statewide homeschooling associations promoting a distinctly Christian approach to parental responsibility and education in general.

The doctrine of the separation of church and state, which originally was intended to forbid the government from establishing an official state religion, has been reinterpreted by some judges and educators to mean the separation of state from religion or a belief in God, particularly the God of the Bible. This has led to such extreme measures that in one county in Kentucky, school bus drivers were warned not to say Merry Christmas to any of the children. Presumably, they could say "Happy holidays," but not Merry Christmas for the obvious reason that pronouncing the name Christ in Christmas violated the now sacred separation of church and state.

John Leo reported in *U.S. News & World Report* (December 12, 1996) that the principal of Loudoun High School in Virginia told student editors to keep the school newspaper as secular as possible and "to be careful that they don't associate the upcoming holiday with any particular religion." Leo further reported that some schools allow only instrumental versions of traditional Christmas carols for fear that the words might contaminate the students' minds with religious sentiments. Schools in

Scarsdale, New York, actually forbade the singing of "Jingle Bells" and "Frosty," which is an indication to what length some public schools will go to keep out of their classrooms any reference to biblical religion, although it can hardly be said that "Jingle Bells" or "Frosty" have any serious religious connotations.

Many parents believe that to omit the spiritual dimension from education is a serious mistake. They believe that children, indeed, have a spiritual component in their makeup that must be nurtured, if the child is to develop into a well-rounded, moral human being. Robert Coles, author of *The Moral Life of Children* and *The Spiritual Life of Children*, writes of how children learn the common spiritual and moral values of their society through church attendance, Bible stories, or the example of committed adults. Thus, reading books that promote moral character can be an excellent way to promote spiritual values. Thomas Lickona, author of *Educating for Character*, writes, "If we want to raise good children, we must help them fall in love with what is noble and good."

A very good book that can help homeschoolers and educators to inculcate moral values is *Books That Build Character* by William Kilpatrick and Gregory and Suzanne Wolfe. The book is a guide to teaching moral values through stories. The authors write:

> Stories, histories, and myths played an essential role in character education in the past. The Greeks learned about right and wrong from the example of Ulysses and Penelope, and a host of other characters. The Romans learned about virtue and vice from Plutarch's *Lives*. Jews and Christians learned from Bible stories or stories about the lives of prophets, saints, missionaries, and martyrs. And new research suggests that they were right. In the June 1990 issue of *American Psychologist*, Paul Vitz, a professor at New York University, provides an extensive survey of recent psychological studies, all pointing to "the central importance of stories in developing moral life." Narrative plots have a powerful influence on us, says Vitz, because we tend to interpret our own lives as stories or narratives.

How right Professor Vitz is. We do tend to see our own lives as stories and narratives, and that's why parents are so concerned over what their children see on television or in the movies or read in school textbooks. Indeed, many Jewish and Muslim parents are also beginning to realize that homeschooling is a viable alternative to the present antireligious public schools. The secular curriculum has tended to undermine the religious beliefs of all children, Christian and non-Christian alike. Even some Unitarian parents, who have traditionally supported public education, have joined the homeschool movement and created their own support association. When even Unitarians begin to express dismay at the way the public schools are educating their children, one can believe that homeschooling is bound to grow among the more secularized of our population.

In other words, whether or not you believe in God, there are plenty of other reasons why parents should remove their children from the public schools and teach them at home. One of the oldest homeschooling groups is written about in John Holt's *Growing Without Schooling*, which approaches homeschooling from a secular viewpoint. Holt was deeply concerned with how the bureaucratically run state education machine was destroying the minds of countless children. He felt that the school, as a kind of self-serving institution, had become an actual obstacle to learning and that it thrived on failure because failure got it more money. He wrote in *A Life Worth Living*, a compilation of letters edited by Susannah Sheffer:

> I hardly think any more that it's possible to be a full-time teacher, I don't care [in] what kind of school or institutional setting, without somehow corrupting the relationships between oneself and other people... In the last year or two I have found myself really *hating* schools with an intensity that seemed to me almost irrational, and that I could hardly explain even to people who agree with me a lot.... (p. 216)
>
> My deep and long-range concern is not just to get children out of schools but to help knock down all the barriers we have put up between children and the world of serious adults.... (p. 230)
>
> It is *extremely* difficult to talk to people in education—and most difficult of all at the college or university level—without getting into an unpleasant kind of verbal battle.... (p. 231)
>
> A school is a place that exists only to take care of kids, and *as such* is more likely than not to be more bad than good for kids, no matter who is running it.... (p. 233)
>
> Most of the people in teaching, and I mean something like 90% or more, are incurious, unintelligent, mentally lazy people who distrust, dislike, fear, and even hate kids.... In most schools the kids don't like or trust any adult. Their unspoken and

perfectly justified question to you would be, "If you're such a good person, what are you doing in this stinking place?" (p. 250)

Holt had come to the homeschool movement through a purely secular process. His teaching experience, in which he saw how bored and frightened the children were, led him to believe that the schools had to be reformed. He argued that the school's big mistake was in thinking that it had to make children do what they naturally wanted to do, and knew how to do, namely learn about the world around them. Consequently, he became active in the free-school, or alternative-school, movement of the 1960s in which it was thought that schools could become places where children could be independent, self-directing learners. But by the mid-1970s many of the alternative schools had closed, and the basic ideas behind them had been absorbed into the mainstream school establishment. But none of this was enough to reform the system.

With the failure of the free-school movement, Holt was attracted to the deschooling movement sparked by the sociologist Ivan Illich, whose book *Deschooling Society* was published in 1970. To Illich deschooling society not only meant doing away with the physical school but also doing away with society's schooling mentality, which gave schools their credentialing power. Thus, it was this schooling mentality or mindset that maintained these self-serving, debilitating institutions in which children unlearned their natural desire to learn.

Once Holt had decided that the schools could not be adequately reformed because of their intrinsic bureaucratic, antihuman nature and that deschooling was the only way to restore sanity to education in America, he began to think of how this radical change could be brought about. He decided that home education was the best way to go, because parents would not have to wait for others to do the reforming for them, and home education would demonstrate that parents and children could teach and learn and make their way in the working world without the need of an institution called a school. And so, in 1977 Holt launched *Growing Without Schooling* magazine, which has become one of the world's leading publications promoting the liberation of children from state schooling. When John Holt died in 1985, homeschooling was already well established as a viable alternative to the ever unreformable public school.

Meanwhile, on the Christian front, the Rev. Rousas J. Rushdoony, a leading Calvinist theologian and author of *The Messianic Character of American Education,* had been persuading parents through his writings and lectures to abandon the state schools and put their children in good Christian schools or educate them at home. Although mainline Christian churches still supported the public schools, young Christian parents were being attracted to more fundamentalist churches which generally advocated a biblical approach to education. Many of these parents decided to homeschool as they found that only through home education could a new Christian family lifestyle be achieved. In such a family, the father assumed spiritual leadership, there were daily devotions and prayers, there was a suitable division of labor in which everyone had something useful to do, and children absorbed the values of their parents. And because in such a family, the parents lived in obedience to God's law as taught in the Bible, disciplining children was not at all difficult. When children saw their parents living in obedience to God's law, it served as a model whereby the children could see their own need to submit to the authority of their parents.

Therefore, religion has become the backbone of the Christian homeschool movement and given it an ideological cohesion and purpose that parents need when they decide to defy common practice and make a clean break with society's statist institutions. But this is the kind of quiet revolutionary action that is required if the American Christian family is to be restored to its full purpose as a carrier of Christianity to its own children. People often wonder how it was possible for the Jewish people to survive persecution and maintain their religion through the centuries, deprived of their own land, and forced to live among other nations with other religions. It was done by one generation transferring its values to the next generation through daily, consistent family practice and education. Ironically, in America, where Jews have had the greatest freedom to thrive as human beings, secular education has done more to destroy religious belief among young Jews than any other influence, proving that once the religious bridge between generations is destroyed, the next generation is unlikely to inherit its parents' values.

Homeschooling has done much to restore religion to family life; it has also restored spiritual values to education. As long as the doctrine of separation of church and state prevents the teaching of religion in public schools, it will make it impossible for public education to transfer the spiritual values of one generation to the next. Which suggests that the only way to restore spiritual values to schools is to privatize them by getting the government out of the education business. In other words, the separation of school and state should be as desirable as the separation of church and state. If that were done, Americans would have a much greater choice of schools for their children—secular schools, Christian schools, Jewish schools, Islamic schools—eliminating the never-ending conflict over who is to control the government schools.

But by the time the American people are willing to accept that separation, technology and homeschooling will have made the school as a teaching institution totally obsolete. It is unlikely that those who have been homeschooled will choose schools for their own children, for they will have learned firsthand how much better a family is that educates its own children, and how much better off are the children when they are educated at home by loving parents in the context of a happy family life. There is no better preparation for adulthood than that.

-15-

Homeschooling and
the Community

Although the number of children being homeschooled is still quite small compared to the 45 million in public schools, most people are unaware of how influential the homeschoolers are becoming as a social and political force as their movement grows larger and stronger. Most homeschooling parents merely want to be left alone so that they can carry out their parental responsibilities with as little interference from the government as possible. But it is the tendency of bureaucrats not to want to leave people alone, especially if there is a regulation to be enforced.

Compulsory school attendance laws give some bureaucrats a kind of license to enforce regulations as if they were laws. Nor have the courts been very helpful in this matter. In fact, one of the things that homeschoolers have learned in their dealings with the courts is how ignorant judges can be not only of education laws but of the U.S. Constitution to which many homeschoolers turn for protection from unwarranted violations of family privacy and parental rights.

All of which means that homeschoolers have been forced to become interested in politics because it is now evident that educational policies are not made by bureaucrats or truant officers but by legislators who pass laws which affect parents and children. The National Education Association, the largest and most powerful labor union in the United States, has been hostile toward homeschooling ever since educators began to fear it as a future threat to the government's virtual monopoly on education. The N.E.A. would like nothing better than to get state legislatures and the Congress to put homeschoolers out of business. And because they have professional lobbyists working full time to get their legislative agendas passed, homeschoolers have had to start worrying about the men who are elected to state legislatures and the Congress. Several years ago, this writer asked a legislator in Alaska what his stand was on parental rights. He confessed that he had none and didn't even know that parental rights might become an issue. Thus, the need to educate legislators.

Meanwhile, networks of activists, concerned with the ongoing crisis in American education, have begun to monitor what is going on in the state legislatures and Congress and are using phones, faxes, and letters to contact their representatives and let their views be known. That's how it became possible for a small group of activists to alert the network when an amendment was added to an education bill in Congress that would have required homeschoolers to be certified teachers. The Congress received so many phone calls and faxes from homeschoolers across the nation that the telephone system shut down due to overload. And believe it or not, the entire alert was initiated by an activist in New Jersey who had phoned her congressman and asked if such an amendment had been put in the bill.

The phone and fax barrage was enough to force the congressmen to reconsider the amendment and delete it from the bill. That's the kind of strength and political power the homeschool movement has quietly built up and which only now is beginning to be felt in state capitals and the halls of Congress. In other words, out of necessity, many homeschoolers have become political activists because they have come to realize that their freedom is not guaranteed by a Constitution which is so routinely ignored and violated by judges, bureaucrats, educators, and legislators.

Thus, the homeschool movement is gradually beginning to change our political and educational culture. Homeschoolers believe that the state, through compulsory education laws and child-protection agencies, has invaded the realm of the family and, in many cases, deprived families of their fundamental rights to bring up their own children in accordance with their own values. That is why the Home School Legal Defense Association has become active in trying to limit what the state can do to affect family life.

And so, if you intend to become a homeschooler, be prepared to get involved, through a state association or a local support group, in political and community activities. This is necessary if homeschoolers are to make their neighbors sympathetic toward homeschoolers and politicians aware that homeschoolers are a force to be reckoned with. Of late, more and more newspapers and magazines are publishing sympathetic stories about homeschooling. But because homeschooling "is not for everyone," it is still considered by many as more of a curiosity than a viable alternative to public education. The establishment still promotes the idea that the schools can be reformed and improved, and that is why the vast majority of Americans still go along with that notion, and almost every state legislature in the Union has passed expensive, radical education reform programs that are supposed to end the education crisis but won't.

Yet, while homeschooling, as we are constantly reminded by its detractors, "is not for everyone," there are thousands if not millions of parents who would be willing to try it if they knew more about it. That's where home educators can help by spreading the word about the benefits of home education. Some state associations have gotten their governors to proclaim a Home Education Week, during which homeschoolers can set up tables in public libraries and elsewhere to inform the public about homeschooling, distribute literature, do workshops, have student recitals, etc. The public should also be made aware that homeschoolers, by educating their children at home at their own expense, are saving the community lots of money. If it costs the state $5,000 to educate a child in a public school, five thousand homeschoolers would be saving the state $25 million! That's the kind of information that would make the taxpayer appreciate what homeschoolers are doing.

In addition, homeschoolers are producing competent, literate young adults who will be less inclined to rely on government help and subsidies for their advancement. Homeschoolers tend to be entrepreneurs because of their sense of responsibility and self-reliance which home education by its very nature inculcates. They tend to be active self-starters and participants rather than passive watchers of the game. They are high on morality and practically zero on delinquency. Thus, the homeschooling movement is contributing productive, honest, generally ambitious young adults who will be a credit to any community.

There are many things homeschoolers can do to make the community aware of the home education movement. Take your child to the state legislature and let him or her watch the lawmakers at their business. Afterward, have your kids meet their representative. A homemade pie, or cookies, presented to the representative and his staff will make a lasting, favorable impression. Everyone loves wholesome, well-behaved kids. In fact, the best advertisement for homeschooling is homeschooled kids. Take a group of homeschoolers to visit the mayor or the governor. Politicians understand the need to appear benevolent toward children if they want to be reelected.

Also, do not be afraid to take your children to the supermarket or mall during hours when other kids are in school. If anyone asks how come your kids aren't in school, just tell them that you are a homeschooling family and that you make your own schedule. This may surprise or even shock some citizens. But actually one finds that more and more people have heard about homeschooling and that some of them may even know of a family that is homeschooling. You might hand the questioner a little brochure describing the benefits of homeschooling, prepared by your support group. And you might inform an interested parent about when the next homeschooling convention or workshop is taking place in your area. In other words, become a proselytizer for home education. It will get Americans to start questioning their assumptions about education, particularly the notion that education can't take place without school and that parents are not qualified to educate their own children. It is this public school mentality that keeps so many parents from enjoying the benefits and pleasures of home education.

One of the great pleasures of parenthood is the sheer delight in transferring to one's own children the knowledge and values that one holds dear. But when parents put their children in public and sometimes even private schools, strangers impart their own values to the children under their care, and children generally accept them even though they may conflict with the values of their parents. That's how teenage rebellion often gets started.

In any case, the contribution that homeschoolers will be making to our country in the decades ahead can only be seen as positive. Some of them will become legislators or lawyers or judges, and that's when we shall see some really significant social and cultural changes taking place in America.

-16-

A New Family Lifestyle

During the past few years much has been written about the breakdown of the American family. Unwed motherhood, single-parent families on welfare, rampant divorce, child abuse, and spouse abuse have just about put the American family on the endangered species list. Even the word *family* itself is undergoing redefinition. But in the midst of all of this gloom about the increase in dysfunctional families, a brand new model of a happy family is emerging in America. In fact, one of the most positive developments of the homeschool movement is the emergence of a new family lifestyle centered on child rearing and education.

In the homeschooling family, education becomes the cement of family togetherness, a dynamic kind of togetherness that adds a new intellectual, spiritual, and cultural dimension to family life. Because the emphasis is on knowledge and the development of creative and productive skills, the family becomes a rich source of intellectual discussion and experience.

In homeschooling, the family becomes a place where everyone learns. The younger children learn by hearing and seeing the older children being taught. And parents learn by teaching their own children subject matter that they may have forgotten or may never have learned. In a way, homeschooling parents learn more than the children because they are in a position to expand their knowledge from a broader base that includes life's experiences.

The new family lifestyle is shaped by the fact that parents and children get to know one another very well. They spend more time together, they do more things together, they become aware of each family member's idiosyncrasies, talents, and difficulties. The children, because of all the direct attention they get from their parents, develop a greater sense of emotional security and a knowledge that they are especially loved and appreciated because mom and dad are willing to devote so much time to them. Thus, family bonding is stronger and deeper than in the nonhomeschooling family.

When the children grow up and leave home, family ties remain as strong as ever, because they are based on the special bonding that produces rich, lifelong friendships among siblings. And when home-schooled chidren get married, they have a model of family life that permits them to duplicate what they enjoyed as children and to pass it on to their own children.

The importance of family ties cannot be overestimated. We all know of adopted children who spend years trying to find their biological parents. And we've seen on television some of these emotional reunions in which mother and child who haven't known or seen one another in twenty or thirty years embrace each other in a way that seems uncanny. The yearning to be connected with one's blood relatives is the same yearning that connects us to the human race. Some children, abandoned at birth on a church doorstep or in a garbage can, will in adult life go to great lengths to find some knowledge of the mother who abandoned them. What a scar such abandonment leaves on the psyche of the child who becomes, as an adult, so obsessed with his or her origin.

And that is why the homeschool family lifestyle represents such a powerful force, for it is a family lifestyle that is child-centered and child loving. Bringing up kids becomes the focal point of family life, and that is why the children are so well adjusted and emotionally secure. Homeschoolers tend to enjoy kids and want to have many of them, because each act of creation produces a new human being who adds joy to the family. When a new son or daughter or sister or brother enters the family, that gives each family member an additional blood relative with whom to bond and share life's experiences.

Homeschooling families seldom experience the traumas of teenage rebellion which occur when children develop values that conflict with the values of their parents. In homeschooling, parents transfer their values to their children. In public schools, the values of that institution tend to replace the values taught at home, and today's public schools place great emphasis on changing children's values to conform with the values of the school. Social scientist Prof. Benjamin Bloom of the University of

Chicago, made that objective very clear in his book, *Taxonomy of Educational Objectives*, first published in 1958. He wrote:

> By educational objectives, we mean explicit formulations of the ways in which students are expected to be changed by the educative process. That is, the ways in which they will change in their thinking, their feelings, and their actions. . . .
>
> The evidence points out convincingly to the fact that age is a factor operating against attempts to effect a complete or thorough-going reorganization of attitudes and values. . . .
>
> The evidence collected thus far suggests that a single hour of classroom activity under certain conditions may bring about a major reorganization in cognitive as well as affective behaviors. We are of the opinion that this will prove to be a most fruitful area of research in connection with the affective domain.

In other words, the educators have made it very clear that their goal is to "effect a complete and thoroughgoing reorganization of attitudes and values" that the kids bring from home. Apparently, the educators disapprove of the attitudes and values that children acquire from their parents. And so, what the educators do is sow the seeds of rebellion and familial conflict.

Fortunately, the homeschooling family need not worry about conflicting values which lead to teenage rebellion. The new family lifestyle is one of harmony and basic agreement between parents and children when it comes to values. This is particularly true among religious families where daily devotions and Bible readings create a strong spiritual unity among parents and children alike. In such families, where according to the orthodox tradition, the father is the spiritual leader of the family, his authority is respected because it relies on God for its source.

Obviously, therefore, the kind of lifestyle a homeschooling family will have will depend greatly on its philosophical foundations. But all homeschooling families have several things in common. The most important thing of all is that the homeschooling family is master of its own time. The children of the family are no longer captives of the state, confined in the school during the best hours of the day, requiring the family to plan its activities in accordance with the school's schedule. And much of that time in school is spent being dumbed down, not educated.

Being free to determine how one is going to spend the day, gives homeschoolers an exhilarating sense of freedom and independence. The family, not the state, decides how to spend its time. It can actually be spent learning and developing one's intellect. Thus, the emotional and psychological benefits of declaring one's own independence from the state school gives the family an understanding of what freedom is all about. Freedom means being free of government coercion. That is the freedom that the founding fathers fought to obtain for all Americans. To them, the purpose of government was to secure the unalienable rights of life, liberty, and the pursuit of happiness for all Americans.

Freedom also provides economic benefits for the family. For example, homeschoolers can take advantage of the off-hours at skating rinks, or will get a better rate from a music teacher who might otherwise not have students until they get home from school. In addition, the homeschooled children have more energy for these activities. They are not exhausted and listless because of a day of confinement in the suffocating atmosphere of the public school. On the other hand, public schoolers, if they are involved in extracurricular activities, must do the work in the late afternoon when their energies and enthusiasm are not at their highest. The best hours of the day are spent in the drudgery of the classroom, and the worst hours of the day are given over to what children really like doing.

All of that is changed in homeschooling. The academic work is usually completed by noon and the rest of the day can be spent at whatever activities the family wants to engage in. Sometimes, if a morning field trip has been planned, the academics can be done at some other time. Also, the family can take advantage of off-season vacations or travel, thus avoiding crowds and saving money. The family goes on vacation or takes trips when Dad is free, not when school is closed. The calendar revolves around the family's needs, not the school's schedule.

Another important aspect of the homeschooling family's lifestyle is its social life. In the family committed to public schooling, parents tend to develop their own social lives, and the kids through school friendships and activities tend to develop social lives of their own. This divides the family in a way that can cause serious problems. Kids can get into a great deal of trouble because of peer pressure in the school, and parents are often kept in the dark about what their children are really up to with their friends. Many children begin to develop intense friendships; some creating their own secret language in order to hide from their parents what they are doing with their friends, particularly of the opposite sex. Dating can lead to premarital sex, which may lead to unwanted pregnancies, diseases, abortions, unwed teenage motherhood, emotional traumas, jealousies, and physical abuse. The parents are the last to know that their son or daughter is in deep trouble. Children may get involved with drugs or gangs, which is the kind of desperate social life that has claimed the lives and souls of many youngsters.

In contrast, the social life of the homeschooling family is positive and delightful. It is not a divided social life, but one built around a united family. Homeschooling parents join support groups or develop friendships with other homeschooling parents, and the kids are always there unless they are engaged in some activity with other homeschoolers. The kids have no secrets to hide from their parents, and the parents' lives are pretty open to the kids. Family members are not outside the family, each going in his or her own direction. Dating is discouraged as an open invitation to dangerous temptation. Courtship is encouraged and parents try to match up their kids with other homeschooled kids. Innocence is often maintained for as long as the children are under their parents' care and protection. The public schooler, on the other hand, is introduced to sex education as early as kindergarten and will start experimenting with sex in the preteen years. And when one examines the dysfunctional family, it becomes obvious that premarital sex is one of the premier causes of social trauma.

This doesn't mean that homeschooled children never get into trouble. What it does mean is that homeschoolers get into much less trouble than their public school counterparts because of the strong moral teaching at home. Homeschoolers tend to be busy, creative, productive, independent self-starters with little interest in the kind of temptations that public schoolers are confronted with every day in school or on the bus. Public schoolers, being among a couple of hundred kids daily, away from parental supervision, and without much moral guidance from the educators, can easily fall prey to the seductive pressures of their friends.

Thus, the lifestyle of the homeschool family gives a sense of security and togetherness that keeps the corruption, temptations, and evils of the greater culture at bay. Parents decide what the children will watch on television, and usually the less TV the better. There are plenty of good videos that parents can get for their kids. This produces a healthy moral environment in which parents enjoy their responsibilities as parents, and children enjoy the safety and warmth of a truly rich and fulfilling family life.

Homeschooling also encourages the development of family enterprises in which all members can take part. Many homeschooling families have built home businesses that have helped make their families economically self-sufficient. This is important during a time of dynamic economic change in America. Homeschoolers are in a good position to take advantage of all the new opportunities that are being created by the new technology. They can use their time to develop whatever interests them. Many pioneering homeschool families have become successful booksellers, magazine publishers, homeschool program developers, clothing designers, software developers, etc.

All in all, the new family lifestyle that homeschooling has created is the most positive social development in America today. The rest of America can learn much from this healthy phenomenon, which a family can enjoy only when it rejects government schooling and discovers the great moral, spiritual, and psychological benefits of homeschooling.

-17-

Support Groups

One of the great sources of moral support available to home-schoolers is the local support groups which have grown up like mushrooms across America. Wherever there are a few home-schooling families, one is likely to find a support group providing these families with mutual help, a place to exchange information and experiences, a sounding board, and plain old neighborly socializing. Support groups provide homeschoolers a means to reach the community at large through open meetings and community projects. The support group can project a very positive image of what homeschooling is all about since it brings together parents who have achieved educational freedom for their families.

At support group gatherings parents can discuss the problems they all have in common: choosing the right curriculum, restricting television, home discipline, testing, relations with local superintendents, experiences in teaching (what works, what doesn't work, finding good books, finding good educational materials and supplies, organizing sports), and the sensitive issue of how to handle their children's socializing with the opposite sex. In a culture awash with sexual stimuli, how does one make sure that one's children are not caught up in the vortex of modern trends? These are matters that parents can discuss in support groups.

The support groups also provide opportunities for homeschooled children to get to know one another, to play together, to go on field trips together. Some support groups organize all sorts of extracurricular clubs for the children. They also provide the means to exchange expertise in particular areas of study. For example, a parent who is an engineer can help students with math. A parent who speaks French or Spanish or any other foreign language can start a club for that study group. A parent or child who is a computer buff can help others learn to use a computer, get on the Internet, or recommend specific equipment to buy. Parents with older children who no longer need certain books or curricula can pass them on to parents with younger kids. In other words, in support groups parents help parents do a better job at homeschooling.

Some support groups organize drama clubs so that the kids can act in plays. They organize team sports, visits to museums and historical sights, and visits to skating rinks at off-hours when the rinks are empty and the price of admission is lower. Thus, the support group is a kind of extension of the family in that it can provide socialization, recreation, expertise, and friendship—all at the same time.

The point is that homeschooling families do not live in isolation from one another or the community. They are eager to join others of like mind to provide their children and themselves with healthful, enjoyable socialization. And, of course, the support groups vary in outlook. Christian homeschoolers will usually join support groups comprised of parents who share their religious values. Jewish homeschoolers have created their own groups for mutual support. In eastern Massachusetts, for example, where there are more than eight thousand children being homeschooled, the support networks include a theater group that meets in Cambridge, a problem-solving group based in Malden, a ski group in Marlborough, a play group for children that meets at the Arnold Arboretum in Boston, a campfire group for boys and girls that meets at the Boston Museum of Science, a chess club, a math study group, and a history club.

Some of the groups organize spelling bees, geography bees, science fairs, craft shows, and musical and dance recitals. Some groups meet in churches, or public libraries, or in the larger homes of the families. Potluck dinners are a staple of support group meetings. Sometimes the children themselves organize an activity, such as reading poems the children have written, putting on a play, baking cookies and bread, reading a favorite book out loud in a circle, publishing a newsletter which includes children's drawings, family biographies, and event calendars. The telephone, the modem, and the fax keep everyone in touch.

Support groups can also have some impact on local politics. Visits to the offices of state legislators, or inviting state legislators to attend a support group gathering, can be a good way to introduce legislators to the homeschooling phenomenon and also to acquaint homeschoolers with the political leaders of their communities. Discussions about the political makeup of the community might inspire some homeschooling parents to run for office and inspire some of the children to become politically active when they get older. A study of the history of our form of government would be an excellent project for any support group. Visits to the legislature, to county courthouses, to the governor's office, to fire and police stations, or to prisons would no doubt be enlightening experiences for the parents as well as the children.

Getting to know how your community is governed would make a great, useful learning project. Have your support group read aloud the Declaration of Independence, the U.S. Constitution, and the constitution of your state. Read the writings of the Founding Fathers to acquaint yourself with their ideas and intentions. I can think of no better activity for a support group than learning about and discussing the philosophical basis of our American form of government. Deciding to homeschool is a political as well as an educational decision. The act of homeschooling is an indication that you believe that America is still a free country in which parents still have the right to determine how their children are to be educated. That act, in and of itself, indicates a very serious and profound understanding of what it means to be an American.

New homeschoolers who are testing the waters of freedom are relieved of their anxieties when meeting experienced homeschoolers in the group who can answer their myriad questions. The first year is always the hardest because it requires such a radical change in educational philosophy and attitude, and it does take courage to make such a change in a society that puts heavy emphasis on conformity and political correctness. But getting to know other courageous parents who have successfully made the transition from public schooler to homeschooler can be greatly encouraging.

How does one go about finding a support group? You won't find them in the phone book. The easiest way is to ask a homeschooling family, if you can find one. They will know a support group, tell you how to get in touch with it, or invite you to the next meeting. Another way is to contact the state homeschool association which usually can direct you to a local support group. In the appendix is a list of state homeschool associations with their phone numbers. The state organizations are usually the best source of information about what is going on in the state. Once you get involved with a support group, be creative. Think of all the wonderful ways that you and your family can enjoy the freedom that comes with homeschooling, and think of ways in which you can bring that message of freedom to others.

-18-

Dating Versus Courtship

One of the most interesting developments among homeschoolers is the shift from dating to courtship as the means of getting their children to establish a relationship with the opposite sex. Dating is probably one of the worst forms of social activity in the United States. Who among adults today can forget the emotional roller coaster associated with the ups and downs, the highs and lows of dating? Who can forget the pain of being snubbed or rejected by the opposite sex in a kind of teenage rat race, better known as a popularity contest?

And then there is the business of going steady, that is, dating the same person over a period of weeks or months, with the growing possessiveness and jealousies, and the pain of being dumped for someone else. Teenage magazines are full of letters from adolescents suffering the anxieties and insecurities of the dating game. Falling in and out of love can create some very painful emotional experiences. And getting involved in premarital sex can ruin a life before a teenager is even out of school.

In fact, premarital sex is probably the cause of more social problems and tragedies in America today than any other social activity. When boys persuade girls to give up their virginity, and the girls say yes because they want to feel loved or wanted, a horrible degradation takes place. Word will get around school that so-and-so has been had. In a society where virginity has lost its value, the girls nevertheless know that something bad has happened to them. They are emotionally and morally confused, and don't know how to say "no," or even why they should say "no."

Fathers and mothers accept the dating game and suspect that their children are engaging in sex but dare not interfere, since the dating game is the sacred ritual of the public school adolescent. The result is that parents keep their fingers crossed and hope for the best and are shocked out of their minds when their daughter comes home pregnant, or find out that she has had a secret abortion with the help of a boyfriend, or find out that her boyfriend has turned her into a drug addict.

Sometimes dating means nothing more than having sex, and going steady is little more than having steady sex with one partner. Occasionally, a girl will dump a boy with whom she has been having steady sex, and this can create a serious problem of jealousy leading to physical abuse and mental abuse. And if it is the boy who dumps the girl for someone else, the girl could even wind up in a mental hospital, especially if she aborted a child which they accidentally conceived.

According to *Parade Magazine* (February 2, 1997), an estimated half-million teens in the United States gave birth in 1995. Why are so many teens having so much irresponsible sex? The girls identified drinking as a major factor leading to sex. Also, some of the girls think they will lose their boyfriends unless they have sex. In other words, girls often trade sex for love, and apparently that is the kind of naive, emotionally driven thinking that pervades so many teen girls in the dating game.

There is no doubt that explicit sex education and condom distribution have contributed to the increase in premarital sex among schoolchildren. The cry of the educators is that you cannot successfully teach kids abstinence because they're going to do it anyway. So why not protect them from unwanted pregnancies and sexually transmitted diseases by giving them condoms and encouraging them to use them? Of course, it is quite possible to appeal to the rationality of the young as to why they should postpone sex until marriage. But since some educators believe that teenagers are incapable of controlling their animal urges, there is little point in appealing to them rationally. After all, teenagers are not rational!

The *Boston Globe* (February 1, 1997) published an article about a much-heralded sex education course being given to public school students in Newton, Massachusetts, an affluent suburb of Boston. The article is worth quoting to give the reader an idea of how explicit the course is:

> No, they're not nervous, insist the ninth graders in Norman Hyett's classroom, as they shuffle, twitch and fidget. They learned about ejaculation eons ago when they took reproductive anatomy, or "plumbing" as it's called around here, back in sixth grade.

But the giggles start as soon as Hyett utters the 's' word: "Let's start our first day together by going over what we will cover in this sexuality course."

Dating and love, contraception, herpes. When Hyett says the phrase "breast self-exam," several girls blush a hot shade of pink. When he mentions "homosexuality," two boys in the back of the room point frantically at each other.

Asked to write why everyone's eyes are suddenly glued to the floor, one girl scribbles the headline, "Why it's Uncomfortable to Talk About Sex." Her top reasons: "We're in a co-ed group; its embarrassing; this is school!!!"

Hyett takes such answers seriously, but his goal is to squelch the squirming. Six months from now, these same Newton South High School students, for a homework assignment, will browse local pharmacies for condoms and diaphragm jelly and turn down sexual advances in classroom skits entitled "Careful on the Couch.". . .

Here, no one utters euphemisms like hanky-panky. Instead, students devote their second class to listing every slang word they can think of for sex and sexual organs. Once they master the more scientific terms—and learn to roll condoms onto their index fingers—it's on to the other graphic topics, such as gonorrhea and date rape.

If ever there were a course to destroy the innocence and natural modesty of youth and arouse dormant, latent sexual interest this would be it. But then America's popular culture is saturated with sex and violence. So what the school does is make sure that the child, who may have missed some of that on TV or not gone to any X-rated movies, gets his or her full dose of cultural explicitness in the classroom. Believe it or not, only 10 out of 375 ninth-graders had parents concerned enough to keep their children out of the course. Perhaps by now these concerned parents have had enough of public education and are homeschooling.

When kids are forced to attend schools in which they are age-segregated and regimented for twelve years, serving in a kind of low-security prison run by the state, they become irresponsible and rebellious in their social habits. Back in the days of single-sex schools, there was no need for sex education. Girls got intimate knowledge from their mothers, and boys either got some advice from their fathers or picked up sexual knowledge from their friends. But now, with coed schools, a kind of pressure cooker dating culture is created in which romantic emotion and lust are elevated over reason and further promoted by a degenerate entertainment industry.

While premarital sex can lead to all sorts of problems and tragedies, one should not ignore the emotional damage that is done by serial attachments and breakups that are part and parcel of the dating game. The worst thing a parent can do is encourage a young child to pair off in a romantic relationship with a "girlfriend" or "boyfriend" a decade before either of them is ready to marry. Children are not capable of sustaining a romantic relationship so early in life. They do not have the life experience or the emotional maturity. Parents may think of such pairings as "cute," but they inevitably lead to crushes, infatuations, and love affairs that will rarely result in marriage but will leave permanent emotional scars.

In a book I wrote some years ago on the subject of feminism, I listed the reasons why a girl should not engage in premarital sex: the loss of virginity, which could have a devastating effect on a girl's self-esteem; the possibility of becoming infected with a lifelong venereal disease like herpes or AIDS; an unwanted pregnancy and the prospect of becoming an unwed teenage mother, or giving up the child for adoption, or having an abortion; the awakening of a sexual appetite which might make sexual loyalty to a husband difficult if not impossible; the high probability of a devastating emotional breakdown if the boyfriend dumps her for some other girl; and conflict with her parents, since she will be engaged in an affair her parents would no doubt disapprove of. Does it make sense for any girl to engage in premarital sex when the consequences could ruin her life? When teenagers engage in premarital sex, they are playing with fire, and all too often they get severely burned.

That is why so many homeschooling parents are turning to courtship as the proper way to lead their young adults toward a happy life. If marriage is the goal of a relationship with the opposite sex, then teen dating is the worst way to get there. An excellent explanation of what courtship is all about is given by Michael Farris, president of the Home School Legal Defense Association, in his informative little book, *The Homeschooling Father.* Farris and his wife Vickie have nine children, all but the toddler homeschooled. He writes:

> We now have two teenaged daughters—one is in her late teens. They are clearly and objectively attractive girls. But neither has ever been on a date.... Our older daughters... have

committed themselves to the idea that they will pursue a relationship with a boy only when it is consistent with these three principles:

1. Both the young man and I are prepared for marriage.

2. I am investigating this particular young man because he appears to meet the spiritual standards my parents and I have agreed upon for a husband.

3. I find him to be personally interesting and attractive.

Farris urges homeschooling fathers to secure their children's commitments to the above three principles and to raise them with the understanding that the entire area of boy-girl relationships is to be reserved for the time of life just before marriage. In other words, if your children are not ready for marriage, they ought not to be getting romantically involved with the opposite sex. Thus, courtship should start when one is prepared to get married. And that goes for both sons and daughters. Farris writes:

> Men who are not ready to work are not ready for marriage.... It is clear to me now that a man is not ready for marriage until he is ready to care for his family.... Marriage and fatherhood go together.... If a man marries unprepared for fatherhood, there is a possibility that he will become an unprepared father.

Obviously, the homeschooling situation makes courtship quite practical. The children can be brought up to understand the principles involved. Since they are not in the public school, they can avoid all of the emotional chaos and confusion that is an integral part of public school socialization. The homeschooling situation permits parents to assert a benign, well-reasoned authority over their children in matters pertaining to boy-girl relations. This is virtually impossible in the public school situation. And perhaps nowhere better than in the contest between dating and courtship is the revolutionary nature of homeschooling demonstrated. And nowhere better than in the dating-versus-courtship contest are the different views of socialization dramatically demonstrated. In homeschooling, boys and girls are raised to be responsible and devoted husbands and wives, fathers and mothers. The prospects of a happy, productive, healthy life are thus assured.

Of course, this is the ideal. It would be foolish to believe that some homeschooled children will not get into trouble. Human nature being what it is, we can expect some children to go astray. But what is significant is how well homeschooled children have turned out thus far. Perhaps the movement is still too young and it's too early to tell, but this writer has been in many homeschooling homes, and met many of the children, and it is refreshing to see how different they are from the public schoolers. This is particularly true of Christian homeschoolers who have the advantage of a strong moral and spiritual foundation on which to build their family. But it is obvious that the principles that guide Christian homeschooling parents are universal in their application. Thus, non-Christian homeschoolers can learn much from the religious pioneers who have made homeschooling a new way of life.

-19-

Special Needs and Homeschooling

One of the questions often asked by parents is whether or not a special needs child can be homeschooled. The answer, of course, is yes. How you do it depends on the nature of the child's disability. Obviously, if the child is either hearing or sight impaired very special methods will have to be used. If the child is physically disabled and confined to a wheelchair but is otherwise mentally normal, academic homeschooling would not be any different from that of an unimpaired child's.

If the child has a learning disability which appears to have had its genesis in a school's faulty teaching practices, then the best thing a parent can do is remove the child from the school and teach that child correctly at home. If the child remains in school and is put in a special-ed class, that child will suffer not only a loss of self-esteem but may wind up permanently disabled by the school's faulty remediation program. A school that creates learning problems is hardly the place to get them cured.

Of late, many parents of special needs kids have wanted to have their children mainstreamed in the public schools where, it is thought, they will get healthful socialization and good teachers if they are taught in the same classrooms with normal kids. The reality, however, is quite different. Many parents of normal children resent the fact that their kids are being shortchanged by the greater attention that must be given to the impaired children. Some of the special needs children require the full-time attention of a teacher, and in fact in some states there are publicly funded private schools which specialize in educating severely disabled children at a cost of $35,000 a year. But if the child is in a public school, it is unlikely that a teacher who is miseducating normal children will not also be miseducating the special needs children.

So what is a parent to do? In the past, kids with special needs were educated in private schools created by dedicated individuals to deal with such problems. But this meant that only those parents who could afford the tuition could get their special needs children educated. The states that now mandate that the public schools must educate special needs children relieve parents of the need to pay for such education in private schools. But it doesn't save their children from all the other problems that afflict the public schools. Also, the publicly funded private schools that were created to relieve the public schools of the burden of educating the severely disabled are required to be certified and conform to state-mandated standards.

In addition, when a special needs child is rejected by the public school and parents are given the option of putting their child in one of the approved publicly funded private schools, the atmosphere of that school might be worse than anything the child would encounter elsewhere. For example, at the private Helden School in Charlestown, Massachusetts, director Janice Brenner observed to a reporter from the *Boston Globe* that the students the Boston public schools used to send her were non-compliant, mouthy, and disrespectful. Now the behavioral problems the school must deal with involve violent crimes, sex offenses, guns and knives. Putting a special needs child in such an environment would do more harm than good.

The simple truth is that special needs children need what all children need: the care and nurture of a loving family. One suspects that the reason why many parents put their special needs children in public or private school is because they want to be relieved of those children for some hours of the day. They may sincerely believe that the child will be better served in a public or private school, especially if the normal children in the family are in school. But as the failures of public education become increasingly obvious, more and more parents are turning to homeschooling as the best means of educating and raising all of their children, including those with special needs.

We know this to be the case from reports in *Nathhan News*, the quarterly publication of the National Challenged Homeschoolers Associated Network (NATHHAN). This organization, which was founded in 1990 by several homeschooling moms, now has a membership of over 5,500 families with special needs kids. Many of these families adopted children with special needs ranging from learning disabilities to multi-physical handicaps. Their love of these children and their love of family life has made homeschooling the natural way to go.

The result of this growing interest in special needs homeschooling has been the development of all sorts of services and small businesses to help such families. For example, one mother in Minnesota, Tammy McMannus, designs attractive, stylish clothing for special needs kids who must wear body jackets, leg braces, knee braces, body braces, sanitary undergarments, and feeding/drainage tubes. In her ad in *Nathhan News* Tammy writes:

> I decided to open my company after listening to some of my friends' tearful descriptions of long shopping expeditions that all too often resulted in poor fitting clothes. These kids have a right to clothing that suits their individual needs, and yet is attractive, stylish, well made, and actually fits!! They deserve to have clothes that make them feel good about themselves! When a special needs child can look in the mirror and exclaim, "MY CLOTHES ARE SUPER!!", I get a tingle from a job well done.

Another company, Love and Learning, founded in Michigan by parents of a child with Down's Syndrome, offers books and audio and video tapes to help parents teach reading and conversational skills to special needs kids. There is also a round-robin style newsletter for parents with autistic children called PREACCH, an acronym for Parents Rearing and Educating Autistic Children in Christian Homes. A common theme which runs through NATHHAN is the need for God's help when seeking the best ways to educate special needs children.

Obviously, it takes a great deal of courage, patience, and love to homeschool a special needs child. But these children seem to thrive in homeschooling because the parents and siblings who live with them and know them best are willing to seek the best teaching programs for their children. For example, in an article about educating her deaf child, Rhonda Robinson writes in *Nathhan News* (Summer 1994):

> We have hacked our way through the jungle of philosophies of deaf education (to sign or not to sign, ASL, SEE . . .). After wading deep into their philosophies we found that there are so many opinions concerning teaching the deaf and each camp has their own success stories and horror stories of the neighboring

camp. Our conclusion: there is no magic formula. Nothing they could do would make her a "normal hearing" child. So we set out to find what would work best for Chelsea....

I am so thankful we kept her home. I can't imagine what she would be like if she was not homeschooled.

All parents of special needs children go through the same process of trying to determine what is the best way to educate their children. The constant experimentation and discussions that go on among special needs educators suggest that the field is fraught with confusion and uncertainty. But what is probably the most certain thing that can be said of special needs children is that each one of them is unique and requires a one-on-one approach. Obviously, the success that homeschooled special needs children experience is due to the fact that their teacher, their parent, knows them better than anyone else. Putting such a child in a school where the teacher has never known the child is sort of like playing educational Russian roulette. The parent who has seen the child develop from day one, and has lived with the child, is probably more qualified to educate that child than the professional who obtained his or her knowledge from books. And that is why it can be disastrous to put a special needs child in the hands of a teacher right out of college. It takes the professional years of hands-on experience before he or she has seen enough deaf or blind or disabled children to know how best to serve them.

VACCINES AND INOCULATIONS

One of the areas of concern among parents in general and homeschooling parents in particular is that of infant inoculations, vaccinations, and immunizations. There is no doubt that some of these shots can cause permanent neurological damage in some children. This is another case of playing Russian roulette with a child's health by way of inoculations. There is even talk now of adding shots for Hepatitis B for children. One begins to wonder how many children have developed health problems because of the many shots administered to them so early in life before anything is known about their allergies.

Are we now in a situation of inoculation overkill? Obviously, the time has come for a thorough examination and review of this whole area of health care. We read more and more about contaminated sera and the severe reactions that some children have to these inoculations. Are we placing too many children at serious risk by administering shot after shot with no knowledge of what the child may be allergic to? Are more children permanently damaged by DPT (diphtheria-pertussis-tetanus) shots than the disease the shots are supposed to prevent?

In January 1997, about one hundred scientists met in Washington, D.C., to discuss whether or not a monkey virus known as SV 40 contained in early doses of the polio vaccine, and injected into 98 million Americans forty years ago, may now be causing cancer. Although government officials and manufacturers found out about this SV 40 contamination back in 1960, it was decided not to tell the public about it and to continue using the tainted vaccine until 1963. But now new research is linking the virus to human brain, bone, and lung cancers. What's more, it is now believed that the virus can be transmitted from infected mothers and fathers to their infants, some of whom have developed brain cancers in infancy.

Howard Urnovitz, an independent microbiologist in Berkeley, California, was quoted in the *Boston Globe* (January 26, 1997) as saying, "Here is a known cancer-causing virus that almost a hundred million Americans were exposed to through a government-sponsored vaccine program. But for over thirty years, there's been virtually no government effort to see if anyone's been harmed by the exposure."

Barbara Loe Fisher, cofounder and president of the National Vaccine Information Center in Vienna, Virginia, shares Urnovitz's concern. She has served as the consumer member on the National Academy of Science's Institute of Medicine Vaccine Safety Forum. Her organization has long pushed for more government research into and disclosure of the little-studied harmful effects of vaccines upon some recipients. According to the *Globe* article:

> Fisher argues that government agencies like the FDA have an inherent conflict of interest because of their mandate to promote universal vaccination on the one hand and regulate vaccine safety on the other.
>
> Nowhere is this more obvious than with polio vaccine whose revered status, she says, has kept the government from carefully scrutinizing its potential hazards. "Why haven't they been

willing to investigate this whole issue of cross-species transfer of potentially dangerous animal viruses into humans through contaminated vaccines? Who's minding the store when the FDA has allowed drug companies to produce vaccines grown on contaminated monkey kidneys?" Fisher asks. "What happened to protecting the public health?"

What happened, indeed! What all of this really means is that neither the government nor the drug manufacturers can be completely trusted by the public and particularly by parents of newborn children when it comes to vaccines and mandated inoculations. Americans had better start thinking twice about passing laws requiring everyone to be inoculated against everything. No one in a free society should be forced to accept the injection of any foreign substance into his or her body by a government that has made too many mistakes to be trusted.

An excellent book on the subject of immunizations and the risks involved is *A Shot in the Dark* by Harris L. Coulter and Barbara Loe Fisher (Avery Publishing Group, Garden City Park, NY). As many as 57,000 children a week across America receive the controversial DPT vaccine. The law requires it, and most children will receive the vaccine four times before the age of two. In some children the DPT shots have caused convulsions, high fever, high-pitched screaming, persistent crying, brain damage, and even death. But what is equally, if not more, disturbing is the growth of government's role in the field of health. Federal health agencies aggressively promote a vaccine they know to be highly reactive but have failed to conduct the kind of large-scale clinical tests needed to insure safety. We also have state governments passing laws requiring every child to be injected with a vaccine of unknown toxicity as a prerequisite for attending school, thereby abolishing a parent's right to decide freely whether or not a child should be vaccinated. All of this is indicative of the bureaucratic tendency to want to control more and more of a citizen's life. Only homeschooling offers parents the freedom once more to exercise the duties and responsibilities of parenthood in protecting their children from the excessive zeal of government bureaucrats.

In 1982, a group of parents banded together and formed a national organization with the fitting name Dissatisfied Parents Together (DPT). This nonprofit organization operates the National Vaccine Information

Center and has distributed information to thousands of parents. It also collects data on the many hundreds of cases of children severely damaged by the DPT vaccine. (For information about Dissatisfied Parents Together, write to the National Vaccine Information Center, 512 West Maple Ave., Ste. 206, Vienna, Virginia 22180, or call 703-938-DPT3 or (800) 909-SHOT.)

-20-

Homeschoolers and College

Ever since 1982, when Grant Colfax, the homeschooled "goat-boy" from California, was accepted by Harvard—and subsequently his two homeschooled brothers were also accepted by that venerable institution—homeschoolers have been looked at by many colleges and universities as bright prospects for higher education. One should never forget that a college or university is a business which must fill its classroom seats with students if the trustees and professors are to continue enjoying the lifestyle to which they've become accustomed. In fact, at many homeschool conventions, one will now find colleges and universities renting booths, dispensing glossy brochures about their leafy campuses with an eye to recruiting some of these bright homeschoolers.

For all practical purposes, the Colfax family paved the way for homeschoolers to achieve a kind of special reputation for independence and academic excellence among college admissions officers, who appreciate students who don't need remediation in their freshman year. In 1973, Micki and David Colfax had bought forty-seven acres of undeveloped land in the mountains of Mendocino County, California, where they decided to homestead. Their saga is described in their book, *Hard Times in Paradise*, published in 1992—and hard times they were. David Colfax, a college professor, had been blacklisted for his radical political activism on campus.

And so, after considering different options, the Colfaxes, with the enthusiastic urging of their sons, agreed to build a life for themselves on a remote mountain. Trying to subsist in raw nature required all the ingenuity and physical strength they could muster. After all sorts of trials and errors, young Grant Colfax finally found raising and breeding high-quality goats to be the best way to earn money, and the other two boys,

Drew and Reed, did as well in their own endeavors. It was an education for all of them that no money could buy.

Their homeschooling came as naturally as everything else they did. Since their parents were college educated, they knew what had to be learned. The Colfaxes write:

> There was never any doubt in our minds that the boys were *learning*, right alongside us much of the time, questioning, exploring alternatives, working out solutions as we worked on one and then another project and confronted one challenge after another. The *World Book Encyclopedia* was there when, in the process of working on a clogged carburetor on the generator, one of the boys asked what, exactly, a carburetor did, and when, as we were thinning out redwood groves for poles for the garden, somebody asked if redwoods grew only in this part of California. Now that all three of them could read, and as their questions became more difficult, the encyclopedia and dozens of science and nature reference books came to occupy a central place in our lives.

What was truly wonderful about the Colfaxes is how they enjoyed doing things together as a family. Their time was their own, and everything they did was to help one another succeed in making their lives happy and fulfilling despite the physical hardships. Their lifestyle was even reflected in the Christmas gifts they gave the boys. They write:

> Drew, who never became anywhere near as engrossed in sheep raising as Grant did with his dairy goats, didn't take long to develop an interest of his own: astronomy. It had begun the Christmas when he was thirteen. It had become a tradition that our gifts to the boys had to be educational or immediately practical. There were always books, of course—favorite authors, books relating to their special interests, reference volumes, and, one year, a new encyclopedia set—and starkly utilitarian items such as stainless steel milk buckets for Grant, wood-carding brushes and woodworking tools for Drew and Reed, a set of rabbit-watering bowls for Garth. That year...we thought we would get them all a good telescope, only to discover that they were so expensive as to be out of reach.

So what did the Colfaxes do? With the help of an optical shop owner, they bought at much less cost all of the components needed to build a telescope. Over the next year Drew spent hours grinding the telescope mirror. And finally the boys built a sliding roof observatory. Drew spent hours scanning the sky and even discovered a comet, which he reported to a major observatory that confirmed his sighting. That's homeschooling at its best. Here's how the Colfaxes describe their home education philosophy:

> From the outset it was apparent that the boys' natural curiosity provided the motivation to learn and that our job was to be there to provide support, materials, and, when it was requested, direction. We seldom *taught* the boys in the conventional sense of the term. We learned together, and we *talked*— about politics, literature, religion, and economics, about breeds of cattle and brands of feeds, about arts and crafts. Initially, when they were younger, they relied upon us for information and direction, but as they grew older they'd turn more and more to each other as they carved out their different areas of special competence, Grant becoming our livestock expert, Drew the botanist and astronomer, Reed the athlete and musician, and Garth the naturalist-artist.

And, as usually occurs among homeschoolers, the older child helped the younger ones. Sometimes the materials they used didn't work. They write:

> We all recalled the year that [Grant] had used the "new math" text we had selected only because it was assigned in a University of California correspondence course and had come perilously close to becoming convinced that he was "bad at math." (We switched to another series that guided him—and, subsequently, his brothers—almost painlessly through precalculus.)

Eventually the Colfaxes had to begin considering the future. They write:

> It wasn't until Grant was sixteen that we began to think seriously about his—and the other boys'—off-the-land future. We didn't have any reason to worry about how well they might do in college.... Because they were self-directed and enjoyed learning—whether it was building a house or solving a math problem—we were confident that they would have no trouble managing whatever they might encounter in a college setting.

Grant took the SAT and scored in the ninety-ninth percentile. In 1982 the family drove to the East Coast so that Grant could be interviewed by Haverford, Princeton, Yale, Brown, and Harvard. In place of a school transcript Grant had written a letter describing his "unique educational background," his course work, and a list of textbooks used during the past four years. He provided a half dozen letters of recommendation from fellow dairy goat breeders, 4-H project leaders, etc. He had also been doing volunteer work at a health center and had decided that he wanted to become a doctor.

Soon after Grant had been accepted by Harvard, the *San Francisco Examiner* got wind of the story and sent two reporters up to the mountain to interview the "backwoods scholar" heading for Harvard. In a short time the young goat-breeder and his family became national news. Grant was talked about by Paul Harvey and invited to appear on the *Today Show* and on the *Tonight Show Starring Johnny Carson,* and for the first time Americans were hearing about something called homeschooling.

Grant graduated from Harvard with high honors in biology, got an award for his senior thesis and won a Fulbright Fellowship to spend a year in New Zealand, and then entered Harvard Medical School. His brothers Drew and Reed followed him into Harvard.

So, not only do homeschoolers get into college, but they usually do very well in an environment where independence, self-direction, and self-motivation are rewarded with success. And so, if you are a parent intending to homeschool, you can start planning your child's college education anytime you want. Of course, much has changed since Grant Colfax entered Harvard, in 1983. As college tuition fees have risen and computer technology has developed to the point where professors can bring their courses to anyone who has a computer, a modem, or a CD-ROM, it soon may no longer be necessary to live on a campus or sit in a classroom to get a college degree.

Why should anyone travel long distances, pay over $30,000 a year plus the cost of room and board, merely to be able to sit in a classroom in an old ivy-covered building and listen to an assistant instructor tell you what you can read in a book or get off the Internet at home? Rarely do any of the great professors teach classes any more. At one time, before computer technology, you had to physically attend a college to get the instruction needed to get a degree. But that's no longer the case when it comes to your typical liberal arts education. Medicine, law, and engineering still require attendance at a university. But if one is not going to pursue the kind of career or profession that requires extensive postgraduate study, then one should think twice about shelling out $120,000 over four years for the college experience and most likely the burden of a long-term college loan debt.

However, if a homeschooler is going to pursue a profession requiring a college degree and attendance at a campus, then he or she must start thinking about and planning for it as early as the freshman year of high school so that in the next four years he or she can complete the courses required for admission. Have your son or daughter start making inquiries, get college catalogs, write to admissions officers, and talk to the alumni of the college that he or she wants to attend. Find out what scholarships are available and if the college provides opportunities for part-time work.

High school is also the appropriate time to start thinking about what one is truly interested in. Note that Grant Colfax became interested in medicine after working as a volunteer at a health center. His brother Drew became interested in botany and astronomy. Reed took to music, and Garth to art. Each child, if sufficiently stimulated by all that is fascinating in the world, will find areas of interest. This is particularly true of homeschoolers who are encouraged to become self-motivators.

Have your homeschooler keep track of all the courses taken and the books read during high school so that when it comes time to present his or her qualifications for college, all of that information is readily at hand. An easy way to keep tabs on what has been studied and read is to keep a journal or a daily log on one's homeschooling activities so that important and colorful details are not forgotten. Also, keep a file folder for each year with the pertinent information. Another good idea is to have the homeschooler start saving money as early as possible for college tuition. Part-time and summer jobs are obvious ways to earn money.

Taking achievement tests is an important part of the college preparatory process. The ACT or SAT are required for college admission. The maximum score on the ACT Assessment (American College Testing Program) is 36. The ACT includes four tests: English, Mathematics, Reading, and Science Reasoning. Testing time is 2 hours and 55 minutes. More information about the ACT and the other tests is in the appendix.

The maximum score on the SAT (Scholastic Aptitude Test) is 1600. It is comprised of two parts: Verbal and Mathematics. The SAT was recently renormed and revised. Multiple choice has been replaced by "student-produced responses," and the use of calculators is now permitted in the math section. Some colleges require homeschoolers to take the GED (General Education Diploma). Find out from your local school board when and where the GED can be taken. The PSAT (Preliminary Scholastic Aptitude Test) is a sort of practice run for the SAT. The maximum score is 160. It is combined with the NMSQT (National Merit Scholarship Qualifying Test). The National Merit Scholarship Corporation and colleges and universities use the scores on the PSAT/NMSQT to determine eligibility and qualifications for scholarships. There are books and courses about how to take these tests; they are generally available online and in your local public library.

Have your homeschooler carefully read the various college catalogs to see what is required in the way of tests and how to qualify for scholarships. More and more colleges and universities have come to recognize homeschoolers as a sizable group of students requiring special attention. When a student identifies him- or herself as a homeschooler when applying for admission, he or she will get that special attention.

Not every homeschooled child has to or ought to attend college. Basic liberal arts subjects can be studied at home. Home businesses provide plenty of opportunities to develop work and entrepreneurial skills. Apprenticeships can be sought out for valuable work experience. Also, there are plenty of jobs for highly competent homeschooled high-school graduates whose knowledge is certainly equal to if not better than that of many of today's college graduates. Most liberal arts colleges have simply become arenas of mindless social activities that boil down to drinking and partying and experimental recreational sex interspersed with boring classes taught by faculty promoting their own political and social agendas. Most of the students are there to get a valuable credential known as a college diploma. Some of them will remain in academia for the rest of their lives, becoming part of the vast educational establishment.

Incidentally, it is not necessary to attend a college in order to get a degree. In fact there are many accredited schools that offer bachelor's, master's, doctorates, and even law degrees by home study. More and more schools are making their courses available by correspondence, home study, through cable television, over home computers linked to the university computer, and by videos and CD-ROMs. Many of these courses are listed in a directory called *The Independent Study Catalog,* published by Peterson's Guides, Inc. You can contact the publisher by phone at (800) 338-3282.

No doubt the best book available on how to get a college degree at home is the guidebook written by John Bear and his daughter Mariah Bear entitled *College Degrees by Mail.* The Bears list one hundred educational institutions that offer home study courses leading to degrees. They include Boise State University, Brigham Young University, Colorado State University, Regent University, Skidmore College, Syracuse University, University of Massachusetts at Amherst, University of Oklahoma, and many, many more. For example, Auburn University in Alabama offers an almost totally nonresident M.B.A. and Master of Engineering degrees in such fields as aerospace, chemistry, computer science, and industrial engineering. The courses are taped in the classrooms and mailed to distance students who are required to maintain the same pace as resident students. Regent University at Virginia Beach, Virginia, offers a Master's degree in business administration or management with only two weeks of attendance on campus. There is even an Electronic University Network which uses the America OnLine computer bulletin board service to connect students with instructors, other students, and support services such as a library and student union.

In short, there are plenty of opportunities to earn a degree while remaining at home. The Bears' *College Degrees by Mail* provides a wealth of information and advice on how to choose the right school, how to get credit for life experience, how to prepare for equivalency exams, etc. See the appendix for information on how to order the book.

The Bears have also written another highly useful book, the *Bears' Guide To Earning College Degrees Nontraditionally.* First published in 1974, it is now in its twelfth edition and contains an incredible amount of information about every aspect of nontraditional higher education. They write: "Since the mid 1970s, there has been a virtual explosion in what is now commonly called 'alternative' or 'nontraditional' and 'external' or 'off-campus' education—ways and means of getting an education or a degree (or both, if you wish) without sitting in classrooms day after day, year after year." The book is arranged in four parts: Part One: Important Issues in Nontraditional Education; Part Two: Alternative Methods of

Earning Credit; Part Three: The Schools; and Part Four: Miscellany and Reference. There are nonresident programs, short residency programs, correspondence law schools, health-related schools, etc. For home-schoolers interested in home-study vocational programs, such as meat-cutting, appliance repair, and the like, the Bears recommend contacting the Distance Education and Training Council at 1601 18th St. NW, Washington, D.C. 20009. As for information on ordering the Bears' book, see the appendix.

A homeschooler who enters the world of work after high school will have a great headstart in learning about the working world, while the average college student may face great disappointment as he or she seeks a job with diploma in hand. Unless you are an outstanding student at an Ivy League university with corporate, establishment, or good family connections, finding a good job will require all of the skills one can muster. There are many self-made entrepreneurs in America. But their success is due more to their love of the challenges they face and their inner need to deal with them than to what they learned in college. Many of them are so eager to get started that they often drop out of college in order to take advantage of the opportunities that the real world of work and creativity have to offer.

The average public schooler sees college as a way of delaying the day when he or she will have to face the real world. They are attracted by a collegiate social life which includes fraternities and sororities, football games, dances, parties, drinking, and drugs. It is said that bulimia and anorexia are now common disorders among young women in college and public high schools because of the enormous pressures to be attractive and popular in the dating game on campus. However, it is believed that the homeschooler does well in college because he or she has greater self-discipline and the moral convictions that make it possible to resist the temptations of college social life.

In any case, technology will undoubtedly change the way higher education is conducted in America. Futurist Lewis Perelman writes:

> [S]ome people may still speak in the twenty-first century about "schools" and "colleges" and "students" and "teachers." But the hyperlearning systems of the imminent future in reality will bear less resemblance to old-fashioned classrooms than the M1A1 Abrams tank bears to a Roman chariot.

What will life be like in a society without schools, without what we would recognize as an institution of education? The cultural details of that coming society are as unpredictable as fuzzy dice, tail fins, low-riders, drive-in movies, Levittown, and a host of other features of automotive culture would have been in the 1890s.

However, as of now, the great universities and colleges that dot the American landscape will probably be around for as long as it takes the new technology to change the education habits of a nation.

-21-

Can Homeschooling Cure ADD?

The *New York Times* magazine (February 2, 1997) published an article about homeschooling in which the writer, a college professor, confessed that he had a hard time conceiving of education anywhere but in a school. He wrote:

> My American sense of rightness of school, the inevitability of school, the hegemony of school, is akin to my sense of the rightness of the oceans, of rivers, of rain. . . .
> Still, there's something noble—if perhaps quixotic—in refusing the culture's assumptions about school, in marching into the fray alone, an individualism distinctly American.

One gets the impression that the professor hadn't been in an elementary school classroom for a very long time. Otherwise, he might have had a somewhat different sense of the rightness of what goes on in today's classrooms. Perhaps he's not aware that, according to *Teacher* magazine of December 1996, four million American schoolchildren take the stimulant drug Ritalin every day so that they can sit in their classrooms and do their work. Although the kids are encouraged to "Dare say no to drugs," they must say "yes" every morning to a very potent drug that alters their physical and mental behavior. The reason for the drug? Attention Deficit Disorder, formerly known as Minimal Brain Dysfunction.

What exactly is Attention Deficit Disorder, or ADD as it is usually called? *Business Week* (June 6, 1994) identified the disorder as "an often-hereditary biochemical condition." The *Ladies Home Journal* (September 1993) said it was "a neurochemical disorder in the areas of the brain that regulate attention" as well as "a lifelong, genetically based affliction." A July 1994 *Time* magazine cover story remarked that fifteen years ago no one had ever heard of ADD, but now it was the most common behavior disorder in American children. How could a genetically based affliction suddenly arise out of nowhere? *Time* had no answer.

By the way, there are two types of ADD, one with hyperactivity and one without. The one with hyperactivity is known as ADHD, and it afflicts, according to *Time*, as many as three and a half million children, or five percent of the entire student population under eighteen. The symptoms include distractability, impulsiveness, knee-jiggling, toe-tapping, inability to sit still. For many of the afflicted, these symptoms continue into adulthood. The result is that prescriptions for Ritalin are going through the roof.

There is even an advocacy and support group called CHADD (Children and Adults with Attention Deficit Disorders), which is generously supported by the drug firm that manufactures the stimulant. Yet, nobody fully understands how Ritalin and other drugs such as Thorazine, Dexedrine, Cylert, or Prozac work. Nor do doctors have a very precise idea of the physiology of ADHD.

Meanwhile, books about ADD are sprouting out all over the place. One of the latest and most comprehensive is *Driven to Distraction* by two M.D.'s, Edward M. Hallowell and John J. Ratey, who have diagnosed themselves as having ADD. Hallowell writes:

> I'd been called in grade school—"a daydreamer," "lazy," an "underachiever," "a spaceshot"—and I didn't have some repressed unconscious conflict that made me impatient and action-oriented.
>
> What I had was an inherited neurological syndrome characterized by easy distractibility, low tolerance for frustration or boredom, a greater-than-average tendency to say or do whatever came to mind (called impulsivity in the diagnostic manual), and a predilection for situations of high intensity.

And so the authors are committed to the notion that ADD is a neurological condition, genetically transmitted. They elaborate:

> ADD lives in the biology of the brain and the central nervous system. The exact mechanism underlying ADD remains unknown.

But one thing we do know is that virtually every ADD case history discussed by the authors involved some traumatic experience in early education. The authors are very vague about which came first, the traumatic school experience or the ADD. They write:

> Due to repeated failures, misunderstandings, mislabelings, and all manner of other emotional mishaps, children with ADD usually develop problems with their self-image and self-esteem. Throughout childhood, at home and at school they are told they are defective. They are called dumb, stupid, lazy, stubborn, willful, or obnoxious.... They are reprimanded for classroom disturbances of all sorts and are easily scapegoated at school. They are the subject of numerous parent-teacher conferences.

In other words, to the primary symptoms of distractability, impulsivity, and restlessness are added the secondary symptoms of cognitive confusion, academic failure, low self-esteem, depression, boredom and frustration with school, fear of learning new things, impaired peer relations, sometimes drug or alcohol abuse, stealing or even violent behavior due to mounting frustration, exasperating forgetfulness, disorganization and indifference, underachievement, and unpredictability.

We wonder how many of today's adult ADD patients attended the once-controversial open classrooms in their primary school years in which they were subjected to wall-to-wall bedlam. Why should it have been expected that children under such conditions would be able to calmly concentrate on learning the complex abstractions of alphabetic writing and arithmetic being taught in a fragmentary, disorganized manner by an equally distracted, befuddled teacher with noises of all sorts coming from all directions? How could any normal child fail to be distracted and annoyed by the din of activities around him or her and by the constant interruptions inherent in such a learning-hostile environment?

Yet, apparently, none of the experts on ADD has bothered to investigate the possible school causes of attention deficit disorder. Perhaps they surmise that since many students have emerged from that classroom turmoil without ADD, those who were affected by the environment were biologically predisposed. And that might well be the case. But the point is that schools are supposed to be healthy environments for all children, not only for those with nerves of steel.

Everybody knows that no two children are alike. Some children can tolerate loud noises, others cannot. I know that I have always been unnerved by loud noises and can concentrate only on one thing at a time. Am I ADD? Some children, like me, require silence in order to concentrate, while others can listen to rock-and-roll on earphones while reading or doing homework. But American schools have become increasingly chaotic not only in curriculum and teaching methods but also in the classroom configuration. The doctors write revealingly:

> Many people with ADD point to school as the first place they realized that anything was different about them.

So what is the cure or treatment for ADD? First, the doctors insist that the patient be told that he or she has a neurological condition which is the source of the individual's nonconformist behavior. Then come the drugs and psychotherapy. The drugs, of course, do not always work, and sometimes they have to be discontinued because of intolerable side effects. The possible side effects of Ritalin, a stimulant, are suppression of appetite, loss of sleep, increased blood pressure and heart rate, nausea, headaches, and jitteriness. Rarer but more severe side effects include involuntary muscle twitches, growth suppression, and alteration in blood count or other blood chemistries.

As for the antidepressants used to treat ADD, Norpramin, the most commonly used, produces dry mouth, mild urinary retention, and sporadic lowering of blood pressure when standing up, resulting in dizziness. Norpramin can cause cardiac arrhythmias and in rare cases sudden death. We occasionally hear of a young student athlete suddenly dropping dead on a playing field or in a gym. But we're never told whether or not that student was taking one of these ADD drugs. Other antidepressants include Pamelor, Tofranil, Wellbutrin, Ludiomil, Prozac, and Catapres.

Since the drugs do not eradicate the basic ADD condition but only alleviate some of the symptoms, the doctors also include psychotherapy in their treatment. And what does that psychotherapy consist of? Surprise! The essence of their therapy is to bring structure into the life of the patient. They write:

> Structure is central to the treatment of ADD. . . . Structure makes possible the expression of talent. Without structure, no matter how much talent there may be, there is only chaos. . . .
> Structure refers to essential tools like lists, reminders, notepads, appointment books, filing systems, Rolodexes, bul-

letin boards, schedules, receipts, in and out boxes, answering machines, computer systems, alarm clocks, and alarm watches. Structure refers to the set of external controls that one sets up to compensate for unreliable internal controls.

The ADD student needs a structure of external controls. That's what we had when I was going to public school in New York City, back in the 1930s. We were all seated in rows in desks bolted to the floor. The desks did not have lids that could be slammed down. We slid our papers and books in the storage space below the top. And we had inkwells with real ink. But I never saw or heard of anyone tossing an inkwell around the room. We were all dressed according to the school's dress code. Boys wore white shirts and a red tie and long trousers and girls wore middy blouses with a red scarf and skirts. The teacher sat at her desk at the front of the room. All eyes were on her. She was the focus of attention. She used rational, traditional teaching methods that included rote memorization of the arithmetic facts, and we all learned the same things. There was no such animal as an individualized learning plan. And there was silence. The pupils were not permitted to speak to one another during class. The walls were bare except for a picture of George Washington and an American flag. There was no litter and no graffiti. You couldn't possibly have attention deficit disorder in that class. Your attention was focused on the teacher; there were no distractions, and your mind was engaged.

Contrast that scene with what you have in today's primary classrooms. You walk in and what do you see? The children are seated at movable tables, facing one another, chatting with one another, pestering one another. The teacher is wandering around the room. She is no longer the focus of attention. She is a facilitator with a cluttered desk in a corner somewhere. The walls are covered with every possible distraction: cartoons, dinosaurs, posters, decorations. Then there are fish tanks, gerbils, rabbits, and other creatures, and from the ceiling mobiles dangle and drift. In addition, everyone is learning something else because each pupil theoretically has his or her own individual learning plan. One child may be reading a book under a table. Another may be sprawled on the floor drawing something. Another may be staring into space while several others may be noisily working on a project. And the curriculum being used—whole language, invented spelling, the "new" new math— is the most irrational and harmful ever devised by so-called educators. It's a miracle that more children don't have ADD in such noisy, untidy classrooms. Who can possibly concentrate with so many distractions?

If the ADD child needs structure, the last place he will get it is in today's chaotic, irrational classrooms. Not only must there be structure in the physical environment but also in the curriculum and teaching methods. That's why homeschooling is the best environment for the ADD child. At home, not only can structure be created but the parents can use the best, most effective and rational teaching methods devised by man. And one-on-one instruction helps the child focus his attention on the lesson at hand. Also, the freedom to pursue activities and studies that interest the child will greatly enhance the child's self-esteem as a self-directed learner.

How do normal kids manage in the chaotic school? Teen idol Leonardo DiCaprio described his trials and tribulations in the March 1997 issue of *Teen*:

> I was frustrated in school—I wasn't happily learning things. I know it's up to you to a degree, but a lot of times school is just so dull and boring, it's hard for a kid to learn in that environment. You go to school, you go to this class, study this, study that, get your homework, go home. There's hardly any vibrance there. I could never focus on things I didn't want to learn. I used to do break-dancing skits with my friend at lunchtime. I had this one science class where the teacher would give me 10 minutes after the class ended and I would get up and do improv. I needed to go to a place where I was excited about what I was learning. For me, it's all about getting a person interested in a subject by linking a lot of happiness to it, a lot of joy in doing it. That was lacking for me—and maybe for a lot of other kids in this country.

The poor fellow sounds like a prisoner, grateful for having been given ten minutes in which to do something he enjoyed. That's the essence of the public school rip-off. The system kills the most precious commodity you have—your time. Obviously he had a high tolerance for boredom or else he would have wound up on Ritalin.

It is this writer's contention that the present configuration of the American classroom, plus the irrational curriculum that produces learning frustration, and the constant psychological probing of the child's feelings, beliefs, and values, are enough to create serious emotional and behavioral problems for many children which are then diagnosed as symptoms of ADD. We are all capable of becoming ADD under certain conditions that rattle our nerves and cause extreme frustration. The writer of the article in the *New York Times* magazine described a potential ADD situation that was nipped in the bud by homeschooling. He wrote:

> During Darcy's first year at a progressive Montessori pre-school, her teachers noticed she couldn't concentrate in a roomful of kids. Her parents were unhappy with the changes they saw in her: she was coming home agitated, stressed out. She developed nervous habits and slept poorly. Her parents launched an exhaustive search of alternative schools and private programs, hoping to find schooling that would allow their daughter to learn and concentrate in her own way.

After reading several books by John Holt, the parents decided to try homeschooling. Almost immediately Darcy's agitation diminished, her nervous habits began to disappear and, as her father remarked, "Suddenly this frustrated child could learn." Obviously, Darcy was a candidate for the ADD label, and had her parents not been wise enough to take her out of school, she probably would have been put on Ritalin. Darcy's mother says:

> In school, a kid like Darcy is road kill. . . . Kids who are different really get it from other kids. And teachers, even the best teachers, don't have time to protect a more tender child. Sometimes they're as mean as the kids. Darcy is a very deliberate child; she speaks slowly, she learned methodically, she's sensitive. Even her sisters are tough on her.

Luckily for Darcy, her parents were fast learners. Can homeschooling cure ADD? It certainly is worth a try.

-22-

Bureaucrats and Legislators

In a previous chapter we touched on the need for homeschoolers to get involved politically because educational policies are not merely determined by district superintendents of schools and local judges but by legislators enacting laws in state capitals and in Washington, D.C. The very existence of the U.S. Department of Education, with its multibillion-dollar budget and federal programs affecting education in every school district, makes it imperative for homeschoolers to monitor everything being done by the Congress and the bureaucrats that will affect their freedom in the future to educate their chidren at home without government interference.

In 1994 more bills concerning education were introduced in Congress than in all previous sessions. While most of these bills never got out of committee, some of them were enacted and have had an enormous impact on state education reform programs. These include the School-to-Work Opportunities Act, the Goals 2000: Educate America Act, and the Improving America's Schools Act which is a reauthorization of the Elementary and Secondary Education Act of 1965. It was this latter act which contained the amendment requiring all teachers to be certified which was later deleted from the bill because of the phone and fax blitz initiated by homeschoolers.

Both the School-to-Work Opportunities Act and the Goals 2000: Educate America Act are potentially dangerous to the future health of the homeschool movement. Both acts, crafted by individuals who think that the government ought to be planning the lives of all of its future adults, call for changing traditional liberal education into a kind of glorified vocational training that will begin in elementary school. An important component of these reforms is a massive computerized data-gathering system in the National Center for Education Statistics—a part of the Department of Education—in which highly personal, intimate, and sensitive information about every aspect of an individual's life will be stored. This information will be made available to just about anyone who wants it. The questions we must ask are, first: Does the government of a free people maintain detailed and extensive dossiers on the private lives of all of its citizens? Second: Who will own this information? And third: To what use will it be put?

Where do such un-American, totalitarian ideas come from? They come from such think tanks as the Carnegie Corporation of New York or the National Center for Education and the Economy. The president of the latter organization, Marc Tucker, has described his school reform scheme, funded by the School-to-Work Act, as a "Human Resources Development System" which will "create a seamless web of opportunities to develop one's skills that literally extends from cradle to grave and is the same system for everyone—young and old, poor and rich, worker and full-time student." When he says that it's a system for everyone he means it. In other words, homeschoolers will be brought into the system through some means. This all-inclusive idea was reiterated by J. D. Hoye, the White House director of the National School-to-Work Office, who said in 1994: "Our issue is it's for all kids. And all means all—all does not mean some."

Perhaps now you see why homeschoolers must become politically active. The legislators who enacted these laws—which, if uncontested, will put an end to educational freedom in America—must be made aware of what they are doing. The sad fact is that many of the legislators do not even read the bills they enact. They simply take their cue from the party leadership. But the homeschool activist network makes it a point to read all of the education bills that come before Congress. And therefore they are able to discuss these bills intelligently with their representatives and their aides, and state why they oppose them.

Once you decide to become an activist, find an activist network in your local area. There are literally hundreds of such groups across America, with all sorts of newsletters monitoring the legislative scene. There are also national conferences being held which deal with education issues. One of the handiest tools you can get is a U.S. Congress handbook, which contains the names and phone and fax numbers of all the members of Congress. The handbook will give party affiliation, committee membership, staff names, and other useful information. Thus, you'll be able to send your congressman or woman a fax urging him or her to vote for or oppose a particular bill. Politicians who want to be reelected pay attention to the letters they get from voters back home. You can even create a committee of one or several activists and produce a letterhead which will get even more attention from the legislator.

You may wonder how so small a group can wield so much clout when it comes to influencing legislators. The reason is simple. Homeschoolers may be small in number, but virtually all of them tend to be activists and vote in elections, while the vast majority of those who send their children to public schools tend to have less interest in getting involved politically—they don't have to, with the powerful teachers unions doing the politicking for them.

Another important area for homeschoolers to monitor is their state legislature. The state teachers organizations will be quite active in trying to expand their power and, if possible, get the legislature to enact laws requiring homeschoolers to register with the state, or require homeschooling parents to be certified, or require homeschooled kids to be tested, or require home visits by local superintendents, or require supervision of the homeschool by a state-certified teacher. The public educators have been able to get such regulations passed because they've been able to convince the legislators that homeschooling parents cannot be trusted.

Many homeschoolers have been quite willing to have their children tested because they know how much better educated their children are compared to the public schoolers. But many of these testing regulations state that if a homeschooled child does not score at his grade level, he or she may be forced to attend a public school. The irony here is that millions of public school children score below their grade level on achievement tests, yet the schools are not punished for their poor jobs of educating. In other words, homeschoolers are held up to a much higher teaching standard than the teachers in the public schools.

Sometimes, superintendents, armed by some state-mandated regulation, will try to intimidate homeschoolers. A letter to the superintendent from the Home School Legal Defense Association (HSLDA) will usually be enough to get the superintendent to back down. If not, lawyers from the Association will contest the superintendent in court. That's why it is worthwhile for homeschoolers to join the HSLDA. It provides the kind of legal protection that is sometimes necessary in dealing with the state or school district.

Also, join your state homeschool association if it is a membership organization. The homeschool movement in America is now very well organized, and there is power in numbers. You may even want to become an officer of the association. Most of the state associations are about ten years old, and many of the original founders are beginning to pass on the baton of leadership to others. What were once small organizations with mimeographed bulletins are now larger and more sophisticated, with glossy monthly magazines, big conventions, homeschooling handbooks, and all sorts of services for members. And they will become even larger in the years ahead.

All in all, it is important to remind superintendents and legislators that they are your public servants. They are not your masters, since it is your taxes that pay their salaries. So many bureaucrats and politicians seem to have forgotten that the taxpaying, law-abiding public is their master. And so, it is sometimes necessary to gently remind them of the facts of American political life. Only by such constant vigilance will we be able to preserve the free system of government handed down to us by the preceding generation.

-23-

Why Public Schools
Can't Be Trusted

I f you have any doubts as to what a public school can do to harm your child, read this chapter and weep.

On March 27, 1990, the *Detroit News* published the sad and tragic story of an eight-year-old boy who hanged himself at home after seeing a film about suicide in school. The newspaper wrote:

> An 8-year-old boy hanged himself on 3/24/90 in Canton, Michigan, one day after seeing a film on suicides shown to his class. Stephen Nalepa was found by his brother Jason about 9:30 p.m., Saturday, dangling by a belt from his bunk bed, his feet barely an inch off the floor.
>
> Stephen's shocked parents, Larry and Debby Nalepa, said their son's hanging may have been an accident inspired by a movie on suicides shown to his class Friday at Gallimore Elementary School in Canton.
>
> "A sequence in the movie depicts a child who is depressed trying to commit suicide by hanging from a belt and being saved at the last minute," Debby Nalepa said. "Less than 24 hours later, this happens."
>
> Stephen had never played with belts before and wasn't depressed like the child in the movie, said his mother, a nurse at Garden City Osteopathic Hospital, who tried in vain to revive him.
>
> "He was always imitating and mimicking because he was always so adept at everything," she said. "The principal told me the essence of the movie is to show that life is worth living, but

what really angers me is she admitted she had not even screened the film to see if it is appropriate for 8-year-olds."

Three officials at Plymouth-Canton Community Schools said they had never heard of the movie and refused to comment.

Debby Nalepa said Stephen stayed home to watch a vintage movie, *Titanic*, but became bored and went upstairs to play. About 9:30 p.m., she sent her older son, Jason, to get Stephen.

"That's when we heard this blood-curdling scream," Larry Nalepa said. "I ran upstairs and found Jason trying to hold Stephen up."

"His feet were only this far from the floor," Nalepa said, holding his forefinger and thumb barely an inch apart. "I took him down, and Debby started CPR (cardiopulmonary resuscitation) while Jason dialed 911. EMS came quickly and worked on him a whole hour, but it was too late."

Stephen, who had an IQ of 130, was an outgoing child who played soccer and basketball, collected baseball cards and took art and music classes.

Was the school responsible for Stephen's death? The parents thought so, and so on November 8, 1990, the Nalepas filed a wrongful death cause of action in Wayne County Circuit Court against the following parties involved in the production, distribution, and showing of the film: Encyclopedia Britannica (distributor), Osmond Productions (producer), the Wayne Oakland Library Federation (which obtained the film from defendant Wayne County Intermediate School District, and which distributed the film to the Plymouth-Canton Community Schools), the Plymouth-Canton School Board, Dr. Jacqueline Hisey (school psychologist), Shirley Spaniel (executive director of elementary education), Jane Armstrong (Stephen's teacher), Norma Foster and Alice Brown (the second-grade teachers who showed the film to three second-grade classes). On May 16, 1991, the Nalepas' attorneys requested a trial by jury but were denied it by the court. This should have warned the Nalepas that they would never see justice done in the case of their son's death.

What was this lethal film about? Entitled *Nobody's Useless,* it is about a child named Andy who had a leg amputated after falling in a barn where he was forbidden to play. In the film, Andy attempts to commit suicide twice, once by having a friend push him into a body of water while tied inside a burlap sack, and once by attempting to hang himself with a noose around his neck, attached to the rafters in a barn. Andy's friend attempts to push the bale of hay on which Andy was standing so that Andy would be hung. In the movie, Andy was saved by his friend's older brother, who happened to walk into the barn at a fortuitous moment. The movie ends with Andy enjoying new-found acceptance from friends and family.

On March 23, 1990, Stephen Nalepa's second-grade class viewed the film along with two other second-grade classes. Encyclopedia Britannica had recommended the film for grades 4 through 9. So why was this film about amputation and assisted suicide shown to second graders, and why weren't the parents notified that the film was going to be shown? Were the teachers engaged in some kind of experiment to see what kind of reaction second-graders would have to seeing this film?

Both Shirley Spaniel, the executive director of elementary education and the plaintiffs' expert Dr. Burnis Hall Jr., of Wayne State University, agreed that the film was not an appropriate resource for use in Stephen's second-grade social studies curriculum. According to Professor Hall:

> Using, or permitting the use of, the film *Nobody's Useless* for second-grade students, without previewing, without requiring or receiving approval ot without preparation of students would constitute a serious breach of duty amounting to gross negligence on the part of the teachers and administrators who are Defendants in this lawsuit.

According to the complaint:

> All of the rules were broken when the film *Nobody's Useless* was shown to the second-grade students at Gallimore School without preview, without approval from the principal and with questionable, if any, relationship to the curriculum it was supposed to support.... Attempted suicide is a confusing concept to introduce to young minds. It is an understatement to say that the introduction of attempted suicide is controversial. Defendants had certain procedures to follow if potential confusion or controversy might arise from the use of certain "educational materials." None of these procedures were followed and the most devastating personal injury to an elementary student followed.

What about Stephen Nalepa? Was he at all suicidal? At the insistence of Debby Nalepa, Stephen had been referred to the school's psychologist,

Dr. Jacqueline Hisey, for testing because he was a "bright boy with poor work production." The testing was done in November 1989 using the Wechsler Intelligence Scale (WISC-R), Bender-Gestalt, and the Kaufman Test of Educational Achievement (K-TEA). The report states:

> The kindergarten teacher... found that Stephen was enthusiastic, as well as an interesting, creative boy when involved in activities that he enjoyed, such as art. However he needed to "tend to work."... He was seen by the agency social worker who diagnosed "performance anxiety" and who thought Stephen might qualify as Emotionally Impaired under special education guidelines. Stephen is now a second grader and continues to have the same problems that prompted the initial Child Study referral. His present teacher, like his previous teachers, describe him as a bright boy with good skills who produces very little.
>
> ... Stephen approached the performance items with logic and insight. His language was mature and thought processes well organized and devoid of any loose tangential thinking.... In the interview he stated that school was "too easy" but then he didn't know why he had trouble getting his work done.... His stated interests are age appropriate. He likes hockey, soccer and collecting baseball cards. When confronted about some inappropriate language at school he said he learned it from an older boy.
>
> Stephen, on the WISC-R, obtained a Verbal IQ of 123, in the Superior range, a Performance IQ of 132, in the Very Superior range and Full Scale IQ of 131, also in the Very Superior range of intellectual functioning.... His performance in Object Assembly is outstanding and Stephen's explanation was "I like to do puzzles." The high was a result of motivation, superb planning strategies and puzzle experience.... He has good understanding of cause/effect and can sequentially put events together into a meaningful whole.... In essence, Stephen is very well endowed intellectually and uses his intelligence efficiently.

How Stephen would have thrived had he been homeschooled! He had what it takes to become a self-directed, self-motivated learner. As expected, he found school "too easy" and was bored out of his mind. If he produced very little it was probably because what the school required of him offended his logical mind. That's easy to understand, considering that the Plymouth-Canton Schools had adopted an Outcome-Based

Education and Mastery Learning curriculum in 1982. In fact, a six-page Board of Education Policy Statement of Oct. 26, 1982 (Policy No. 3709) outlined the district's Philosophical Principles and Practices. It states:

Mastery Learning assumes that virtually all students can learn, and that learning can be improved greatly, providing favorable learning conditions are present. In its "Statement of Philosophical Principles Underlying Outcome-Based Schooling," the Network for Outcome-Based Schools claims that almost all students are capable of achieving excellence in learning the essentials of formal schooling and that the instructional process can be changed to improve learning.

The fact that Stephen found school to be "too easy," is an indication that he was bored with the dumbed-down OBE-Mastery Learning curriculum. Mastery Learning is the application of B. F. Skinner's behavioral conditioning, animal-training techniques to the teaching of children. Because it requires no intellectual engagement on the part of the child who is being trained, it can become a deadly bore to a bright child or a dumbing-down, mind-numbing exercise for an average child.

In Stephen's case he was so turned off by the curriculum that Debby Nalepa had him tested on the morning of his death to see if he qualified for the Talented and Gifted Program. If he were suicidal, certainly there would have been some indication of deep emotional trouble that morning. But there wasn't, for, according to his parents, Stephen was not at all suicidal. He died of asphyxiation by hanging, in an act of imitative but self-injurious play.

And Stephen was not the only child who had tried to imitate what he had seen in the film. The Nalepas had obtained an affidavit from Mary Jane Egan, another parent who had a son at the Gallimore School. In the affidavit, Mrs. Egan said in sworn testimony that while her son Jimmy was a student at the Gallimore school, he was shown the movie *Nobody's Useless*. Shortly thereafter her daughter telephoned her at work and said that Jimmy had just tried to kill himself by climbing on top of a freezer in the basement, tying a noose around his neck and pretending to jump. When she came home and asked her son why he had done this, he replied that it was because the boy did it in the movie he had seen in school. Mrs. Egan then went to the school and told the principal, Joyce Deren, what her son had done at home. Mrs. Deren asserted that Jimmy's actions couldn't possibly be connected to the movie and suggested that Mrs.

Egan was making far too much of the situation. Furthermore, Mrs. Deren said that the school board believed that *Nobody's Useless* was an excellent film.

What does that tell you about the judgment of school boards and principals? Apparently, the film had been shown for a number of years with no concern on the part of the educators for its possible negative effects on the students. An affidavit from Encyclopedia Britannica stated that the film was released for distribution in 1980 and that by 1990 it had been shown to at least 1,800,000 children without a claim ever having been made by anyone against the distributor. But does that mean that no child had been psychologically harmed by the film? What if the child had committed suicide six months after seeing the film? Would anyone have made the connection then? Some emotional traumas can gestate for months before they lead to tragedy.

Despite Encyclopedia Britannica's assertions, an affidavit from child psychiatrist Dr. David Shaffer, of Columbia University's College of Physicians and Surgeons, left no doubt that a film of this kind, which he had viewed, could indeed produce tragic results. Dr. Shaffer stated:

> I have conducted extensive research and studies on adolescent suicide and foreseeable acts of imitation and have examined the incidence data for suicide among eight-year-old children....
>
> It is my professional opinion that there is a probability that under appropriate circumstances an elementary school student who viewed the film *Nobody's Useless* could attempt to imitate the suicide scenes depicted in the film. It is my professional opinion that the death of Stephen Nalepa on or about March 24, 1990, resulted because he viewed the film *Nobody's Useless* the previous day.
>
> My conclusion is based on an examination of the incidence data for suicide among eight-year-old children in the United States; the similarity between Stephen's death and the scene depicted in the film and the close proximity in time between Stephen viewing the film and his death.
>
> It is my professional opinion that Stephen Nalepa's death on March 24, 1990, would not have occurred had he not viewed the film *Nobody's Useless* the previous day. It is my professional opinion that there is nothing in the psychological autopsy which I conducted of Stephen Nalepa which would suggest that he was suicidal or that his death would have occurred had he not seen

the film *Nobody's Useless*. It is my professional opinion that prior to viewing the film *Nobody's Useless* Stephen Nalepa was not suicidal and that his death constituted an act of imitation.

It seemed like an open and shut case. The educators were guilty not only of negligence in their failure to protect the health and safety of a student but they were guilty of educational malpractice in showing a film to second-graders which the distributor had recommended for fourth- to ninth-graders. In addition, the educators had failed to obtain parental approval before showing this obviously emotionally charged film. Also, a parent had warned the principal of the fact that her son had imitated the suicidal child in the film and had almost killed himself. And considering the fact that educators are constantly reminding us that they are the experts and how much better they understand child psychology than those of us without degrees, one would have expected them to be especially cautious in what they exposed their students to. Thus, the picture we get of the Plymouth-Canton educators is one of ignorance, incompetence, irresponsibility, carelessness, and unprofessionalism. And they were all certified! No wonder the public is losing its faith in public education.

In addition, we expect educators of very young children to be able to foresee the possible consequences of school activities that arouse strong emotional reaction on the part of the students. And inasmuch as Stephen was compelled to see the film, and that the relationship between Stephen and the educators was custodial, their duty was to make sure that they did nothing that could harm any child in their charge, including one who might imitate the character in the film and hang himself.

One of the reasons why the news media in recent years have tended to play down teen suicides is because of the copycat effect. It is widely known that even adults are subject to the copycat effect. But children are forever imitating others in their games and play. For educators to pretend that such imitation is so rare that no cautions need be taken to protect children from their own imitative impulses is to suggest that either the educators were incredibly ignorant or that other motives were involved in their lapse of ordinary caution and common sense.

Early in the litigation, the court dismissed the case against Encyclopedia Britannica because its relationship to the deceased was too remote. They were not Stephen's custodians. That was the same argument used by the manufacturers of "Dungeons and Dragons" in *Watters v. TSR* (1990), in which parents of a youngster who had committed suicide blamed "Dungeons and Dragons" as the cause. The court ruled in favor of the manufacturer because the latter was not the custodian of the youngster at the time of his death or at any other time in proximity to his death.

However, in Stephen Nalepa's case, the educator-custodians actually showed Stephen the film that taught him the behavior that led to his death. But shouldn't Encyclopedia Britannica have warned the educators of the possible negative effects of the film on very young children, just as drug manufacturers dutifully warn users of the possible side effects of a drug, and cigarette manufacturers are required to explicitly warn smokers of the harmful effects of smoking?

To sum up the Nalepas' case: the educators were guilty of gross negligence of their custodial duty to care for the well-being of their students; the educators failed to foresee the possible harmful consequences of showing the film to impressionable eight-year-olds; and the defendants could not possibly seek the protection of the First Amendment in this case since the child had been compelled to view the film and the film itself was recommended for older children.

How did the educators defend themselves? Their attorneys first cited the court's summary dismissal of the case against Encyclopedia Britannica which ruled that the defendant "owed no duty to Plaintiffs and that imitative suicide is not a foreseeable risk of harm as an act of self-destruction breaks the chain of legal causation." The attorneys then argued: "Allowing the civil action to continue and/or the imposition of civil damages against these Defendants would violate the right of free speech guaranteed by the First Amendment of the United States Constitution, resulting in self-censorship of educational materials falling within the curriculum of the school district." In their Argument, the attorneys wrote:

> The Defendant teachers involved in this litigation, including Jane Armstrong, Norma Foster and Alice Brown, are likewise entitled to summary disposition as no duty existed on their part to refrain from showing the film in question. The conduct of the Plaintiffs' decedent simply was not foreseeable to give rise to such a duty. The teachers herein cannot be held liable for the self-destructive act of Plaintiffs' decedent. . . .
>
> The complaint filed by Plaintiffs herein alleges duties that resemble teacher malpractice and not those dealing with personal

injury proximately caused by a teacher. . . . However, . . . Michigan law does not recognize teacher malpractice as a theory of recovery.

And so, the defendants' case rested on the denial of the duty to protect the child from possible harm resulting from viewing the film, that such duty resembled teacher malpractice which the state of Michigan did not recognize as a theory of recovery, and that requiring the teachers to engage in censorship of instructional materials violated their First Amendment rights to freedom of speech. Would a jury have absolved the defendants on the basis of these flimsy, tortured arguments? In any case, the court ruled in favor of the educators.

In clearing the Encyclopedia Britannica, the judge wrote:

> The question involved is then whether defendant distributor [Encyclopedia Britannica] was under a duty to warn as articulated in plaintiff's complaint to avoid the contingency of an imitative suicide as allegedly occurred in the instant case. No legally compelling nor logically persuasive authority has been presented by the plaintiff tending to establish the type of duty involved herein. The weight of authority in cases of this sort rejects imposition of such a duty, finding that no duty to warn exists, that susceptibility to suicide is not foreseeable in such circumstances and that the act of self-destruction typically constitutes a break in the chain of legal causation. . . . Accordingly defendant Encyclopedia Britannica's motion for summary disposition shall be granted. (Signed Samuel A. Turner, Circuit Judge, Feb. 28, 1992)

On November 9, 1992, Judge Turner dismissed all of the complaints against all of the other defendants. He insisted on viewing Stephen's death as a simple suicide and not an imitative act resulting in accidental death by asphyxiation. All of the evidence indicates that Stephen had no intention of killing himself. Nevertheless, the judge, in a semiliterate opinion, wrote:

> First, although defendants herein owed plaintiffs' decedent a duty of reasonable care, as a matter of law that duty did not include an obligation to view and thereafter decline to exhibit the subject film based on the contingency that a student might resultingly commit suicide.
> Second, on the basis of the record as made the Court finds

that the result that in fact occurred (i.e. the suicide) was not as a matter of law foreseeable.

Third, the suicide, as a matter of law constituted a break in the chain of causation.

The judge also agreed with the defendants that they were protected by the First Amendment to the Constitution. He wrote:

In response to plaintiffs' claims defendants-movants submit 1) that they are not beholden to any duties such as those alleged by the plaintiff and 2) the free speech clause of the US Cost, Amend I enjoins the type of action herein sought to be maintained. Inasmuch as the first issue is, of itself, dispositive, the constitutional question need not be reached.

The Nalepas were devastated by Judge Turner's opinion, and took the case to the Court of Appeals. There had been many difficulties in this case. For example, the Nalepas had great trouble obtaining documents from the educators, such as the lesson plans of the teachers who had shown the film. The complaint states:

[The] Defendants are attempting to justify the use of the film by representing that it was a supplemental resource used to support the Social Studies curriculum. There is clearly a fact question as to what curriculum the film allegedly supported. If the film was utilized as a curriculum resource, Plaintiffs are entitled to know whether Defendants Foster, Armstrong, and Brown referred to any specific curriculum in their lesson plans or in the summary of their plans. Clearly Plaintiffs have substantial need of any written explanation or justification regarding why the film was shown, why it was unpreviewed and why second graders were required or permitted to view it.

In addition, Plaintiffs are unable, without undue hardship, to obtain the substantial equivalent of the written explanations by other means. The three Defendants testified at deposition that they destroyed their lesson plans. Thus, the only evidence pertaining to the lesson plans and/or why the film was shown would be found in documents supplied to the investigator employed by the Defendants' insurer in or about March, 1990.

At her August 1991 deposition, Defendant Foster admitted that she had prepared a write-up, in March 1990, which is a close recollection of what was in her lesson plans regarding the showing of the film. She then destroyed her lesson plans. When Plaintiffs' counsel attempted to inquire as to the contents of the write-up, defense counsel objected and *refused to allow Ms. Foster to answer* the question.

Foster admitted that she copied both Social Studies and Health curriculum when she prepared a write-up of activities surrounding the showing of the film. Indeed, Foster herself confused the written summary with her lesson plans and subsequently changed sworn interrogatory answers. Initially, Foster said she gave her lesson plans to her principal then changed and said she gave a written summary of the plans to her principal.

Defendant Armstrong [Stephen's teacher] also testified at deposition that she had destroyed her lesson plan book for the 1989–1990 school year. She has no recollection of what was in her lesson plan book for the day the film was shown, March 23, 1990.

Defendant Brown testified at desposition that she had prepared handwritten notes regarding why the film was shown and gave them to Ms. Deren, the principal of Gallimore School. The handwritten summary included pages from the curriculum which dealt with the subject, and this came out of her lesson plans, but she could not recall the content of the summary. She has not retained her lesson plans.

Since when do teachers deliberately destroy their lesson plans, especially when they are involved in a case where these plans may serve as crucial evidence? Obviously, the lesson plans were destroyed because they contained incriminating evidence. Such destruction of evidence is known as "obstruction of justice" and is a criminal offense. Half of President Nixon's staff went to jail for that, and Nixon himself was forced to resign because of that serious crime. Yet, the court let the teachers get away with it.

However, on August 9, 1991, the court ordered the defendants to produce copies of all written explanations, descriptions, justifications, or writings of any kind prepared by the defendants pertaining to the showing of the film. It was revealed that the film had been shown in conjunction with the second-grade health curriculum—in particular, the feelings and emotions section. The feelings and emotions section is part of Outcome-Based Education's affective domain. Prof. Benjamin Bloom, who formulated Outcome-Based Education, asserted that it was necessary to get to the children as early as possible in order to have the strongest influence on their values, beliefs, and behavior. He wrote in his *Taxonomy of Educational Objectives* concerning the affective domain:

> The evidence points out convincingly to the fact that age is a factor operating against attempts to effect a complete or thorough-going reorganization of attitudes and values. . . .
>
> The evidence collected thus far suggests that a single hour of classroom activity under certain conditions may bring about a major reorganization in cognitive as well as affective behaviors.

Were the educators at Gallimore School trying to prove the correctness of Professor Bloom's theory by showing the film to second-graders? Was this part of an effort to effect a complete reorganization of attitudes and values in these second-graders as part of a larger experiment? Indeed, we wonder what was in their lesson plans that was so incriminating.

And now comes the shocker. On November 23, 1994, four years and eight months after the death of Stephen Nalepa, the Court of Appeals announced its decision. It dismissed the Nalepas' case against all of the defendants. The court had decided that the school district and the superintendent were "entitled to absolute governmental immunity from tort liability when acting within the scope of their authority. . . . The film dealt with mental health issues, about which our state has evinced a concern." Concerning Encyclopedia Britannica and the rest of the defendants, the judges wrote:

> We find that Encyclopedia Britannica did not undertake a service to benefit the schools or the children. Thus, we agree with the circuit court that defendant Encyclopedia Britannica did not owe plaintiffs or Stephen a duty of care.
>
> With respect to the remaining defendants—the principal, teachers, counselors and other staff members—we conclude that although a duty of care exists, that duty does not extend to the actions of these defendants, which allegedly caused Stephen's death.
>
> Although Michigan recognizes a teacher's common law liability for a student's injuries proximately caused by the teacher, public policy must be considered in determining to what type of actions that duty extends. . . . Michigan law is clear that the duty does not extend to educational malpractice. . . .
>
> The rationale for declining to recognize claims of teacher malpractice stems from the collaborative nature of the teaching

process. *See Ross v. Creighton University.* . . . For a positive result to obtain, both teacher and student must work together. The ultimate responsibility for what is learned, however, remains with the student, and many considerations, beyond teacher misfeasance, can factor into whether a student receives the intended message. . . .

Even if the harm appears to flow from the alleged malpractice, for public policy reasons, we would still decline to recognize a duty. We agree with the Supreme Court of Wisconsin's statement in another educational malpractice case:

"Even where the chain of causation is complete and direct, recovery may sometimes be denied on grounds of public policy because . . . allowance of recovery would enter a field that has no sensible or just stopping point." . . .

Further, we conclude that recognizing this cause of action could lead to a flood of litigation which would be detrimental to our already overburdened educational system. . . . Finally we do not wish to embroil our courts into overseeing the day-to-day operations of our schools.

We conclude that the decision to show the film was based on academic factors. Therefore, any cause of action arising from that decision must fit within the educational malpractice genre. As a result, we agree with the trial court that the remaining defendants' duty of care did not extend to utilizing an allegedly improper teaching device. . . .

Plaintiffs' complaint is dismissed.

Are you shocked? What the judges' decision means is that, short of actual physical damage, educators can cause irreparable harm to a child and get away with it because the court does not recognize educational malpractice to be a cause of legal action. Apparently, educators need all the protection they can get, because what is being taught in sex education can lead to harmful consequences for many students, and how reading is taught in most public schools clearly causes the reading disability known as dyslexia, and the drugging of children with Ritalin and other drugs may also cause serious harm to some children. So the educators need whatever immunity the court can give them as they engage in blatant and outrageous educational malpractice. The state judicial system operates not to protect children or provide justice but to protect educators.

Thus parents should be aware that when it comes to public education, the cards are stacked against them. By putting and keeping their children in public schools they are placing their children at great risk. In fact, the Nalepa case provides parents with the strongest justification to remove their kids from the public schools and educate them at home. Educators can do just about anything they want to your child and get away with it because the court will protect them. Parents can no longer assume that their chidren are safe in school. If the educators want to use your kids as experimental animals in pursuit of some psychosocial goal, you can't stop them. The only thing you can do is take your kids out.

The Nalepa case also provides homeschoolers with a very strong argument against any government regulation of their children's education, for the government education establishment cannot be trusted and cannot be held liable for educational malpractice.

Let me end this chapter with a last look at little Stephen Nalepa. On Saturday morning, March 24, 1990, the last day of his life, Stephen was tested to see if he qualified for the talented and gifted program. Terri Michaelis, the program coordinator, provided an account of how Stephen behaved. She wrote:

> Mrs. Nalepa also asked me to comment on my recollection of Stephen during the testing on March 24. I picked up the students at the front of the school. Stephen first came to my attention when I called the roll from my list to see if I had everyone I should. Stephen self-confidently corrected my mispronunciation of his last name. He sat directly in front of my desk. He was active during testing with a lot of moving in his seat during the test. There were three short breaks while testing, during which he moved about with others and chatted at my desk. He tried hard and seemed to want to do well. He finished the test. The whole group left chatting and my memory is that Stephen was glad the test was over and as eager as the rest of the group to go home and play on a sunny Saturday. My memory of Stephen is that of a bright energetic second grader.

Despite all that the courts did to clear the educators of any wrongdoing, Debby Nalepa knows that if Stephen had not seen that film in class on March 23, 1990, he'd be alive today.

-24-

How Bad Can Public Schools Get?

Much has been written about the failures of the public schools: declining test scores, violence, drug trafficking, academic chaos. But what is even more disturbing is the changing mentality of public educators. At one time they were considered dedicated public servants who would never violate the trust that parents had vested in them. However, all of that has changed. Superintendents and principals now display a disdain for parents whenever the latter start complaining about school practices. For example, in New Hampshire the parents of a child were told that unless the child was put on Ritalin, the child could not attend school. In other cases, where parents have protested their children being exposed to highly explicit sex education, the schools have largely ignored the parents' concerns and continued doing whatever the educators wanted to do.

But the most egregious outrage we know of took place in March 1996 when fifty-nine sixth-grade girls at a middle school in East Stroudsburg, Pennsylvania, were forced to strip and subject themselves to an examination of their genitalia without the knowledge or consent of their parents. As expected, the incident caused a considerable outcry among parents. Here's an account of the story from the *Pocono Record* (March 22, 1996):

> Police Thursday investigated parents' complaints about physicals given to some J. T. Lambert Intermediate School sixth-grade girls. Some parents told school officials that their daughters were given an internal gynecological exam Tuesday. School officials, as well as the East Stroudsburg pediatrician who performed the exams, say there was only an external examination of genitalia—with some touching—which is within parameters set by the State Department of Health.

State police from Swiftwater came to the same conclusion. Some parents who acknowledged that their daughters were given an external genital exam said even that went too far in school. Several parents called the Pocono Record Thursday, saying their daughters were traumatized.

Katie and Paul Tucker of Bushkill said their 11-year-old daughter was touched internally. "She said most of the girls were crying. She tried to be brave.... She didn't go to school today because she was afraid," Mrs. Tucker said.

Mr. Tucker said, "I know her regular doctor would not have... done (that). She knows enough about her private parts. When she says no, she means no. Why not just rape her and deny it?"

Parents who called the paper told a similar story: Girls were asked to wait while partially clothed; some asked not to have their genitals examined, but they were told they had to; some started to cry, and at least one was denied a call home.

Dr. Ramlah Vahanvaty, who performed the exams, said no one was forced. At least one school nurse was present. "What it involved is an external examination of the labia to see if there were any warts or vaginal lesions. You can't see these if you don't retract the (labia)," Vahanvaty said....

Elaine Schneider of Bushkill said her daughter came home and said, "I'm never going through that again."

"Had I known, I would have taken her to a family doctor," Schneider said.

Vahanvaty said there was a lot of apprehension among some girls, but that she explained each part of the exam. When asked if some of the girls were crying, she said, "I don't remember."... Later she said, "Even a parent doesn't have the right to say what's appropriate for a physician to do when they're doing an exam. Parents were sent letters home saying they could be there. Few chose to show."

Dr. Vahanvaty said that few parents chose to be present at the exam, when in fact no parents were present. Also, the idea that a parent doesn't have the right to say what's appropriate for a doctor to do to that child, is evidence of an arrogance that has become standard behavior among bureaucrats and educators. On March 25, 1996, a meeting was held at the school, during which parents voiced their complaints and asked school officials to suspend the nurses who presided at the exams and asked that

Dr. Vahanvaty no longer be used by the district. The *Pocono Record* (March 26, 1996) reported:

> Vahanvaty, who did not attend the meeting, said in a telephone interview late Monday night that every physical was conducted "within strict professional standards. There was absolutely no internal exam." . . . The state Department of Health lists an examination of genitals as part of its guidelines for the physicals, mandated for all sixth-graders who have not seen their own doctor.
>
> A Department of Health spokesman said last week that each doctor has discretion over the extent of the exam. The two school nurses also did not attend Monday's meeting, one on the advice of her attorney, according to a school official.

It would be interesting to find out how many parents of school-children in Pennsylvania actually know or even suspect that their state Department of Health has mandated that all sixth-grade girls undergo an official, state-sanctioned examination of their genitalia. Is this what any state government ought to be doing in the name of education? And who, by the way, wrote these mandates? Were they debated and approved by the state legislature? Did the governor sign them into law? Or were they written by several bureaucrats in the Department of Health who had nothing better to do that day? The newspaper report goes on:

> More than fifty parents attended Monday's meeting at J. T. Lambert, and many angrily voiced their opinion that school nurses and Vahanvaty were callous and that the genitals of sixth-grade girls should never have been examined. . . .

Such forced examinations are usually called "sexual molestation," a criminal offense for which perpetraters are often sent to jail. Obviously, Dr. Vahanvaty and the two nurses considered themselves to be good public servants just doing their jobs. The story continues:

> Several sixth-grade girls told the crowd Monday that they asked not to have their genitals examined, but were told the exam had to be done. Some also said they were denied a call home. Susie Tucker, 11, broke down before Monday's crowd while describing the fear many girls felt while waiting half-clothed for the exam. Addie Bianco, a mother of a sixth-grade

girl who was not examined, told school officials that the exams had "raped the girls of their dignity."

Note how parents characterized these exams as "rapes." Granted, these were emotional reactions on the part of parents who viewed forced genital examinations by school officials as offensive and unwarranted in a free society. But what parents today are apparently unaware of is the erosion of that free society into a bureaucratic, controlled society in which our public servants have adopted the mentality and psychology of public masters. They routinely act as such and are somewhat taken aback when citizens balk at their edicts. Thus, the district solicitor in East Stroudsburg said that he would investigate the situation and that further exams would be put on hold, and school officials pledged to set new guidelines. That's what is known as bureaucratic damage control. Sometimes the public masters have to beat a hasty retreat, only to regroup and reassert their authority at a later date.

Meanwhile, local physicians came to the support of fellow physician Vahanvaty with a letter to the school board. The *Pocono Record* (March 28) reported:

> Eight area doctors sent a letter supporting Dr. Ramlah Vahanvaty to the East Stroudsburg School Board Wednesday. . . . In their letter, the doctors said they considered a genital exam a "very important part of the physical."
>
> "In our own practices we perform many school physicals daily. Sixth-graders are going through pubertal development and most of them are reluctant to show that area to doctors," the letter said. However, "Often we find some girls with physical deformities which may get worse with sports activities, and others with contagious conditions that require immediate medical treatment." Also, "Without any specific policy, all school physicals should be complete and comprehensive based upon the examining doctor's own practice." . . .
>
> They ended the letter saying, "We truly believe in the medical and moral standard of Dr. Vahanvaty who returned to provide a much-needed pediatric service to the community where she grew up." . . .
>
> Officials at one other area school district say they include an examination of genitalia for sixth graders. J. C. Mills Intermediate School in the Pleasant Valley School District included a visual

exam of genitalia on sixth-graders this year, Principal Sandra Fellin said. She added that, according to the school nurse, it's a practice that has continued for many years.

I'll bet that was news to a lot of parents! According to Ms. Fellin, genitalia exams have been going on for a long time and nobody's ever complained about it. Either Ms. Fellin is lying, or the people of Pennsylvania are a bunch of dolts who'll let the bureaucrats do anything they want to them. But I think not, for Pennsylvania has one of the fastest growing homeschool movements in the country. As for the doctors' defense of their colleague, nothing in the letter explained why the girls were not permitted to call home or why parents were not adequately informed of the pending exams. In short, the whole unsavory incident provides even more incentive for parents to get their kids out of the public schools and for citizens to get the government out of the education business. Dr. Vahanvaty's disdainful view of parents' rights is typical of the new public master who believes that the public school now owns the children who attend it. Gone is the respect that public educators once had for parents. Gone is the notion that schools served American families *in loco parentis*. And that's one of the reasons why thousands of parents are turning to homeschooling rather than have their children remain in a system that has become increasingly unfriendly, deceptive, and contemptuous of them.

The aunt of one of the students sent the following letter, describing all the gory details, to the American Civil Liberties Union, which agreed to look into the case:

> On Tuesday, March 19, 1996, all of the sixth-grade girls at J. T. Lambert in East Stroudsburg, PA were forced to take a physical exam, which included an examination of their genitalia. The students in each homeroom class were given numbers and called sequentially down to the nurse's office for the exam. There were six to ten girls at any given time, waiting in the nurse's office for the exam. They were required to strip down to their underwear and socks and wait to be called to see the doctor. The girls were subsequently individually called into the doctor's office, where they were required to remove their underwear, lay on the table and spread their legs for the exam. Many of the youngsters protested that they had already submitted proof of physical exams taken by their private physicians. They were told

that the school had lost these doctor notes and consequently the student had to take this exam. Many other students protested that they and their parents were unaware of the physical exam requirement and that they were both frightened and unwilling to undergo this exam without first contacting their parents. Some students complained this exam was not just external, but also internal. These students were denied the right to call their parents and told that they were required to submit to this exam.

Picture this. Eleven-year-old girls told to strip, lie down on a table and spread their legs despite vigorous protests. The school loses the doctors' notes. Just what you'd expect in a well-organized school system. Parents are not informed. The girls are denied the right to call home. Just shut up and spread your legs, they're told. Does this sound like the public school you went to way back when? Does this sound like the school system of a free society? Or does this sound like something out of Nazi Germany? The letter goes on:

> It is true that the school district rules require that students be given "a comprehensive examination upon entering the school district as well as in the sixth and eleventh grades," but the nature of the term "comprehensive" was not made clear to the parents. School officials allege that they sent home notices about the physical exam requirements as well as parental permission slips to take the exam in school. The school officials, showed a copy of this notice, which was allegedly sent and pointed to a paragraph which states, "... Failure to return this notice signed by the parent will be considered to be proof of the parents' permission for their child to receive this exam in school and not to opt to have it given by the child's (private) physician.["] The school was unable to present any proof that parents ever received such notices.
>
> I want to go on record to state that I did not receive the aforementioned parental form, nor any information about the scope of such an exam, or the rationale for it. ... Finally, the only communication I received was a notice informing me of the exam that had already taken place, without my permission, informing me that I could come to the school to voice my concerns.

What do we learn from this outrageous violation of the right to bodily privacy, of parents' rights to guard their children from such violations and their right to expect educators to act within the bounds of propriety and common sense? We learn that not only do the educators lack common sense but common sensitivity as well. These people are supposed to know something about human psychology, but they act as if they know nothing. In short, they have created ugly new standards of behavior that are alien to our way of life. We also learn that the educators are becoming bolder and bolder in their disregard for individual rights. To subject eleven-year-old girls to a forced, humiliating examination of their private parts by government officials is to inform them that they are now owned by the state. And, by the way, are the boys having their genitals examined to see if they have any diseases? Perhaps condoms are supposed to take care of that problem.

As far as we know, none of the girls had any genitalia problems that warranted this gross violation of their privacy. When people in a state of freedom have problems with their private parts they go to private doctors for such intimate exams, diagnoses, and treatments, the records of which patients expect to be kept confidential. It is unheard of in this country for perfectly healthy individuals to be forcibly herded into a nurse's room, told to strip and lie down on a table for an examination of their genitalia. No adult in his right mind would put up with such a situation. Many would resist with violence.

During World War II, when Jews and others were rounded up and sent to concentration camps, the first thing their captors forced them to do was strip. The purpose of the stripping was to deprive these captives of any notion of privacy or personal dignity. The stripping meant that they were now the property of their captors who could do anything they wanted to them. The educators in East Stroudsburg may not be Nazis but their behavior suggests that they really don't understand the difference between a totalitarian society and a free society. If they are indeed so deficient in their understanding, then we have much more to worry about than we'd like to admit.

Meanwhile, as of June 1997, seven families have filed suit against the East Stroudsburg school system for violating their parental rights and inflicting emotional trauma on their daughters, and a bill has been introduced in the Pennsylvania legislature providing stronger protection for students and parents rights.

- 25 -

African-American Homeschoolers

One of the most exciting developments in the homeschool movement is the growing number of African-American families that have decided to join it. They represent a vanguard of families that have come to the realization that government educational institutions have done more to stunt the intellectual growth of minorities than any other force in American culture. One of the reasons why black Americans have tended to shy away from homeschooling is the belief that without a recognized school credential, a diploma, they would not be able to get the jobs that require such credentials. But as more and more homeschoolers have demonstrated that you can get into college and get a good job without the traditional school diploma, black families now realize that their children can get a better education at home, and that their abilities will get them the careers they want. Indeed, as Grace Llewellyn writes in her book *Freedom Challenge:*

> As scary as it can be to challenge the system and risk going without formal credentials, black people may—as a group—stand to benefit more than anyone else from the opportunities homeschooling can offer.

And her book bears that out. In it you will find fascinating accounts of homeschooling by African-American families, stories which really say more about the homeschooling experience in general than about racism or race consciousness. What clearly comes out in this book, however, is that many black Americans are convinced that black children, particularly the boys, are being deliberately dumbed down and shortchanged by the public schools. They see this as a manifestation of a general racism that is endemic to American society. What they don't seem to see is the fact that white children are being as dumbed down and shortchanged as the minorities. In short, all American children are at risk in the public schools, not just the minorities. Most of the girls at the East Stroudsburg school who were forced to strip and submit to a genitalia exam were white. Stephen Nalepa who was shown a film on suicide in class and hanged himself the next day was white. Of the four million children on Ritalin, the vast majority are white. The public schools are an equal-opportunity destroyer.

Also, there seems to be a great deal of confusion concerning race consciousness and racism. In America, where we have so many diverse races and colors, everyone is race conscious or has an awareness of racial differences. After all, that's one of the major themes on TV talk shows. But very few of us are actually racist in the sense that we want to harm or penalize or disciminate against people because of their color. Indeed, there seems to be far more color consciousness among people of color than among whites. One of the black homeschooling moms, married to a white Frenchman, spoke of her young daughter's color consciousness at a discussion among homeschoolers of color:

> Kids are very color conscious, I think, especially around five and six years old. I think children are really trying to figure it out, you know. We went back East just recently and she was explaining to my family in Massachusetts about all her friends. . . . And she put all the colors out. She said, "One friend, he looks just like me. His mama is *this* color and his daddy is *that* color, but *we* look a lot alike." They begin to see that it doesn't always make sense, but that's the way it is. And it stops being weird, and I think she's feeling more grounded in her sense of self, and she fits in a couple of worlds. We've got lots of French relatives this summer—it's August, they've come. So she's really getting that too.

Color consciousness and racism are facts of life, but homeschooling permits children of color to grow up in an atmosphere of warmth and support and gain all of the benefits of educational freedom. And more and more African-American parents are discovering this. But what has held back most African Americans from enjoying the homeschooling lifestyle is a self-inflicted inhibition. One of the moms in the discussion put it this way:

I think the problem is that we don't *feel* as free [as whites]. When you grow up, you have a psyche that confines you. . . . [W]e have to break our own barriers.

But those families that have broken the barriers are enjoying educational freedom for all it's worth, and their children are thriving. What all of these families have in common is a true love of their children and a desire to see that they get the best education that parents can provide. They also have the courage to test the boundaries of American freedom. Pamela Sparks, a homeschooling mom of four children, writes in Grace Llewellyn's book:

> I've heard homeschooling called the "mothers' milk" of education. And I think it's a fitting analogy. For years, we as a society were convinced by "experts" that formula feeding was superior to nursing for both baby's nutrition and mother's convenience. Now we are coming full circle with the realization that nothing comes close to mothers' milk for overall nutrition, immunoproperties, brain development and emotional bonding from the experience of nursing. We've been similarly duped, only far more so, educationally. What can compare with an artificial institution, to the natural education of living and learning within one's family and the world?
>
> Homeschooling is empowering. It means taking control and making decisions for one's own family and one's children instead of abdicating these rights and responsibilities to others or simply complying with societal norms. Particularly for African Americans, schools are by and large failing our children even while they have convinced us that they know best. And societal norms are not effective in supporting our chidren to be happy, strong, and smart.

It is exhilarating to read these firsthand accounts of homeschooling by African-American parents and children. One senses the tremendous potential for black Americans to excel in our society, if only they will feel courageous enough to opt for educational freedom. Pamela Sparks's ten-year-old daughter Whitney writes:

> I have some advice for parents who are just starting to homeschool and that is: you don't homeschool like a school. Homeschooling is not parents tutoring their kids. When you homeschool, parents are simply sharing their experiences with

their kids, ways to learn about new things, ways to learn about everyday living. . . .

The main reason you would choose to homeschool is so you can free your mind to do anything you want to do. . . . I don't think I would have been able to get interested in names and Greek myths if I hadn't had time to follow my own interests. . . . And once I got onto Greek myths I studied and am still studying all the gods and goddesses in the myths and their similarities and connections to Egyptian and Roman myths and gods and goddesses. And this helps me study the meanings of words.

There can be no doubt that this ten-year-old has caught the essence of homeschooling and is making the most of the time that freedom has given her. Her nine-year-old brother, Brandon, writes:

[W]hen you're being taught at home, you're your mom's or dad's main focus—you're the only person, the entire class. And I think parents have a certain bonding with their kids.

Even a nine-year-old can understand the essential benefit of homeschooling! It's mom and dad being there. He says further:

I think everything could be a learning experience. You just have to know *how* to make it a learning experience.

Smart kid that Brandon! It's amazing how intelligent kids can be when they're being homeschooled. Indira Curry, now twenty years old, left a public high school at fifteen to be homeschooled. She said in an interview:

For me, having experienced both worlds, I could compare a school to jail. Coming out and going into homeschooling, it was like that jail door opened and I had freedom to walk out when I wanted to. I think new homeschoolers would benefit from thinking of it that way: they are now out of jail. They can now go and explore things that they may not have had the privilege of knowing about while in school because the teachers had a set curriculum. Explore everything. Follow your interests.

At seventeen, Indira received a diploma from Clonlara's Home Based Education program. Her goal is to become an architectural engineer.

Donna E. Nichols-White is a dynamic force in the African-American homeschool movement. She is the founder and publisher of *The Drinking*

Gourd, a multicultural magazine for homeschoolers. She writes:

> When I began to homeschool I depended on a structured curriculum for security, but only for three months. I quickly discovered just how much the kids could learn without it. I may use one again in the future but it will be as a supplement—not a life.... Ours is a curriculum of independence.... We have proven that schooling is not necessary, and this we have discovered through trial and error.... Schooling damages Black students the most; no other group of students fail in school at the rate they do.... African-American people could not possibly be the least intelligent people on the planet. I think the institution of education in America is designed to turn us into failure....
>
> Homeschooling is our family's way of life. We like it and we enjoy being a family. I love being a mother. We live a good life. At this moment, we have no need for institutionalized education; we're happy with things just the way they are.

Homeschooling just doesn't get better than that! Some African-American homeschoolers have really taken educational freedom to heart. Tanya Khemet writes:

> We start *our* school day with music and dance; that's our P.E. class. We use drumming to learn the times tables. This is all a learning process for me as well as my students, because it's not the way I was educated, and it is very easy to fall into the trap of presenting the material the way it was presented to me.... If there is a math concept I can't get across, I just use an example that involves money, and suddenly mud becomes crystal clear....
>
> Yes, make no mistake about it, there is a *battle* raging for the very hearts and souls of our children. The weapons I bring to this struggle are my love for my children, every talent and skill I possess, all the wisdom I have acquired, and the courage to take this leap of faith and do what I know is right.

It does indeed require a leap of faith to leave the institutions that government has used for over a hundred years to impose social control over the American people. But these institutions were modeled on the Prussian education system and imposed on America in the mid-nineteenth century by a messianic elite who were convinced they knew how to lead Americans to moral perfection. The system worked until the progressives took it over and implemented their radical reforms. Although the experiment overall has been a colossal failure, the monopolistic edifice the reformers built has not only become the greatest single tax burden on the American people but the greatest retardant of American intellectual development. It is said that a monopoly forces people to pay the highest price for the poorest goods. And that is a perfect picture of the American public school system.

One of the happiest families in Grace Llewellyn's book are the Pogues, a military family of six. It was during one of the family's moves across the country that Cherie Pogue first heard about homeschooling. The children were spending time with her mother-in-law in Pensacola, and Cherie had to drive from California to Virginia to meet her husband coming out of Officer Candidate School. Together they would pick up the kids. She writes:

> With all those hours to myself, I had plenty of time to think about stuff like "what is life all about," and "why am I here." Somewhere in Utah on Interstate 70, I found the Lord, via Christian radio, among the purple-crimson-orange plateaus illuminated by jagged streaks of lightning. Suddenly everything was different. My world was renewed, alive, and suddenly I realized that I knew nothing....I heard some kooks talking about how "ungodly" the public schools were, and how they were teaching their children at home.

But it wasn't until the family was transferred to Okinawa that Cherie and her husband Michael decided to homeschool. They tried a variety of homeschooling programs, but finally decided that "each homeschooling family must find what works for their own children." The day finally came when they were transferred back to the states. And it was during the eighteen-hour flight across the Pacific that Cherie could see the difference between her homeschooled kids and the schooled kids. The latter were bored and turned the airplane into a raucous playground, annoying everyone. The Pogue kids behaved differently, and Cherie explains why:

> The real difference...was that our children had had plenty of time alone throughout the years to amuse themselves quietly while I'd work with one of their siblings. We had dumped the

television three years ago, so they didn't complain on the flight that they were missing their favorite show. . . .

Bottom line: Our children had been responsible for providing their own entertainment for the past three years, and given the responsibility and freedom to choose, they could occupy themselves peacefully for eighteen hours if necessary. Surprisingly, the "toy" the children used the most was their individual notepads. Each child drew, wrote, copied, scribbled, and colored at will. The work in this notebook, in fact, resulted in some of the best "compositions" that the children had ever written.

In other words, the children had learned to use their minds. Another happy family in Grace Llewellyn's book are the Rhues, a biracial couple with three boys. Dad Toby Rhue, who works for the Forest Service, writes:

There has never been a question as to whether we would homeschool; it was a given. Chris and I agreed early on homeschooling, even though we knew little about what we had agreed on. We just knew in our hearts that there had to be an alternative to public education and the high cost of private schooling. . . .

My kids are free to be whatever they want to—maybe explorers, by looking through the pages of *National Geographic* or encyclopedias; maybe chefs, in which case I get the extreme pleasure of sampling their culinary works; or they may dream, inspired by books Chris or I have read to them. If my boys attended public school, it would be impossible to afford them large blocks of time to go deeply into any activity. We have learned that even "doing nothing" is important. "Doing nothing" allows the time needed to assimilate or put meaning to what they have learned during busier moments.

My role in homeschooling is to be as supportive and enthusiastic as I can in challenging the boys to want to learn through having fun—not through the drudgery I experienced in school.

Chris Rhue, the Caucasian half of the union, writes:

I had a mostly traumatic elementary and secondary school experience. I then went on to become a special education teacher and taught for four years. I sometimes tell people—truthfully— that these experiences, as student and as teacher, caused me to vow that my children would never go to school.

The really wonderful thing is that Toby has always completely supported me and has offered all the help he can. This is
what I see as one main difference between us and many other
homeschoolers. We often hear that the husbands are skeptical,
unsupportive, or downright against it. When I hear this, I am
always grateful that we are together in this. Especially as we are
unschoolers, and must trust in the children—not in paperwork
and test scores. . . .

On the question of why so few African-American families are
homeschooling, Chris writes:

> Sometimes I don't think minority peoples are aware of the
> alternatives (and their benefits), or of the true freedoms that they
> do have.

Obviously, African Amercians would benefit immensely from homeschooling. It would give them the sense of freedom they so badly need,
convinced as they are that some great malevolent force is holding them
down. If there is such a force, it is public education which is turning
thousands of young African Americans into frustrated, angry functional
illiterates with crippled intellects, many of whom then find their relief in
gangs, drugs, and violence.

The true models of sanity, learning, and ambition are those African-
American homeschooling families who have discovered, as have other
homeschoolers, that happiness has its genesis in the loving family where
parents and children share their lives with one another and not with an
alien institution called a school that undermines family togetherness.
Homeschooling has helped Americans rediscover the family as it should
be, not the conflict-ridden, divorce-prone household where schooling and
television reign supreme as cultural values, but where love and commit-
ment are the binding forces that create a lifetime of joy and wonderment.

Grace Llewellyn's book provides a wealth of information about how
families homeschool, the methods they use to find the right curriculum
or noncurriculum, the freedom they enjoy to build their lives around
their own needs, interests, and opportunities. And what becomes so clear
in these stories is that when public education is removed from the life of a
family, happiness becomes real, palpable, and sustaining. For information on how to get the book, see the appendix.

-26-

What Do Homeschoolers Do?

Most public schools are pretty much alike. A high school in Anchorage, Alaska, is not much different from a high school in Miami, Florida. They generally use the same textbooks, the same curriculum, the same government-funded programs, the same teaching methods, and they also have the same problems: drugs, violence, ADD, low test scores, etc. One of the reasons for the Charter School movement is to get away from the homogenized sameness of the public system. But even charter schools are public schools and must adhere to certain mandated guidelines.

The reason for the sameness is due to the fact that the education establishment is organized on a national basis. The National Education Association, the Council of Chief State School Officers, the National Association of Secondary School Principals, the Association for Supervision and Curriculum Development are just a few of the establishment entities that have nationalized and homogenized American public education. It is no accident that the headquarters of many of these major organizations are located in and around Washington, D.C.

On the other hand, no two homeschooling families are alike. They have tremendous freedom to tailor their home education practices to their own needs. Thus, there is great curiosity among homeschoolers to know how other families do it. That's why homeschool conventions, workshops, and support groups are so popular. They give homeschoolers the opportunity to find out how others do it. However, there is now a book by Nancy Lande, *Homeschooling: A Patchwork of Days,* in which thirty homeschooling families describe a day in their lives, which will go a long way to satisfy not only the curiosity of other homeschoolers but of those parents who are thinking about homeschooling and would like to know what it's like in practice.

What we learn from reading Nancy Lande's book is that homeschooling families come in all sorts of shapes, sizes, and colors. There are large families and small families, religious families and secular families. Most are middle-class families living on limited budgets, and most live in suburbs, in the country, or on farms. While most of the families in the book live in various parts of Pennsylvania, the other families live in Kansas, Alaska, Vermont, Nebraska, Indiana, Texas, and New Mexico; and in other parts of the world—Quebec, Australia, Scotland, and Senegal. The family in Senegal are missionaries who are homeschooling their two boys.

In short, the homeschooling lifestyle can be practiced successfully just about anywhere. It does help to have a large house if you have lots of kids. But even cramped apartment dwellers in big cities could no doubt homeschool if they put their minds to it. For most homeschoolers, the library is their main resource for books and videos, and cities have many wonderful places to visit, such as zoos, parks, botanical gardens, concert halls, museums, historical sights, monuments, courts, newspapers, radio and TV stations, sports arenas, skating rinks, bowling alleys, shopping malls, exhibitions, conventions, colleges, universities, etc.

That so many homeschooling families live in small towns may be due to the fact that small-town, rural life is more conducive to having large families than city life. There is more room in the country, more family self-reliance, more dependence on the love and comfort that family life provides. Homeschooling families are happy families. That's not to say that they don't have problems, such as the birth of a sickly child. But they usually don't have the kinds of problems that afflict public school families, such as drug addiction, alcoholism, child abuse, spouse abuse, venereal disease, teen pregnancies, gangs, crime, and suicide. The dysfunctional family is usually a public school family.

Homeschoolers seem to have developed a special sense that tells them what will make a family happy and a willingness to make whatever adjustments are necessary to insure that happiness. Usually mom and dad have a good marriage and love the idea of having a large family. Their desire to homeschool grows out of their knowledge that public schools do not produce happy children. Nancy Lande writes in her Introduction:

My husband and I watched our older two children gradually lose their spark for learning after attending public school for several years. . . . But it's one thing to be unhappy with a situation and quite another to create an alternative.

That summer we heard a lecture by a well-known advocate for home education. Everything he discussed about education rang true and we realized then that homeschooling was the answer for the changes we urgently sought.

And so Nancy and her husband got as much information about homeschooling as they could find and then took the plunge. She writes:

Our first year of homeschooling was one of trial and error, wonderful and wasted purchases, changes in styles and routines, too many group activities, and the growing happiness of our family. We wondered if we had to be [sic] what the schools do and do it better. Or could we do something that had no resemblance to "school"? . . .

At the end of our first year, after hundreds more hours of readings, phone calls, workshops, tapes, discussions, and now *actual experience,* we had begun to answer some of our questions and to find our own style of home learning which still continues to evolve.

But then, Nancy thought, wouldn't it be wonderful if there were a book from which homeschoolers could learn from the experiences of other homeschoolers and new homeschoolers could learn from the experiences of longtime practitioners? The result is a book that does all of that, as you will see from the quotes in this chapter.

So what do we learn? We learn that just about every homeschooling family goes through the same learning period of trial and error, for each family adjusts to the new home education lifestyle in their own way. They learn how to set aside certain areas of the house for homeschooling. They learn how to assign chores to the kids so that things are picked up, food prepared, dishes washed, clothes folded, etc. They learn how to schedule time. They learn that each child is different and learns differently and that you have to learn what works and doesn't work. They learn how to handle television, either banning it or limiting it to certain times and certain programs. Most of them start out with highly structured programs and then decide to loosen up in the second year when they notice how marvelously children learn. That's always one of the great discoveries that homeschooling parents make: their children enjoy learning when given the freedom to follow their own interests. They find that they can choose among many different study courses and programs as their children grow, and they are not averse to trying a new program to see if it will work better than the one they have been using.

Homeschool homes are cheerful, lived-in places. Nancy, a mother of four in a Philadelphia suburb writes:

> Home is where we have over-filled bookshelves in every room, inviting chairs and sofas in which to read and talk, lots of cheerful quilts on beds and walls, a woodworking shop and a well-supplied art room in our basement, a kitchen area that is the center of activity where we all gather to cook, bake, can, clean, learn, play, think and most often—talk. . . .
>
> The use of our rooms continually changes, as does our homeschooling itself. From the beginning of homeschooling, as the children grew to relax and become comfortable working around each other, they quickly found that they all preferred to work in the living room or at the kitchen table. For concentrated focus, they can retire to a quiet corner of the house. . . .
>
> Also in the living room are the piano, violin, cello, and percussion instruments, along with one of our three networked computers, the TV and video machine, CD and stereo equipment, copy machine, and baskets on the floor for well over a hundred library books. Our book shelves hold thousands of books, games, math manipulatives and things we have forgotten about.

What public school could compete with that home for comfort and equipment! There is no limit to what homeschoolers can do to make their homes warm, cheerful centers of learning. On a smaller scale, a mother of two describes her homeschool:

> Our school room is a converted one-car garage that is attached to our house. One side is taken up with bookshelves that are bulging with books, and my desk and chair. On the opposite side are our silent teachers—posters on the wall, a filing cabinet, our computer, a long work table where the children work most of the time, and some storage for curriculum and other school supplies. The children's beanbag chairs are on the floor in front of the bookshelves where they sometimes work.

Just about every homeschooling family has a computer. Many are on the Internet and receive and send e-mail. One family with four kids in Pennsylvania runs a small mail-order catalog business. Mom writes:

> Our home business that serves homeschoolers has its office on our second floor—a hi-tech room with four computers, a photo-copier, laser printer, comb-binding machine, a fax phone machine, scads of file cabinets. . . . My husband Howard is up here most days when he's home, and the kids often find their way into the old easy chair in one corner.

What are the children doing during school time?

> Jesse, seventeen, might be upstairs reading in his bunkbed or typing on his computer in the office. Jacob, fourteen, is usually found at his computer in the project room. Molly, eleven, might be sprawled on the sofa reading or on the floor somewhere involved in some new art project. Hannah, age seven, might be playing up in her bedroom or the finished-off attic, or talking with me in the kitchen as I do dishes, or doing French with me up in my bedroom (that way the tape recorder won't distract the other kids downstairs).

Think of it, no bells, no rushing from one classroom to another, no spitballs to dodge, no silly students causing a ruckus in the classroom, no shoving on the cafeteria line. Learning at home is an absolute pleasure and delight. A mom of two in Texas writes:

> Homeschooling takes place all over the house. It has been at the kitchen table, at a card table in the living room, on the floor of whoever's room is picked up, and both at a table and on the floor of a converted garage that I use as a library. . . . The more formal parts of schooling are done between breakfast and lunch, but time on the computer is anytime the children want it.

As for chores, everybody learns to do his or her share. A mom of two girls in Pennsylvania writes:

> I believe in not doing things for children that they can do themselves. Jennifer, eleven, and Michelle, nine years old, sort, fold and put away laundry, unload the dishwasher, help set and clear the table, help plan and prepare meals, help make grocery lists and shop, clean their rooms, and help straighten the living and dining rooms. Sometimes the girls help wash the car and clean

the windows, plant and water the garden, weed and harvest the garden. Jenny is learning to drive the tractor and cut the grass.

A homeschooling dad of four in Nebraska writes:

> One of the most important reasons we are homeschooling, and a part of the values we are trying to teach our children, is to teach responsibility and hard work.... I finally decided that a list of things to do for each child was important. So, I sat down with each one and we came up with a list. Katy, twelve, now has to do things like vacuum the living room carpet (which has her dog's hair on it), empty the kitchen trash, sweep the basement, vacuum the stairs. Colleen, seven, now has a list that has things like bring Eamon's, age one, laundry upstairs and put it away.... Ethan, five, now gets to do things like dust... take hangers to the laundry room, pick up Eamon's toys in the living room.... Oh, a final thing about chores: do them or you don't get dessert.

In rural Alaska, a homeschooling family with three kids uses their computer to connect with the world. The mother writes about how she spends the early morning before the kids are awake:

> I take advantage of the quiet time to have some personal time for myself and check my e-mail. There are some messages waiting for me from homeschoolers around the world. I enjoy the homeschool mailing list I subscribe to and find the opinions and messages as varied as the snowflakes falling outside.... We have a "Home Page," which is a document with text and pictures telling about our family on the World Wide Web. I have "met" more homeschoolers through the computer than I have at our local homeschool support group.... The people and messages have been like rays of sunshine on dark and cold days.... [T]he Internet has allowed me to "visit" the world from my desktop and the adult interaction has been a life-line of communication....
>
> Caleb, ten, has [an e-mail] letter from his friend in the Ukraine! We saw a posting on the Internet Usenet from a nine-year-old Ukrainian boy who was looking for an English-speaking pen pal. Caleb responded and we have all had a wonderful time learning about him and his family.

Homeschoolers have taken to the Internet like ducks to water. They are way ahead of public schoolers in their use of the new technology, not only because they have computers in their homes but because they have the *time* to use them.

Although moms do most of the homeschooling, the importance of dads is emphasized. Nancy Lande writes:

> Though I am the one who spends most of the day with the children, Gary fully supports our homeschooling with his input, guidance, supplies, field trips, computer support, financial backing for our family, and his constant love for all of us. . . . He guides us to keep on track, hears our frustrations, helps us find solutions, and always comes up with the most wonderful resources. . . . It was important to Gary and me, even before we started our family, that Gary would choose to work at home so that he would be an integral part of our family life, being a father who is a visible role model and who is available to his children.

Another mom writes:

> My husband is all for homeschooling. I am trying to include him in more of the learning, though as of today, he has worked thirty days straight and some of those days are twelve-hour days!

A homeschooling dad in Pennsylvania writes:

> We have committed ourselves to homeschooling four very different children. To do so, we have had to make many sacrifices. Putting the boys in school might seem easier, but would force us to sacrifice what we are unwilling to sacrifice: strong and active involvement in the lives of our children. To accomplish this, we have decided that I will be the primary "bread winner," while Nancy will be the primary teacher and "housekeeper." . . . I do the grocery shopping . . . all the laundry, clean the bathroom, and jump in when necessary with cooking, meal clean-up, and whatever else needs to be done. . . . I think that the most important role that a homeschooling father can assume is that of nurturing his wife.

That's the attitude it takes to have a successful, happy homeschooling family. Another mom writes:

> Homeschooling isn't easy—nor is it impossible! A husband who is the sole bread-winner has a great responsibility in that fact alone. My husband's willingness to be such enables me to stay at

home and teach. This *is* important; this *is* support. It entails lots of sacrificing of the extras that a second paycheck could offer. Lots of men won't go *that* far today.

On the matter of how children learn at home, one Pennsylvania mom writes:

> There are many things I've learned from the ten years of homeschooling my kids: . . . that allowing children to make their own decisons and follow their own path can be as painful to a parent as it is rewarding and is filled with self-discovery for the child. . . . It's not been easy stepping back and trusting the kids to work through the difficult stuff without my labored breathing down their necks; it's sometimes impossible to believe that one bad math day or an indifferent, toss-away science report does not mean the end of life on earth. Even if the girls may not do something the way I'd like to see it done, I have learned that they will be able to meet their own goals when they have the need or the desire, or will adjust their aspirations accordingly.

That's the kind of hard-learned wisdom many parents acquire when homeschooling, particularly those parents who start off by thinking that they must replicate the schoolroom in their home. The most relaxed homeschoolers are those who have adopted John Holt's unschooling philosophy. An unschooling mom in New Mexico writes:

> Our daily plans are nebulous, and although we might schedule a trip to the zoo . . . we don't have something scheduled on most days, and we don't "educationalize" trips to zoos and museums and such. We just go, and what we read or see is discussed, but not in a scheduled, checklist way.

In the unschooled home, the child learns what he or she wants to learn when he or she wants to learn it. That's the educational philosophy of the famous Sudbury Valley School in Massachusetts, where children learn what they want to learn when they want to learn it. But, in reality, unschoolers are not that loose. They generally do stimulate their children to learn by having lots of books, tapes, games, and other materials in the home.

However, most homeschoolers believe that some sort of scheduling and some sort of definite educational objectives are necessary if the child is to acquire the knowledge and skills needed to pursue a career and/or go to college. Homeschoolers stress the need to learn to read, write, do math, know grammar, think logically, know history, geography, the sciences, literature, etc. The families in Nancy Lande's book are constantly seeking new materials, new approaches, new books to make sure that their children are indeed getting the best educational experience that they can possibly get anywhere. Since homeschooling is about education, that's what homeschooling parents are concerned with most. They learn rather quickly, certainly after the first year, that their children learn best when they are interested in the subject being taught and can, more or less, go at their own pace. A mother in Quebec writes:

> We try as much as possible to let the children determine what they want to do.... Our daughter is just approaching adolescence and has only just recently shown any interest in "formal" learning. It seems much easier to let our children play and explore while they're young without imposing "lessons." Later, when they have the interest, discipline, maturity and brain development for abstract concepts (yes, the three Rs I would include in that category!), their learning in that area will be very fast and effortless.

Another mom writes:

> One of the easiest motivational techniques is to see what each child is interested in and pursue this interest in any and all ways. Possibly take out library books on the topic or invest in the material needed.... The motivational tool I use to teach reading is to read to the children.... I'm learning that a child feels loved when he is read to.

One very wise mother of seven kids in Indiana writes:

> I became a staunch believer in watching my children and waiting for them to show signs of readiness before I pushed them or panicked that they were not learning something as fast as I thought they ought. Since then I have taught three more children to read and have been amazed by how different their timetables have been for learning....
>
> We are freer in our structure. I still have structure, but I allow more input from my children about what they want to learn and how they want to learn it. We still use workbooks, but only the ones my children choose. On the surface, our day looks a lot the same as it did last year, but underneath there had been a

major shift as I quit worrying I would fail my children and
allowed them to learn and grow according to their abilities. . . .

As I talked with other mothers and observed their families'
tempos, I realized that each family has to find its own pace, its
own rhythm. . . . I am beginning to understand that just as each
child has his own rate of learning, each family has its own
rhythm. There is no one way to homeschool, just as there is no
one way to live.

What do homeschooled kids think of homeschooling? Will they
homeschool their own kids? *New Attitude* (Vol. 4 No. 4), a Christian
magazine for teen homeschoolers, asked their readers these questions and
got an overwhelmingly positive response. Of the forty respondents, only
a few said that they would consider public school as an option for their
own kids. The rest were grateful for the experience of being homeschooled and enthusiastic about doing it with their own kids. Several of
them stressed the importance of parents imposing structure and scheduling. One girl wrote: "I seemed to find freedom in a set schedule and
assignment." Another girl wrote: "I wish there had been more account-
ability in my earlier high school years, that I had been made to work
harder. If only I could get back some of that time I wasted." That raises
an important question: will kids waste a lot of precious time by being
given too much freedom? That surely should be a topic for homeschool
magazines and workshops. Other future homeschoolers in the survey
wanted to be more creative than their parents.

Obviously, there is much more to homeschooling than one book can
cover. But whether one thinks that some homeschoolers are too strict or
not strict enough, or one curriculum is better than another, the main
point is to do what is best for the children and the family. After much
reading, it becomes clear what the ingredients of a happy homeschooling
family are: a devoted husband and wife, a love of children, a willingness
to make whatever sacrifices are necessary to give the children the kind of
education they need, and the confidence that parents can do the job at
home.

To find out how to get a copy of *Homeschooling: A Patchwork of Days,*
see the listing in the appendix. As for *New Attitude* magazine, the editor,
Joshua Harris, decided after four years to discontinue publication and
seek his life in the ministry. But he'll be on the Internet. To learn how to
get back issues, see the listing in the appendix.

The Best Reason to Homeschool

The best reason to homeschool is the present reform movement to change American public education from its traditional function as an academic institution into something called a Human Resources Development System. This system has been described by its chief architect, Marc Tucker, as "a seamless web of opportunities, to develop one's skills that literally extends from cradle to grave and is the same system for everyone—young and old, poor and rich, worker and full-time student." In other words, what the reformers have in mind is an even bigger and more intrusive government educational monopoly than the one we already have.

The various components of this system, which some people recognize as Outcome-Based Education, are presently being implemented throughout the United States. The basic law behind it is called Goals 2000 and was enacted on March 31, 1994, by the U. S. Congress. Kathy Finnegan, in her book on the subject, writes: "GOALS 2000 is raw social engineering, intended to restructure all of American society and not just the schools."

On May 4, 1994, the U.S. Congress enacted the School-to-Work Opportunities Act, which establishes a formal partnership between the U.S. Departments of Education and Labor. The grant money for this education-labor linkup is tied to compliance with requirements outlined in the GOALS 2000 legislation. On October 20, 1994, the Improving America's Schools Act, a reauthorization of the Elementary and Secondary Education Act of 1965, was signed into law. Because of the many overlapping areas in all three laws, they can be viewed as the legislative foundation of the current education reform movement and the source of its funding. Note that all three laws were passed when the Democrats still held a majority in the U.S. Congress. However, in November 1994, the Republicans won majorities in both houses of Congress.

In September 1995, the U.S. House of Representatives passed the Consolidated and Reformed Education, Employment, and Rehabilitation Systems Act, more simply known as the Careers Act (H.R. 1617), by a vote of 345 to 79. In October, the Senate passed its version of the bill, the Workforce Development Act of 1995 (S. 143), by a vote of 95 to 2. Obviously, both bills were passed with overwhelming Republican support. They then went to conference committee for reconciliation.

Conservative activists who had read both bills realized that their purpose was to provide funding and full implementation of Marc Tucker's Human Resources Development System. The alarm went off, and Henry Hyde, representative from Illinois, became the leader of the opposition to the two bills. As of this writing, in March 1997, the two bills have neither been reconciled nor voted on.

Why are these two bills so dangerous? Because they would fund the federal computer data-gathering system developed by the National Center for Education Statistics. It seems that since 1964 the federal government has been working on a system of gathering detailed personal data on every student in America. To standardize the data-collection system, so that every school and every state could provide uniform data, the U.S. Department of Education published a handbook entitled *Public Accounting for Local and State School Systems*. A first version was published in 1964, a second in 1974, a revision of that version in 1976, and the newest version in 1994. This latter version bears the title *Student Data Handbook for Early Childhood, Elementary, and Secondary Education* (NCES 94-303). In other words, the scope of the system has been expanded to reflect Marc Tucker's idea of a system that monitors an individual from cradle to grave. In fact, the new version even calls for data on the gestation of every child. Thus when Gov. Lawton Chiles of Florida remarked that "education starts at gestation," he knew what he was talking about.

A second handbook, *Staff Data Handbook: Elementary, Secondary and Early Childhood Education* (NCES 95-327), "is a major effort to establish current and consistent terms, definitions, and classification codes to maintain, collect, report, and exchange comparable information about staff."

It is this planned data-gathering system for students and teachers that is the dead giveaway of what the planners want: a means of controlling the population through compulsory schooling and remediation. They must have detailed, intimate information about each and every student in order to be able to decide how that student is to be taught or remediated. And they must know as much about each teacher in the system to ascertain if that teacher is loyal to the system's purpose. It is a system in the making for total control.

Do I exaggerate? Here's the kind of information that will be gathered: Identification. Apart from name and address, the handbook calls for driver's license number, health record number, Medicaid number, school-assigned number, Selective Service number, Social Security number, College Board/ACT number, local education agency number, state education agency number, U.S. Dept. of Education number, etc.

Under Religious Background the government will want to know if you are: Amish, Assembly of God, Baptist, Buddhist, Calvinist, Catholic, Eastern Orthodox, Episcopal, Friends, Greek Orthodox, Hindu, Islamic, Jehovah's Witnesses, Jewish, Latter-Day Saints, Lutheran, Mennonite, Methodist, Pentecostal, Presbyterian, Other Christian Denomination, Seventh Day Adventist, Tao, None, Other.

What business is it of the federal government to collect data about your religious affiliation? Why do they need this information and what are they going to do with it? What about the separation of church and state? What about the right to privacy? They will also want to know if you are being homeschooled or attending a private, nonreligiously affiliated school, a private religiously affiliated school, a Montessori school, or an alternative school. And they will want to know why you are homeschooling.

In the category of Assessments, they've designed a whole battery of tests listed and described in the *Student Data Handbook* that will wrench from you every bit of private information the government wants to have about you: Achievement Test, Advanced Placement Test, Aptitude Test, Attitudinal Test—"An assessment to measure the mental and emotional set or patterns of likes and dislikes or opinions held by a student or a group of students. This is often used in relation to considerations such as controversial issues or personal adjustments."

What business is it of the federal government to collect data on your attitudes? What kind of "personal adjustments" are they referring to?

Who will have access to this data and for what reasons? Additional assessments include: Cognitive and Perceptual Skills Test, Developmental Observation, Interest Inventory—"An assessment used to measure the extent to which a student's patterns of likes and dislikes correspond to those of individuals who are known to be successfully engaged in a given vocation, subject area, program of studies, or other activity." Language Proficiency Test, Manual Dexterity Test, Mental Ability (Intelligence) Test, Performance Assessment, Personality Test—"An assessment to measure a student's affective or nonintellectual aspects of behavior such as emotional adjustment, interpersonal relations, motivation, interests, and attitudes." Portfolio Assessment, Psychological Test—"An assessment to measure a sample of behavior in an objective and standardized way." Psychomotor Test, and Reading Readiness Test.

What will the government not know about you when they're through testing you? And who will have access to all of this private, intimate, personal information? And why should the government be collecting it in the first place? All of these tests will have been devised by the nation's leading behavioral psychologists whose theoretical goal is the control of human behavior. Clearly, our limited government is assuming unlimited power to control us.

The *Student Data Handbook* also calls for the collection of an incredible amount of information about a person's health, since comprehensive health care is to be part of the new education system. For example, concerning the individual's oral health, the government will want to know: Number of Teeth, Number of Permanent Teeth Lost, Number of Teeth Decayed, Number of Teeth Restored, Occlusion Condition, with subcategories Normal Occlusion, Mild Malocclusion, Moderate Malocclusion, Severe Malocclusion; Gingival Condition, with subcategories Normal, Mild Deviation, Moderate Deviation, Severe Deviation; Oral Soft Tissue Condition with subcategories Normal, Mild Deviation, Moderate Deviation, Severe Deviation; Dental Prosthetics, and Orthodontic Appliances.

Anyone reading your dossier will have a perfect picture of what's in your mouth! Why should the government know if you have false teeth, or a bad bite, or once wore braces? Why should anybody, except your dentist, be privy to that information?

Your medical data will include Maternal and Pre-Natal Condition, Conditions at Birth, Health History—"A record of an individual's

afflictions, conditions, injuries, accidents, treatments, and procedures."
Also, Medical Evaluations, Disabling Conditions, Medical Laboratory
Tests, Immunizations, Limitations on School Activities, Health Care
Provider, and Other Heath Information—"Information about an individ-
ual's medical or health requirements that are not otherwise addressed
above."

Under the category Student Support Service Type, we read, "Type of
related or ancillary services provided to an individual or a group of
individuals within the formal educational system or offered by an outside
agency which provides non-instructional services to support the general
welfare of students. This includes physical and emotional health, the
ability to select an appropriate course of study, admission to appropriate
educational programs, and the ability to adjust to and remain in school
through the completion of programs. In serving a student with an
identified disability, related services include developmental, corrective,
or supportive services required to ensure that the individual benefits from
special education."

How could anyone fail with so many government services to help?
Under the category Service Provider Type, we learn that the school
Health Nurse is: "Certified, licensed, registered nurse or nurse practitioner who provides any of the following services: 1) case-finding
activities to include health appraisal, screening for developmental matu-
rational milestones, vision and hearing acuity, speech, dental deviations,
spinal deviations, growth, and nutritional disorders; 2) nursing care
procedures that include immunization, medication-monitoring and administration, nursing assessment, and procedures related to the health-
impaired student's Individual Health Plan (IHP)."

Isn't an Individual Health Plan some sort of socialized medicine? It is
assumed that all of these wonderful services will be available to the
student free of charge. The Health Nurse will also be involved with "care
coordination and outreach to children who do not otherwise receive
preventive health care, follow-ups to assure referral completion, home
visits for follow-up planning or home environment assessment, and
interim prenatal or family planning and monitoring." Can you imagine
how many people the government is going to have to hire and train for all
of those home visits and prenatal monitorings?

And there will also be available a certified, licensed Social Worker
who will prepare a social or developmental history on a student with

disabilities, provide group or individual counseling with a student and his or her family, work with those problems in a student's living situation (home, school, and community) that affect adjustment in school, and mobilize school and community resources in order to enable the student to receive maximum benefit from his or her educational program.

Then there is the Psychologist. No student will be able to do without one. Of course, he or she will be licensed or certified and able to administer psychological and educational tests, and other assessment procedures; interpret assessment results; obtain, integrate, and interpret information about student behavior and conditions relating to learning; consult with other staff members in planning school programs to meet the special needs of students indicated by psychological tests, interviews, and behavioral evaluations; plan and manage a program of psychological services, including psychological counseling for students and parents.

And if the Health Nurse, Social Worker, and Psychologist are not enough, there is also the Counselor described as, "A staff member responsible for guiding individuals, families, groups and communities by assisting them in problem-solving, decision-making, discovering meaning, and articulating goals related to personal, educational, and career development."

This is American public education for the twenty-first century, a system that will either turn you into a basket case or make you so dependent on government that you'll barely be able to tie your shoes without the help of your Health Nurse, Social Worker, Psychologist, or Counselor. In the American public education system of the twenty-first century, the government will plan your life for you, and you will be trained to serve the government or the economy. You will never know what it was like to have been raised in a free society, where you planned your own life for your own self without the help of a Health Nurse, Social Worker, Psychologist or Counselor, where your private life was your own and where the inside of your mouth was nobody's business, least of all the government's.

When I attended public school as a child in New York City, in the early 1930s, all they wanted to know was my name, address, date of birth, and my parents' names. That was it. And it was all written by hand on a card. My entire school record was on a single card with my final grades for each subject for each year. That's all anyone needed to know.

If the data-gathering system doesn't convince you that our government is up to no good, nothing else will. But it certainly should convince concerned parents that they'd better get their kids out of this Human Resources Development System before it reduces them to helpless dependents who can't make a decision without the friendly assistance of a government official. What do you call such a government? Your lesson for today is to think up a fitting label.

One last word: Homeschooling is not only about education—it's about freedom. Use it or lose it.

APPENDIX

Homeschool Resources

Magazines

The homeschool movement has seen the growth and development of a number of excellent magazines devoted to the homeschool lifestyle. The ones listed here are national in circulation. There are many local and statewide newsletters and magazines published by state associations and local support groups. By contacting these state and local organizations you should be able to get samples of and subscribe to their publications.

The Teaching Home is "A Christian Magazine for Home Educators." It is an attractive, glossy magazine published bimonthly, with lots of interesting features and ads. It covers the national homeschool scene quite thoroughly. It publishes letters from homeschoolers, legislative news, convention news, and a report by the Home School Legal Defense Association (HSLDA) on legal cases in the various states. Each issue is devoted to a specific area of interest to homeschoolers. The January/February 1997 issue was devoted to the teaching of history. Subscription rate: $15 per year. To order by credit card call (800) 395-7760. Customer Service address: P.O. Box 469069, Escondido, CA 92046-9069, phone: (619) 738-2379. Editorial and advertising office: Box 20219, Portland, OR 97294, phone: (503) 253-9633. Fax: (503) 253-7345.

Practical Homeschooling, published quarterly "for homeschoolers and their friends," is published and edited by the talented and affable Mary Pride, author of *The Big Book of Home Learning,* which comes in four phone-book-size volumes. Mary Pride probably knows more about homeschooling than anyone on the planet. The magazine is chock-full of articles and features on every aspect of homeschooling, features a "Computer Room" and lots of ads, plus a classifieds section, and letters to the editor. Mary Pride writes: "Homeschooling is now clearly *more* sophisticated than classroom education. We have more (and better) resources to draw upon. We can adapt the latest technology more quickly. We are far more committed to finding out what works, as opposed to what sounds impressive on someone's resumé." Subscription rate: $15 for four issues. Can be ordered by phone: (800) 346-6322. Mailing address: Home Life, P.O. Box 1250, Fenton, MO 63026-1850.

Growing Without Schooling is published bimonthly by Holt Associates. It was founded in 1977 by unschooling pioneer John Holt. The magazine publishes lengthy letters from homeschoolers and is therefore an excellent prime source of the homeschool experience, also news and reports about the homeschooling scene, a list of pen pals and their interests, plus a unique yearly, state-by-state directory of homeschooling families that will put you in touch not only with local homeschoolers but with other families around the world. It also has an extensive directory of homeschool organizations. Its orientation is secular. Editor: Susannah Sheffer. Publisher: Patrick Farenga. Subscription rate: $25 for six issues. To order by phone call: (617) 864-3100, or write: Growing Without Schooling, 2269 Massachusetts Ave., Cambridge, MA 02140.

Homeschooling Today is published six times a year. Its motto: "Practical Help for Christian Families." Fine-looking glossy magazine with articles, regular features, and resources, plus lots of ads. Greg Strayer is executive editor. Subscription rate: $16. To order call: (904) 462-7201, or write: P.O. Box 956, Lutz, FL 33549.

Home School Digest, the Quarterly Journal for Serious Homeschoolers. This magazine is full of excellent articles of interest to homeschoolers drawn from a wide variety of sources. Its orientation is Christian. Subscription rate: $18 per year. Back issues are available for $5.00 each. Write: Wisdom's Gate, P.O. Box 125, Sawyer, MI 49125.

Home School Computing, Tools & Technology for Today's Christian Home School. This new bimonthly magazine will help you make good use of your computer for homeschooling and home businesses. Provides extensive reviews of new programs and products. Subscription rate: $20 for six issues. Home School Computing, P.O. Box 116, Blue Rapids, KS 66411. Voice/Fax: (913) 363-7797.

Home Education Magazine is published six times a year. This is a general homeschooling magazine with a secular orientation. Subscription rate: $24 per year. Home Education Magazine, P.O. Box 1083, Tonasket, WA 98855. Phone: (509) 486-1351.

The Drinking Gourd Multicultural Home-Education Magazine, edited by Donna Nichols-White, an African-American homeschooler. The editor writes: "My magazine is called *The Drinking Gourd*. It was named in honor of those brave and determined Africans who refused to accept slavery and escaped to freedom, in honor of the strength of my ancestors." Provides an excellent means of getting to know the concerns and experiences of African-American home-schoolers. Subscription: $15 for six issues. Single issues available for $4.00. Call: (800) TDG-5487 or write: The Drinking Gourd, P.O. Box 2557, Redmond, WA 98073.

Homeschool Associations

The homeschool associations listed are mainly statewide organizations. We have included what we believe are the largest Christian and secular associations in each state. The major statewide organizations have yearly conventions that will provide the new or prospective homeschooler with a view of what the homeschooling movement is all about. There are also many local and regional groups in the larger states. They can be contacted by getting to know local homeschoolers.

Alabama

Alabama Home Educators
P.O. Box 16091, Mobile, AL 36116

Christian Home Education Fellowship of Alabama
Box 563, Alabaster, AL 35007, (205) 664-2232

Homeschool Advocates
6962 Chalet Dr. N., Mobile, AL 36608, (205) 344-3239

Alaska

Alaska Homeschoolers Association
P.O. Box 230973, Anchorage, AK 99523-0973, (907) 333-4840

Alaska Private & Home Educators Association
Box 141764, Anchorage, AK 99514, (907) 696-0641

Arizona

Arizona Families for Home Education
Box 4661, Scottsdale, AZ 85261, (602) 443-0612

Parents Association of Christian Home Schools
6166 W. Highland, Phoenix, AZ 85033.

Phoenix Learning Alternatives Network
8835 N. 47th Pl., Phoenix, AZ 85028, (602) 483-3381

Arkansas

Arkansas Christian Home Educators Association
Box 4025, N. Little Rock, AR 72190, (501) 758-9099

Coalition of Arkansas Parents
P.O. Box 192455, Little Rock, AR 72219, (501) 565-6583

California

California Homeschool Network
P.O. Box 44, Vineburg, CA 95487-0044, (800) 327-5339

Christian Home Educators Association of California (CHEA)
Box 2009, Norwalk, CA 90651, (800) 564-2432

Home School Association of CA
P.O. Box 2442, Atascadero, CA 93423, (707) 765-5375

California has many local homeschool associations which you can find by getting to know local homeschoolers.

Colorado

Christian Home Educators of Colorado
3739 E. 4th Ave., Denver, CO 80206, (303) 388-1888

Colorado Home Schooling Network
7490 W. Apache, Sedalia, CO 80135, (303) 688-4136

Independent Network of Creative Homeschoolers, c/o Woodhouse
724 Victor St., Aurora, CO 80011, (303) 340-3185, (303) 751-6421

Connecticut

The Education Association of Christian Homeschoolers (TEACH)
25 Field Stone Run, Farmington, CT 06032, (800) 205-7844 or out-of-state (860) 677-4538

Connecticut Home Educators Association
P.O. Box 250, Cobalt, CT 06414, (203) 781-8569

Delaware

Delaware Home Education Association
Box 1003, Dover, DE 19903

Tri State Homeschoolers Association
P.O. Box 7193, Newark, DE 19714-7193

Florida

Florida Association for Schools at Home (FLASH)
1000 Devil's Dip, Tallahassee, FL 32308, (904) 878-2793

Florida at Home
4644 Adanson, Orlando, FL 32804, (407) 740-8877

Florida Parent Educators Association
P.O. Box 1193, Venice, FL 34284-1193, (813) 492-6938

Georgia

Atlanta Alternative Education Network, c/o Paymer
1158 McConnell Dr., Decatur, GA 30033, (404) 636-6348

Georgia Home Educators Association
245 Buckeye Lane, Fayetteville, GA 30214, (770) 461-3657

Hawaii

Christian Homeschoolers of Hawaii
91-824 Oama St., Ewa Beach, HI 96706, (808) 689-6398

Hawaii Homeschool Association
P.O. Box 3476, Mililani, HI 96789

Idaho

Family Unschooling Network
1809 N. 7th St., Boise, ID 83702, (208) 345-2703

Idaho Home Educators
Box 1324, Meridian, ID 83680, (208) 323-0230

Illinois

HOUSE, c/o Ann Wasserman
806 Oakton, Evanston, IL 60202, (847) 328-7129

Illinois Christian Home Educators
Box 310, Mt. Prospect, IL 60056, (847) 670-7150

Indiana

Families Learning Together, c/o Jill Whelan
1714 E. 51 St., Indianapolis, IN 46205, (317) 255-9298

Indiana Association of Home Educators
850 N. Madison Ave., Greenwood, IN 46142, (317) 859-1202

Iowa

Iowa Home Educators Association
P.O. Box 213, Des Moines, IA 50301

Network of Iowa Christian Home Educators
Box 158, Dexter, IA 50070, (515) 830-1614

Kansas

Christian Home Educators Confederation of Kansas
Box 3564, Shawnee Mission, KS 66203, (913) 234-2927

Teaching Parents Association
P.O. Box 3968, Wichita, KS 67201, (316) 945-0810

Kentucky

Christian Home Educators of Kentucky
691 Howardstown Rd., Hodgenville, KY 42748, (502) 358-9270

Kentucky Independent Learners Network
P.O. Box 275, Somerset, KY 42502, (606) 678-2527

Louisiana

Christian Home Educators Fellowship of Louisiana
Box 74292, Baton Rouge, LA 70874, (504) 775-9709

Louisiana Citizens for Home Education
3404 Van Buren, Baker, LA 70714, (504) 775-5472

Maine

Homeschoolers of Maine, HC 62
Box 24, Hope, ME 04847, (207) 763-4251

Maine Homeschool Association
P.O. Box 421, Topsham, ME 04086, (800) 520-0577

Maryland

Maryland Association of Christian Home Educators
Box 247, Point of Rocks, MD 21777, (301) 607-4284

Maryland Home Education Association
9085 Flamepool Way, Columbia, MD 21045, (410) 730-0073

Massachusetts

Massachusetts Home Educators
22 Garland St., Lynn, MA 01902, (617) 599-6267

Massachusetts Homeschool Organization of Parent Educators (Mass HOPE)
5 Atwood Rd., Cherry Valley, MA 01611, (508) 755-4754

Michigan

Christian Home Educators of Michigan (CHEM)
P.O. Box 2357, Farmington Hills, MI 48333, (810) 380-3611

Families Learning and Schooling at Home (FLASH)
21671 B Drive N. Marshall, MI 45068, (616) 781-1069

Information Network for Christian Homes (INCH)
4934 Cannonsburg Rd., Belmont, MI 49306, (616) 874-5656

Minnesota

Minnesota Association of Christian Home Educators
Box 32308, Fridley, MN 55432, (612) 717-9070

Minnesota Homeschoolers Alliance
P.O. Box 23072, Richfield, MN 55423, (612) 399-1748

Mississippi

Mississippi Home Educators Association
109 Reagan Ranch Rd., Laurel, MS 39440, (601) 649-6432

Missouri

Families for Home Education
400 E. High Pt. Ln., Columbia, MO 65203, (816) 826-9302

Missouri Association of Teaching Christian Homes (MATCH)
307 E. Ash St. # 146, Columbia, MO 65201, (573) 443-8217

Montana

The Grapevine
P.O. Box 3228, Missoula, MT 59806, (406) 542-8721

Montana Coalition of Home Educators
Box 43, Gallatin Gateway, MT 59730, (406) 587-6163

Nebraska

LEARN
7741 E. Avon Ln., Lincoln, NE 68505, (402) 488-7741

Nebraska Christian Home Educators Association
Box 57041, Lincoln, NE 68505, (402) 423-4297

Nevada

Home Schools United/Vegas Valley
P.O. Box 26811, Las Vegas, NV 89126, (702) 870-9566

Northern Nevada Home Schools
Box 21323, Reno, NV 89515, (702) 852-6647

New Hampshire

Christian Home Educators of New Hampshire
Box 961, Manchester, NH 03105, (603) 569-2343

New Hampshire Homeschool Coalition
P.O. Box 2224, Concord, NH 03302, (603) 539-7233

New Jersey

Education Network of Christian Home Schoolers of New Jersey
120 Mayfair Lane, Mt. Laurel, NJ 08054, (609) 222-4283.

Unschoolers Network
2 Smith St., Farmingdale, NJ 07727, (908) 938-2473

New Mexico

Christian Association of Parent Educators of New Mexico
Box 25046, Albuquerque, NM 87125, (505) 898-8548

New Mexico Family Educators
P.O. Box 92276, Albuquerque, NM 87199, (505) 889-9775

New York

Families for Home Education
3219 Coulter Rd., Cazenovia, NY 13035, (315) 655-2574

Long Island Homeschoolers Association
4 Seville Pl., Massapequa Park, NY 11762, (516) 795-5554

New York City Home Educators Alliance
P.O. Box 1214, Murray Hill Station, NY 10156, (212) 505-9884

New York State Loving Education at Home (LEAH)
Box 88, Cato, NY 13033, (716) 346-0939

North Carolina

The Home Education Association
300 Brown Circle, Rolesville, NC 27571, (919) 554-1563

North Carolinians for Home Education
419 N. Boylan Ave., Raleigh, NC 27603, (919) 834-6243

North Dakota

North Dakota Home School Association
4007 N. State St., Bismarck, ND 58501, (701) 223-4080

Ohio

Christian Home Educators of Ohio
430 N. Court St., Circleville, OH 43113, (614) 474-3177

Home Education League of Parents
3905 Herr Rd., Sylvania, OH 43560, (419) 843-7179

Oklahoma

Christian Home Educators Fellowship of Oklahoma
Box 471363, Tulsa, OK 74147, (918) 583-7323

Home Educators Resource Organization of Oklahoma (HERO), c/o Leslie Moyer
4401 Quail Run Ave., Skiatook, OK 74070-4024, (918) 396-0108

Oregon

Oregon Christian Home Education Association Network (OCEAN)
2515 NE 37th, Portland, OR 97212, (503) 288-1285

Parents Education Association
P.O. Box 5428, Beaverton, OR 97006-0428, (503) 693-0724

Pennsylvania

Christian Home School Association of Pennsylvania
Box 3603, York, PA17402, (717) 661-2428

Pennsylvania Home Education Network
285 Allegheny St., Meadville, PA 16335, (412) 561-5288

Rhode Island

Rhode Island Guild of Home Teachers (RIGHT)
Box 11, Hope, RI 02831, (401) 821-7700

South Carolina

Home Organization of Parent Educators (HOPE), c/o Griesemer
1697 Dotterer's Run, Charleston, SC 29414, (803) 763-7833

South Carolina Home Educators Association
Box 612, Lexington, SC 29071, (803) 754-6425

South Dakota

South Dakota Home School Association
P.O. Box 882, Sioux Falls, SD 57101, (605) 338-9689

Western Dakota Christian Home Schools
Box 528, Black Hawk, SD 57718, (605) 923-1893

Tennessee

Tennessee Home Education Association
3677 Richbriar Ct., Nashville, TN 37211, (615) 834-3529

Tennessee Homeschooling Families
214 Park Lane, Oliver Springs, TN 37840, (615) 435-4375

Texas

Home-Oriented Private Education for Texas
Box 59876, Dallas, TX 75229, (214) 358-2221

Metroplex Middle of the Road Home Educators
1702 S Hway 121, Suite 607-110, Lewisville, TX 75067, (214) 724-1026

Texas Advocates for Freedom in Education (TAFFIE)
13635 Greenridge St., Sugar Land, TX 77478, (713) 242-7994

Utah

Utah Christian Home Schoolers
Box 3942, Salt Lake City, UT 84110, (801) 296-7198

Utah Home Education Association
P.O. Box 570218, Sigurd, UT 84657, (801) 535-1533 or (801) 342-4027

Vermont

Christian Home Educators of Vermont
214 N. Prospect #105, Burlington, VT 05401, (802) 658-4561

Vermont Homeschoolers Association
RD 2 Box 4440, Bristol, VT 05443, (802) 453-5460

Virginia

Community of Independent Learners
P.O. Box 16029, Alexandria, VA 22302, (703) 998-9626

Home Educators Association of Virginia
Box 6745, Richmond, VA 23230, (804) 288-1608

Washington

Washington Association of Teaching Christian Homes (WATCH)
N. 2904 Dora Rd., Spokane, WA 99212, (509) 922-4811

Washington Homeschool Organization (WHO)
18130 Midvale Ave. N., Seattle, WA 98133, (206) 298-8942

West Virginia

Christian Home Educators of West Virginia
Box 8770, S. Charleston, WV 25303, (304) 776-4664

West Virginia Home Educators Association
P.O. Box 3707, Charleston, WV 25337, (800) 736-9843

Wisconsin

Unschooling Families
1908 N. Clark St., Appleton, WI 54911, (414) 735-9832

Wisconsin Christian Home Educators Association
2307 Carmel Ave., Racine, WI 53405, (414) 637-5127

Wyoming

Homeschoolers of Wyoming
339 Bicentennial Ct., Powell, WY 82435, (307) 754-3271

Unschoolers of Wyoming
429 Hwy 230 #20, Laramie, WY 82070

Canada

Alberta Home Education Association, c/o Aine Stasiewich
Box 3451, Leduc AB T9E 6M2

Calgary Home Educators Encouragement & Resource Society (CHEERS)
RR 6, Calgary AB T2M 4L5

Canadian Alliance of Homeschoolers
272 Hwy #5, RR 1, St. George ON N0E 1N0, (519) 448-4001

Canadian Home Educators Association of British Columbia
4684 Darin Ct, Kelowna BC V1W 2B3, (604) 764-7462

Homebased Learning Society of Alberta
8754 Connors Rd, Edmonton AB T6C 4B6, (403) 988-4652

Home School Legal Defense Association of Canada
P.O. Box 42009, Millbourne PO, Edmonton AB T6K 4C4, (403) 986-1566

Manitoba Association for Schooling at Home
89 Edkar Crescent, Winnipeg MB R2G 3H8

Montreal Homeschoolers Support Group
5241 Jacques Grenier, Montreal PQ H3W 2G8

New Brunswick Association of Christian Homeschoolers
RR 1 Site 11 Box 1, Hillsborough NB E0A 1X0, (506) 734-2863

Nova Scotia Support Group, c/o Laura Uhlman
RR 1, Pleasantville NS B0R 1G0

Ontario Federation of Teaching Parents
83 Fife Rd., Guelph ON N1H 6X9, (519) 763-1150

Ontario Homeschoolers
Box 19, Gilford ON L0L 1R0, (705) 456-3186

Quebec Homeschooling Advisory
CP 1278, 1002 Rosemarie, Val David PQ J0T 2N0

Saskatchewan Home-Based Educators
116A Idylwyld Dr. N., Suite 13, Saskatoon SK S7L 0Y7

Yukon Home Educators' Society
Box 4993, Whitehorse YT Y1A 4S2

Australia

Alternative Education Resource Group
P.O. Box 71, Chirnside Park VIC 3116

Brisbane Homeschooling Group
Lot 2, Caboolture River Rd., Upper Caboolture 4510

Canberra Home Education Network
23 Bardolph St., Bonython, ACT 2905

Homeschoolers Australia Pty Ltd
P.O. Box 420, Kellyville 2153, NSW Australia

England

Education Otherwise
P.O. Box 7420, London N9 9SG, phone: 0891 518303

New Zealand

Homeschooling Federation of New Zealand
5 Thanet Ave., Mt. Albert, Auckland, New Zealand.

National Homeschool Organizations

American Homeschool Association, P.O. Box 1125, Republic, WA 99166, (509) 486-2477

Christian Life Workshops, 180 SE Kane Ave., Gresham, OR 97030, (503) 667-3942. Founded by Gregg Harris, who conducts numerous workshops all over the United States.

Holt Associates (Growing Without Schooling & John Holt's Bookstore), 2269 Massachusetts Ave., Cambridge, MA 02140, (617) 864-3100. Founded by unschooling pioneer John Holt. Publishes mail-order catalog and sells books of interest to unschoolers.

Home School Association of Christian Science Families, 445 Airport Rd, Tioga, TX 76271

Home School Legal Defense Association (HSLDA), P.O. Box 159, Paeonian Springs, VA 22129, (540) 338-5600. Provides legal assistance and defense for homeschoolers having problems with their local superintendents. Publishes periodical reports on the legal status of homeschooling in the United States and Canada. See listing under Canada for address of the Canadian affiliate.

Homeschool Support Network, publishes *Home Educator's Family Times,* P.O. Box 1056, Gray, ME 04039, (207) 657-2800. Holds yearly conferences in New England and Michigan. Provides testing services.

Homeschoolers Travel Network, NHA, P.O. Box 290, Hartland, MI 48353, (513) 772-9580

Homeschooling Unitarian Universalists and Humanists (HUUH), c/o Jacki Willard, 3135 Lakeland Dr., Nashville, TN 37214-3312.

Islamic Homeschool Association of North America, 1312 Plymouth Ct, Raleigh, NC 27610

Jewish Home Educators Network, P.O. Box 300, Benton City, WA 99320, (509) 588-2627

Jewish Home Educators Resource, Pam Ernstoff, 6557 Walnut Grove, Columbia, MD 21044, (410) 964-0088

National Association of Catholic Home Educators, P.O. Box 420225, San Diego, CA 92142

National Association of Mormon Home Educators, 2770 S. 1000 West, Perry, UT 84302

National Center for Home Education, P.O. Box 200, Paeonian Springs, VA 22129, (703) 338-7600

NATional cHallenged Homeschoolers AssociatioN (NATHHAN), a Christian, nonprofit organization dedicated to providing encouragement to homeschooling families with special needs children. 5383 Alpine Rd. SE, Olalla, WA 98359, (253) 857-4257. Membership donation of $25 per year includes subscription to *Nathhan News*, a quarterly magazine devoted to special needs children and their parents.

National Home Education Research Institute (NHERI), P.O. Box 13939, Salem, Oregon 97309, publishes the *Home School Researcher*, a quarterly journal of home school studies. Founded and directed by Brian D. Ray, Ph.D. Provides the academic world, media, and homeschoolers with professionally researched papers on subjects related to homeschooling. Individual subscription rate: $25 for 4 issues.

National Handicapped Homeschoolers Association, 814 Shavertown Rd., Boothwyn, PA 19061, (215) 459-2035

Simon of Cyrene Association (Christian African-American Group), P.O. Box 26357, Rochester, NY 14626

Sources of Homeschool Curricula

The incredible variety of homeschool curriculum materials available to families can only be appreciated by a stroll through the vendors' exhibits at a major homeschool convention. And there is nothing more delightful than seeing parents and children poring over books and programs in search of good teaching materials and leaving the convention with arms loaded. All of the companies in this list will send you a catalog if you call or write. The list includes producers of curricula as well as mail-order companies that sell books and curricula through catalogs, often at discount prices. However, at conventions you get a chance to examine the materials firsthand and talk with the representatives and parents who have used the materials. Also, at many homeschool conventions there will be a section with used books and programs for sale at much lower prices. In other words, bargain hunting is alive and well among homeschoolers!

A Beka Book Publications is the national publishing arm of Pensacola Christian College, in Pensacola, Florida. It is a major supplier of textbooks and materials to Christian schools and homeschoolers. Their vendor booth is usually one of the largest at any homeschool convention. The quality of their books is outstanding. A Beka also offers a correspondence school and a video homeschool providing videocassettes that teach a variety of subjects. For catalogs call: (800) 874-3592 or write: Station PH, Pensacola, FL 32523-9160.

Alpha-Phonics: A Primer for Beginning Readers by Samuel L. Blumenfeld. This is an intensive, systematic phonics reading program for children, older students, and adults. Literacy Unlimited Inc., 31724 Railroad Canyon Rd., Canyon Lake, CA 92587, (888) 922-3000 or (909) 244-0485.

Basic Skills Assessment & Educational Services publishes a catalog of its audiocassette tapes of lectures given at its many conferences. Among the speakers are Samuel Blumenfeld, Paul Jehle, Clark Bowers, Chris Klicka, Dennis Peacock, Frode Jensen, Joshua Harris, Gregg Harris, John Blanchard, Brian Ray, Paul Hunter, Barry Byrd, and others. The lectures cover virtually every aspect of homeschooling. For their Home School Educational Products catalog write: Basic Skills Assessment & Educational Services, 19144 S. Molalla Avenue, Suite B, Oregon City, Oregon 97045 or call: (503) 650-5282.

Backyard Scientist, Inc. The Backyard Scientist is Jane Hoffman, the bubbly, exuberant developer of a whole series of delightful science books and projects for homeschool kids. Jane's experimental workshop is one of the most popular and sought-after attractions at homeschool conventions. Each one of her books contains different and stimulating hands-on experiments that can be performed using materials found in the home or readily available at low cost. A wonderful way to introduce science to a child. For information call: (714) 551-2392 or write: Backyard Scientist, Inc., P.O. Box 16966, 14652 Beach Ave., Irvine, CA 92713.

The Big Book of Home Learning by Mary Pride comes in four big volumes. Volume 1: Getting Started; Volume 2: Preschool and Elementary; Volume 3: Teen and Adult; Volume 4: Afterschooling. Mary reviews just about every product available in each category. Mary Pride, mother of eight children, is one of the great homeschooling success stories. She has probably helped more families get into homeschooling than any other promoter of the cause. She is a homeschooling entrepreneur par excellence. If you're going to become a homeschooler, get to know Mary Pride. These books are published by Crossway Books. They can be ordered through Mary Pride's own company: Home Life, P.O. Box 1250, Fenton, MO 63026-1850. For faster service call: (800) 346-6322.

Bob Jones University Press publishes an entire line of traditional textbooks for the homeschool market. BJU is known as the West Point of Christian universities and their textbooks are highly regarded by Christian educators and homeschoolers. BJU Press also provides testing and evaluation services. For a free catalog call: (800) 845-5731 or write: Bob Jones University Press, Customer Services, Greenville, SC 29614-0062.

Builder Books, Inc. is a mail-order distributor of books and materials serving the home education market. To get their discount catalog, call: (509) 826-6021 or write: P.O. Box 99, Riverside, WA 98849.

Calvert School is probably the nation's oldest supplier of secular home instruction materials. It was founded in 1897 to serve families living in remote areas and military families stationed abroad. Calvert publishes a newsletter called *The Calvert Connection.* For a catalog write: Calvert School, 105 Tuscany Road, Baltimore, MD 21210 or call: (410) 243-6030.

Carolina's K-8 Science Source will provide you with all that you will need to teach science at home, from a Raise-a-Frog Kit to a Weather Watch Rain Gauge. To get their colorful, 114-page catalog call: (800) 334-5551 or write: Carolina Biological Supply Company, 2700 York Rd., Burlington, NC 27215.

Christian Liberty Academy offers a full-service program for homeschoolers including a college preparatory program, online computer services, as well as textbooks for every level reflecting America's Christian heritage. CLA has served over 250,000 students during their thirty-year history and has more than 50,000 homeschoolers presently registered. For a free information packet call: (800) 348-0899 or write: Christian Liberty Academy, 502 W. Euclid Ave., Arlington Heights, IL 60004

Christian Light Publications, Inc. publishes and distributes a wide variety of biblically oriented books and materials plus such practical high school texts as *Automotive Fundamentals, Basic Map Skills,* etc. For a catalog call: (703) 434-0768 or write: Christian Light Publications, Inc., P.O. Box 1212, Harrisonburg, VA 22801-1212.

Clonlara Home Based Education Program was founded by educator Pat Montgomery as a curriculum resource for homeschoolers. Pat is a wonderfully dedicated unschooler who believes in the great benefits of educational freedom. For information call: (313) 769-4515 or write: Clonlara, 1289 Jewitt St., Ann Arbor, MI 48104.

Creation Resource Catalog offers books, videos, and CD-ROMs on the creation side of the creation vs. evolution controversy. Some of the books available are *Origin of Life, Science and the Bible, Darwin on Trial, Dinosaurs by Design, Bones of Contention, The Controversy: Roots of the Creation/Evolution Debate.* For their colorful catalog call (800) 778-3390 or write: Answers in Genesis, P.O. Box 6330, Florence, KY 41022.

The Elijah Company offers "Outstanding Teaching Materials for Home Educators." This immensely readable mail-order catalog is produced by the Davis family. Parents Chris and Ellyn have been homeschooling their three boys for ten years, and the books and materials they've chosen to sell reflect their desire to bring the best that's available to other homeschooling families. Their 1995/96 catalog devoted two full pages to an essay on "The Seven Habits of

Successful Home Schooling." To get their catalog call: (615) 456-6284 or write: The Elijah Company, Rt. 2, Box 100-B, Crossville, TN 38555.

Essential Learning Products publishes K through 8 materials on all school subjects. For a free catalog call: (614) 486-0633 or write: 2300 West Fifth Ave., P.O. Box 2590, Columbus, OH 43216-2590.

Family Christian Academy is a unique curricular service founded and run by the Scarlatas, a homeschooling family. According to their catalog, they have several thousand students registered with their school and three retail book-stores. They provide a wide variety of educational materials by mail order, publish a newsletter, sponsor speakers and workshops, and run a summer camp for homeschool families. Their academic specialty is the unit study program in which a topic can be explored in depth. For a free catalog call: (800) 788-0840 or write: Family Christian Academy, 487 Myatt Dr., Madison, TN 37115.

Farm Country General Store publishes an extensive catalog of books and materials on all subjects for the homeschooling family. These include Amanda Bennett's Unit Study Guides, Jane Hoffman's Backyard Scientist series, Bible Study Guides for All Ages, Usborne books, Saxon Math, plus a variety of toys and games, arts and crafts, etc. Most items are at discount prices. For a catalog call: (800) 551-FARM or (309) 367-2844 or write: Farm Country General Store, Rt. 1, Box 63, Metamora, IL 61548.

God's Riches, a mail-order catalog of homeschool resources published by the Rich family. Phil is an electrical engineer and seminary student at Knox Theological Seminary and Debbie is a homemaker with a degree in electrical engineering. They are homeschooling their four children, Billy, Jenny, Jimmy, and Andy. The catalog inlcudes books on the Bible, language arts, parent guides, math, science, social studies, logic and thinking skills. For a catalog call: (305) 667-3130 or write: God's Riches, P.O. Box 560217, Miami, FL 33256-0217.

Greenleaf Press offers a free mail-order catalog of sixty-four pages with over 1,200 titles covering every aspect of education for the homeschooler. They also publish excellent study packages on Ancient Egypt, Ancient Greece, Ancient Rome, and the Middle Ages, plus biographies of such great men as Johann Gutenberg, Erasmus, Martin Luther, John Wesley, and Blaise Pascal. For a catalog call: (800) 311-1508 or write: Greenleaf Press, 1570 Old LaGuardo Rd., Lebanon, TN 37087.

HIS Publishing Company is a home-grown mail-order business founded and run by Jack and Vicky Goodchild, who started homeschooling in 1983. They run this business out of their home with their five children. "Our children are the 'Product Testers' and 'Quality Control Engineers.' In our search to meet their curriculum needs they have inadvertently sifted out, what we believe, is some of the best of what is available to homeschoolers." Thus, you will find in this forty-eight-page catalog just about everything you need to get started. For a catalog call: (954) 764-4567 or write: HIS Publishing Company, P.O. Box 9881, Ft. Lauderdale, FL 33310-9881.

The Home Computer Market, a hardware and software planning guide and product catalog. This excellent twenty-four-page catalog is produced by the Kihlstadius homeschooling family. Like so many mail-order catalogs developed by homeschoolers, it reflects the needs of families for quality products at the best possible prices. Thus, you can be sure that the products in this catalog have been carefully scrutinized for quality and good content. The catalog includes essays on "Twelve Reasons Why You Should Use a Computer in Your Homeschool," "How to Choose a Computer," and "How to Buy a Computer That Won't Be Obsolete in Two Years." It answers many of the questions that beginners need to ask when they start thinking of joining the technology revolution. For a catalog call: (612) 844-0462 or write: The Home Computer Market Corp., P.O. Box 385377, Bloomington, MN 55439-5377.

Homeschool Discount Warehouse is probably the biggest and most comprehensive of the homeschool mail-order catalogs now available. It is published by Great Christian Books, one of the largest, if not the largest, mail-order distributor of Christian books in America. The well-designed catalog of 152 pages lists just about everything that's available, and their discount prices make them quite competitive. For a catalog call: (800) 775-5422 or write: Great Christian Books, 229 South Bridge St., P.O. Box 8000, Elkton, MD 21922-8000.

John Holt's Bookstore is the catalog mail-order division of Holt Associates which publishes *Growing Without Schooling.* As a secular organization, John Holt's Bookstore will be of special interest to nonreligious unschoolers. To obtain a catalog call: (617) 864-3100 Monday through Friday, 10 a.m. to 4 p.m. or write: John Holt's Bookstore, 2269 Massachusetts Ave., Cambridge, MA 02140-1226.

Landmark Distributors is a mail-order book business founded by homeschoolers Alan and Lori Harris, who have four children. They are guided by "The Principle Approach" in what they select to sell through their extensive fifty-five-page catalog. Books are listed under such categories as General World History, Egypt, Greece, Rome, Middle Ages, Christian History, General American History, Pilgrims and Puritans, American Revolution, African-American History, Constitutional History, Philosophy, Music, Science, Mathematics, Grammar, Phonics, Character Development, and more. To obtain a catalog call: (805) 524-2388 or write: Landmark Distributors, P.O. Box 849, Fillmore, CA 93016.

The Learning Edge offers games and toys to enhance home learning. This mail-order company was founded by Bob and Linda Dean, who are homeschooling their four children. They write, "While homeschooling our children we found a need for less 'school room' desk work and more learning opportunities during play. Thus, the Learning Edge began out of our homeschooling needs." This sixty-four-page catalog offers a wealth of toys, games, puzzles, kits, and materials covering every possible subject from a Cartoon Drawing Kit to MathSafari, Harmonica Instruction, Soccer Boingo, Dissecting Kit, Small Bird House Kit, Gardening Unit, Dinosaur Lotto, Rocks Discovery Collection, and lots more. To get a catalog call: (607) 722-6563 or write: The Learning Edge, 4813 East Marshall Dr., Vestal, NY 13850.

Saxon Publishers was founded by the legendary John Saxon, who decided that the New Math being taught in the schools was a disaster. And so, he came up with his own series of math books that made sense. He wrote: "Mathematics is not difficult. Mathematics is just different, and time is the elixir that turns things different into things familiar. Therefore, the most effective way for students to learn is through gentle repetition extended over a considerable period of time." And that is the guiding principle behind the Saxon Math books which start with Math K and go right up through Algebra and Calculus. For a catalog call: (800) 284-7019 or write: Saxon Publishers, 1320 West Lindsey St., Norman, OK 73069.

Timberdoodle Company was founded by Dan and Deb Deffinbaugh, home-schoolers to five kids. They write: "We emphasize practical, real life learning. If children don't see the *why*, the *what* will not be meaningful to them." And so they've put together a delightful catalog of toys, thinking tools, puzzles, art materials, electronics, foreign languages, sign language, keyboarding skills, software, grammar helps, Calculadder/Math Reasoning, etc. To get the catalog call: (800) 478-0672 or write: Timberdoodle Company, E. 1510 Spencer Lake Rd., Shelton, WA 98584.

Understanding the Times is a video-based curriculum that brings over twenty worldview experts into your home. Also included are textbooks, student manuals, and an extensive teacher manual. The purpose of the program is to help young Christians understand the cultural and philosophical forces that are shaping American life. The curriculum is produced by Summit Ministries, P.O. Box 207, Manitou Springs, CO 80829, (719) 685-9103.

The Weaver Curriculum was developed by homeschoolers Ross and Becky Avery for the education of their own children. They wanted the Bible to be at the center of their homeschooling curriculum, and so they developed this K through 12 biblically oriented program that covers all of the subjects from beginning reading to chemistry. For a catalog call: (909) 688-3126 or write: The Weaver, 2752 Scarborough, Riverside, CA 92503.

Whole Heart Catalogue is the production of Clay and Sally Clarkson who are homeschooling their four children. It is another of the many home-based businesses that have come out of the homeschool movement. The Clarksons believe that "real books and real life are the roads to real learning." Thus, this is a book lover's catalog addressed to those who wish to use books as the means of enriching the life of the homeschooling family. For a catalog call: (817) 797-2142 or write: Whole Heart Catalogue, P.O. Box 228, Walnut Springs, TX 76690

College Preparation for Homeschoolers

The following books and catalogs may help your homeschooled child decide whether or not to attend a college or get a degree at home via correspondence. Fortunately there are many options available today.

Bears' Guide to Earning College Degrees Nontraditionally. This is the twelfth edition of another phone-directory-size book by John and Mariah Bear which describes and discusses every known approach to earning a college degree without having to attend classes on some distant campus. Such approaches include getting college credit for life-experience learning, correspondence and online study, and unusual programs. The book lists over 1,600 schools and institutions and tells you where you can get the degree you want. For example, Harvard University offers six hundred courses in over sixty-five fields of study on an open-enrollment basis. You can get a Bachelor of Science in professional aeronautics and a Master of Aeronautical Science with no traditional classroom attendance from Embry-Riddle Aeronautical University at Daytona Beach, Florida. Bob Jones University offers a variety of bachelor's degrees through their extended education programs. If you want the prestige of a foreign degree, you can get an M.B.A. at home from the University of Warwick in Oxford, England, through a distance-learning course. You can get this highly inform- ative book through John Holt's Bookstore or directly from the publisher, C & B Publishing, Benicia, CA 94510, (707) 747-5950. The list price is $27.95, but well worth it.

College Degrees by Mail by John Bear, Ph.D., and Mariah Bear, M.A. This 216-page book, the size of a small city phone directory, provides information about one hundred accredited schools that offer degrees entirely or almost entirely by home study. Among the one hundred are such institutions as Auburn University, Brigham Young University, Central Michigan University, Colorado State University, Georgia Institute of Technology, New School for Social Research, Open University of Israel, University of London, plus at least a dozen state universities. The book also tells you how to apply for a school and how to earn credit for a wide range of nonschool "life experience learning." Some of these institutions not only offer bachelor's degrees by home study but also master's, doctorates, and law degrees. The book's price is $12.95 and it can be ordered through John Holt's Bookstore or directly from the publisher, Ten Speed Press, P.O. Box 7123, Berkeley, CA 94707.

Teenage Homeschoolers: College or Not? by Patrick Farenga, president of Holt Associates. This sixteen-page booklet contains a speech given by Pat at a homeschool conference in 1995. Pat cites books, stories, and articles to show that a college degree is attainable if you need one, but that spending time earning a degree isn't always the best way to pursue one's goals. Available from John Holt's Bookstore, 2269 Massachusetts Ave., Cambridge, MA 02140, (617) 864-3100.

Additional Reading About Homeschooling

The following are books about homeschooling, written from a variety of viewpoints, illustrating the true diversity of the homeschool movement. We've arranged them alphabetically by title:

Freedom Challenge: African-American Homeschoolers, edited by Grace Llewellyn, 1996, 320 pages, Lowry House Publishers, P.O. Box 1014, Eugene, OR 97440-1014. Sixteen African-American homeschooling families tell their wonderfully varied stories about how they got started, what motivated them, and how they do it. As one of the parents writes: "Homeschooling is empowering. It means taking control and making decisions for one's own family and one's own children instead of abdicating these rights and responsibilities to others or simply complying with societal norms. . . . [It] is the beginning of regaining control and making choices about our children's education." The book is available from the publisher or John Holt's Bookstore.

Hard Times in Paradise by David and Micki Colfax, 1992, 284 pages, Warner Books, 1271 Ave. of the Americas, New York, NY 10020. This is the story of how the Colfax family carved out a homestead in California's redwood mountains and homeschooled their kids. It shows how much children can learn when given the freedom to do so. Three of the Colfax boys finally went to Harvard. Available from John Holt's Bookstore, 2269 Massachusetts Ave., Cambridge, MA 02140, (617) 864-3100.

Home Schooling and the Law by Michael P. Farris, 1990, 211 pages, Home School Legal Defense Association (HSLDA), P.O. Box 159, Paeonian Springs, VA 22129, (703) 882-3838. Michael Farris is the founder and president of HSLDA and has defended homeschoolers in many court cases. Part I of the book deals with basic constitutional freedoms, Part II with state homeschooling laws, Part III with practical issues, and Part IV provides state-by-state summaries of homeschool laws. This is a very valuable and informative book to have in your homeschooling reference library.

Home Schooling From Scratch by Mary Potter Kenyon, 1996, 127 pages, Gazelle Publications, 5580 Stanley Dr., Auburn, CA 95603, (800) 650-5076.

This book ought to be titled "How to Homeschool on a Low Budget." The book cover says, "Mary Kenyon has been cited for her penny-pinching ways with grocery bills in Amy Dacyczyn's *The Tightwad Gazette*, Rhonda Barfield's book, *Eat Well for $50 a Week*, and elsewhere. So when it came to homeschooling her own children, she naturally discovered the most economical routes." The book is written in a delightful personal style and has such chapters as "My Journey To Home Schooling," "Beg, Borrow, and Barter," "Low-Cost Activities," "Organize to Economize," "Your Home-Based Business," and more.

The Home School Manual by Theodore Wade and others, 1988, 432 pages, Gazelle Publications, 5580 Stanley Dr., Auburn, CA 95603, (916) 878-1223. This comprehensive book has thirty-one chapters and nine appendix sections. It contains a lot of general information about homeschooling as well as many suggestions on curriculum, teaching, etc.

Homeschooling: A Patchwork of Days by Nancy Lande with thirty families, 1996, 295 pages, WindyCreek Press, 706 Sussex Rd., Wynnewood, PA 19096-2414, (610) 896-7815, e-mail: WindyCreek@aol.com. Nancy Lande got thirty homeschooling families to describe in considerable detail what they do during a day of homeschooling. This is the perfect book for parents thinking about homeschooling who want to know what homeschooling families actually do. They will get great insights not only into how homeschooling works, but how different families work. This is also a great book for homeschoolers who want to know what other homeschooling families are doing

Homeschooling for Excellence by David and Micki Colfax, 1988, 142 pages, Warner Books, New York, NY 10020. The Colfaxes write: "*Homeschooling for Excellence* is intended to provide a picture of one family's part in what has emerged as perhaps the most dynamic and creative educational movement in decades." This book should be read in conjunction with their later book, *Hard Times in Paradise*, which describes the full story of their homesteading experience. Available from John Holt's Bookstore, 2269 Massachusetts Ave., Cambridge, MA 02140, (617) 864-3100.

The Homeschooling Father by Michael P. Farris, 1992, 110 pages, published by Michael P. Farris, P.O. Box 479, Hamilton, VA 22068. This is an excellent little book for Christian fathers who have accepted the responsibility of homeschooling and need the advice of an experienced practitioner. Besides being the president and founder of the Home School Legal Defense Association, Farris is also director of the National Center for Home Education.

The How and Why of Home Schooling by Ray E. Ballmann, 1987, 157 pages, Crossway Books, Westchester, IL 60153. This is an excellent book for Christian parents who are thinking of homeschooling their kids. It has good chapters on what is going on in the public schools, as well as chapters on "How to Begin," "Why Grandparents Should Support Home Schooling," and "Common Questions Asked About Home Schooling." It also has an extensive Select Bibliography.

How to Tutor by Samuel L. Blumenfeld, 1973, 298 pages, The Paradigm Company, P.O. Box 45161, Boise, ID 83711, (208) 322-4440. In this compact book, the author instructs parents in how to teach their children the three Rs: reading by intensive, systematic phonics; cursive writing; and basic arithmetic. The purpose of the book is to give parents the confidence they must have if they are to become effective teachers of their children. That means learning how to teach the basic primary skills effectively. It is especially useful for parents with preschoolers who want to begin teaching the three R's whenever the children are ready to learn them.

The Right Choice: Home Schooling by Christopher J. Klicka, 1992, 410 pages, Noble Publishing Associates, P.O. Box 2250, Gresham, OR 97030, (503) 667-3942. Chris Klicka is a senior counsel at the Home School Legal Defense Association and therefore the book has more information about the legal aspects of homeschooling than other books on the subject. His chapter on the increase of child welfare investigations is a real eye-opener. He writes about how social workers bluff and intimidate parents, the illegality of home visits, and how the Education of the Handicapped Act (EHA) is being improperly applied to private homeschools. There are chapters on homeschooling in the armed forces, parents' rights and the constitution, and how to win in the courtroom. The appendix has a list of colleges that have accepted homeschoolers and a Case Index which lists all of the important court cases dealing with homeschooling. This is a valuable book to have in your homeschool reference library.

Schoolproof by Mary Pride, 1988, 204 pages, Crossway Books, Westchester, IL 60153. This wonderful little book tells you "How to help your family beat the system and learn to love learning—the easy, natural way." What is schoolproofing? Mary explains: "Schoolproofing means making sure your children get a great education, no matter what political or educational theory happens to be in vogue. It means having children who learn to read in an age of illiteracy; who learn to obey legitimate authority in an age of sullen rebellion; who learn to stand against injustice in an age of craven conformity. It means that *your* children will be smarter, more affectionate, less dependent on external rewards and punishments....Schoolproofing means YOU are in control."

No longer will your children have to stand outside in the cold waiting for the big yellow bus to take them for their daily dose of miseducation. Mary Pride is a homeschool genius who knows how to write for the everyday homeschooling mom and dad. Her chapter titles exude her happiness and optimism: "Twenty Ways to Present a Lesson," "Twenty Ways to Show and Tell," "Multiply and Conquer," "Educational Clutter's Last Stand," "Square Pegs and Pigeonholes," etc. This is the kind of delightful book that refutes all of those public-school naysayers who don't want you to take your kids out of their schools.

Teach Your Own by John Holt, 1981, 369 pages, Delta/Seymour Laurence, Dell Publishing Co., New York, NY 10017. This is the classic on unschooling written by its legendary pioneer. It is full of John Holt's wisdom, experience, and philosophy of educational freedom. Holt writes in his Introduction: "This book is about ways we can teach children, or rather, allow them to learn, outside of schools—at home, or in whatever other places and situations (and the more the better) we can make available to them. It is in part an argument in favor of doing it, in part a report of the people who are doing it, and in part a manual of action for people who want to do it." There are chapters on the "Politics of Unschooling," "Living and Working Spaces," "Learning Without Teaching," "Home Schooling and the Courts," "Legislative Strategy," and others equally provocative. The book is available through John Holt's Bookstore, 2269 Massachusetts Ave., Cambridge, MA 02140, (617) 864-3100.

Additional Books Worth Reading

Books That Build Character: A Guide to Teaching Your Child Moral Values Through Stories, by William Kilpatrick and Gregory and Suzanne M. Wolfe, 1994, 332 pages, A Touchstone Book, Simon & Schuster, New York, NY 10020. This is a family guide to classic novels, contemporary fiction, myths and legends, folktales, Bible stories, picture books, biographies, holiday stories, and many other books that celebrate virtues and values. There are more than three hundred titles to choose from, each featuring a dramatic story and memorable characters who explore moral ground and the difference between right and wrong. An excellent, time-saving resource for parents who want to know where the good books are.

Brave New Schools by Berit Kjos, 1995, 308 pages, Harvest House Publishers, Eugene, OR 97402. Berit Kjos is an indefatigable researcher and writer who has provided the most thorough book to date on the forces and philosophy behind the current education reform movement now sweeping through American public schools. According to Kjos, the aim of the movement is to get rid of every last vestige of traditional education and replace it with a new international agenda to prepare American children for the "Global Village" of the twenty-first century. Emphasis in the curriculum will be placed not on the development of academic skills, but on changing the children's values, beliefs, feelings, and behavior to conform with the needs of the global society. Biblical, linear thinking will be replaced by dialectical thinking. Kjos quotes many of the social engineers involved in the movement and provides substantial documentation to prove her points. This book will help parents understand what is going on in the public schools and suggests what they can do about it.

Dumbing Us Down: The Hidden Curriculum of Compulsory Schooling by John Taylor Gatto, 1992, 104 pages, New Society Publishers, 4527 Springfield

Ave., Philadelphia, PA 19143. Mr. Gatto writes: "School is a twelve-year jail sentence where bad habits are the only curriculum truly learned. I teach school and win awards doing it. I should know." This is probably the most honest book ever written about public education by someone in the system. John Gatto spent twenty-six years in the public school system of New York City and in 1991 was named "New York State Teacher of the Year." The speech he gave on the occasion of getting the award, entitled "The Seven-Lesson Schoolteacher," was undoubtedly the most devastating indictment of public education ever uttered by one of its practitioners. This book contains that speech, as well as "The Psychopathic School," and "We Need Less School, Not More." This book ought to be read by any parent who sends a child to a public school, citizens who pay for it, and those educators in the system who still have a shred of integrity left. Available through John Holt's Bookstore, 2269 Massachusetts Ave., Cambridge, MA 02140, (617) 864-3100.

Educating for the New World Order by B. K. Eakman, 1991, 280 pages, Halcyon House, P.O. Box 8795, Portland, OR 97207-8795, (503) 228-6345. Bev Eakman is one of those accomplished writers who has made a distinguished reputation for herself in politics, education, and public affairs. In 1990 she met Anita Hoge, the gutsy mother who stood the whole education establishment on its head and forced the U.S. Department of Education to obey the law. This book is not only about Anita Hoge's struggle to get the truth from the educational bureaucrats about the psychological tests given to her son in school but also about the dubious right of government to use social engineering to mold the minds of its young citizens and maintain a birth-to-death computer file to track the life of every American. The book reveals what is being planned for America in the bowels of the educational bureaucracy in Washington and in the federally funded experimental labs across the country. This is vital information that every citizen should know.

The Exhausted School by John Taylor Gatto, 1993, 120 pages, The Odysseus Group, 295 East 8th St., Ste. 3W, New York, NY 10009, (212) 874-3631. On November 13, 1991, John Gatto staged probably the most unusual performance ever given at New York's famous Carnegie Hall, "The First National Grassroots Speakout on the Right to School Choice." The speakout featured Gatto and seven other speakers, including some of Gatto's former students and Pat Farenga of Holt Associates and Dan Greenberg of the Sudbury Valley School. This book contains the speeches given that night. Gatto writes in his Introduction: "My belief is that conventional schooling preempts the time we need to keep appointments with our developing selves, critical appointments to learn self-reliance, confidence, skill, family relationships, judgment, and a host of other skills without which we never become fully human." Available through John Holt's Bookstore, 2269 Massachusetts Ave., Cambridge, MA 02140, (617) 864-3100.

Goals 2000 by Kathy Finnegan, 1996, 349 pages, Hearthstone Publishing, Ltd., (800) 580-2604. This is an excellent sourcebook for those who want the actual text of the Goals 2000 legislation and a line-by-line critical analysis of it. Kathy Finnegan is one of those indomitable researchers willing to read and examine every line of the most boring bureaucratese in order to make us aware of what is being enacted into laws that will affect us all. Believe it or not, most legislators never bother to read the laws they vote on. They rely on their young aides, fresh out of college, to do the job. And since the young aides have neither the knowledge nor background to understand what they are reading, they rely on the leadership to give them the proper signals. But how well informed are the leaders? These laws are crafted by groups of change agents in some foundation think tank. They come to the Congress to be voted on by lawmakers who may or may not know what they are doing. No wonder bad laws keep being enacted.

Government Nannies: The Cradle-to-Grave Agenda of Goals 2000 & Outcome Based Education by Cathy Duffy, with a foreword by John Taylor Gatto, 1995, 272 pages. If you've wondered what Goals 2000 and Outcome Based Education are about, this book will enlighten you. Cathy Duffy's writing is clear and to the point, and Gatto's foreword provides an excellent historical overview that puts everything in its proper perspective. The chapters on "The Computer Connection" and "National Standards, Enforcement and Money" leave no doubt that we are indeed headed toward the Brave New World, and that homeschooling offers the safest and fastest way out. Noble Publishing Associates, P.O. Box 2250, Gresham, OR 97030, (503) 667-3942.

Intellectual Schizophrenia by Rousas J. Rushdoony, 1961, 141 pages, Ross House Books, P.O. Box 67, Vallecito, CA 95251. This is a book for all seasons written by one of the great theological thinkers of our time. Dr. Rushdoony writes in his typically understated manner: "The purpose of this study has not been either the criticism or praise of the schools as such, but the understanding of the schools and their basic philosophy as cultural manifestations." The book is a great philosophical treat for anyone who enjoys the study of ideas. It has such chapters as "The School and the Whole Person," "The Purpose of Knowledge," "The Unity of Learning," "The State and Education," "The Concept of the Child," "The Mysticism of the Public Schools," "The End of an Age." No doubt Dr. Rushdoony was prescient of our present time when he wrote: "The end of an age is always a time of turmoil, war, economic catastrophe, cynicism, lawlessness, and distress. But it is also an era of heightened challenge and creativity, and of intense vitality. . . . This then above all else is the great and glorious era to live in, a time of opportunity, one requiring fresh and vigorous thinking, indeed a glorious time to be alive."

Is Public Education Necessary? by Samuel L. Blumenfeld, 1981, 263 pages, The Paradigm Company, P.O. Box 45161, Boise, ID 83711, (208) 322-4440. This is Blumenfeld's detailed history of how the government got involved in the education business in America. It starts with colonial times and goes up to the 1850s, when the public school movement had finally overcome the opposition and was well on its way to becoming the monster educational monopoly it is today. Once you understand the basic premises underlying government education, it is easy to understand why the system is in the shape it is today. The long and short of it is that a government education system is interested mainly in the social control of its citizens. Whatever else takes place is incidental to its main purpose. That's why the system must be abandoned if our freedoms are to be preserved.

Marva Collins' Way by Marva Collins and Civia Tamarkin, 1982, 227 pages, J. P. Tarcher, Inc., 9110 Sunset Blvd., Los Angeles, CA 90069. Along with John Holt and John Taylor Gatto, Marva Collins has become one of the great legendary educators of our time. She left the Chicago public school system after twelve years of frustration and decided to start a school of her own where she could educate the same project children who were considered uneducable by the public schools. Her success in educating these children and turning them into the literate leaders of tomorrow has been phenomenal. What is the secret of her success? Using traditional methods that work. Her Westside Preparatory School in Chicago has none of the fancy trappings of the government schools, but the education that takes place there is priceless.

Mathematics: Is God Silent? by James Nickel, 1990, 126 pages, Ross House Books, P.O. Box 67, Vallecito, CA 95251. The author writes: "It may surprise many laymen to realize that professional mathematicians are in a quandary as to the ultimate foundations and meaning of mathematics. . . . The author believes that this mathematical uncertainty is caused by a philosophical prejudice; an assumption that the biblical God is silent in the realm of mathematics." The author uses a historical approach to demonstrate the validity of his thesis. This is a fascinating book for anyone interested in mathematics.

NEA: Trojan Horse in American Education by Samuel L. Blumenfeld, 1984, 284 pages, The Paradigm Company, P.O. Box 45161, Boise, ID 83711, (208) 322-4440. This book, which is now in its eighth printing, has probably woken up more people concerning what is going on in the schools than any book since Rudolf Flesch's *Why Johnny Can't Read,* published in 1955. Blumenfeld gives the history of the National Education Association and shows how it became the instrument of the progressive education movement whose goal it was to create a socialist America. As the NEA has grown in membership, so has its political clout. This book will help you understand why American education has been going in the direction that it has all these years and why parents have been so frustrated in their attempts to get back to basics.

Not With My Child You Don't, A Citizens' Guide to Eradicating OBE and Restoring Education, by Robert Holland, 1995, 316 pages, Chesapeake Capital

Services, 500 Forest Ave., Richmond, VA 23229. Bob Holland won the 1992 Mencken Award given by the Free Press Association for best op-ed column or editorial in the nation. He is Op/Ed page editor of the *Richmond Times-Dispatch* and has written more columns about Outcome-Based Education than any other journalist in America. It all started quite innocently by his first trying to find out about OBE. Soon after, his hard-hitting columns began circulating around the country by fax and copying machines until he became an important source of information for a growing network of concerned parents from coast to coast. This book reprints those columns plus testimonials from parent-activists who are driving school boards crazy all over America. If you want to "get involved," this book is a good place to start.

Outcome-Based Education, The State's Assault on Our Children's Values, by Peg Luksik and Pamela Hobbs Hoffecker, 1995, 207 pages, Huntington House Publishers, P.O. Box 53788, Lafayette, LA 70505. Looking at Peg Luksik you'd never believe that this thin, fragile-looking mother of six is a powerhouse of activism who sends the educational bureaucrats of Pennsylvania running for cover whenever she shows up. She is founder and director of the National Parents Commission and even ran for governor of Pennsylvania in 1996. This book, written with her friend Pam Hoffecker, is the culmination of several years of research on Outcome-Based Education. The chapters have such provocative titles as "Outrageous Outcomes," "Mad, Mad, Mad Testing," "How Do You Spell School? S-T-A-T-E," "Brave New Family," and "What's A Person To Do?" Read the book and learn.

School's Out, A Radical New Formula for the Revitalization of America's Educational System, by Lewis J. Perelman, 1992, 368 pages, Avon Books, 1350 Ave. of the Americas, New York, NY 10019. The main message of this book is that technology has made the school and the classroom obsolete. A lot in the book is futuristic brainstorming, but the basic thesis supports the homeschool view that technology has already made the home a far superior place to learn than the school.

Separating School and State, How to Liberate America's Families, by Sheldon Richman, 1994, 128 pages, The Future of Freedom Foundation, 11350 Random Hills Road, Ste. 800, Fairfax, VA 22030. The movement for the separation of school and state draws many of its most convincing arguments from this timely book. John Taylor Gatto writes of it: *"Separating School and State* makes it clear that even with the best of intentions, force and compulsion set processes in motion which mutilate family life, replace education with indoctrination, and bring the myth of Procrustes to life."* Educational freedom is the answer to our educational problems.

The Whole Language/OBE Fraud by Samuel L. Blumenfeld, 1995, 351 pages, The Paradigm Company, P.O. Box 45161, Boise, ID 83711, (208) 322-4440.

The cover describes this book as, "The shocking story of how America is being dumbed down by its own education system." By now most Americans are aware of this dumbing-down process. The vocabulary of most popular books and magazines is at a sixth-grade level. In this book Blumenfeld explains the how and why and who of the dumbing-down process and the sociopolitical agenda behind it. If you want to know why forty million Americans can't read even though they attended school, this book will tell you.

Why Johnny Can't Read, and What You Can Do About It, by Rudolf Flesch, 1955, 222 pages, Harper & Row, New York, NY 10022. This is the classic book about the reading problem that first informed Americans why Johnny wasn't learning to read—because the educators had replaced alphabetic-phonics with the whole-word, look-say, sight method of instruction that was creating reading disability. Flesch was right on target in 1955, and the book is just as relevant today as it was then. The fact that the educators have kept on teaching reading in the same faulty way leads to the question of why. That's the question Samuel L. Blumenfeld answered in *The New Illiterates,* published in 1973.

Why Johnny Can't Tell Right from Wrong, by William Kilpatrick, 1992, 266 pages, Simon & Schuster, 1230 Ave. of the Americas, New York, NY 10020. Moral illiteracy and the case for character education is the subject of this important book. Kilpatrick is a professor of education at Boston College, where he teaches courses in human development and moral education. Especially useful for homeschoolers is his lengthy "Guide to Great Books for Children and Teens." For example, he writes of *Beauty and the Beast,* that this "is just the right antidote to our modern obsession with looks, surface charm, and casual sex. It speaks volumes about the meaning of true love and true beauty, and about the importance of restraining our animal nature until love has had time to grow." This is an excellent source to have when trying to choose an uplifting book as a gift for a child. Kilpatrick reviews such books as *The Children's Bible, The Children's Homer, The Little Engine That Could, Black Beauty, The Chronicles of Narnia, The Potlatch Family, Captains Courageous,* and many more.

Additional Resources

The following are publications, organizations, and newsletters which home-schoolers may want to use in their educational pursuits.

Aero-Gramme, a newsletter published by the Alternative Education Resource Organization, 417 Roslyn Rd., Roslyn Heights, NY 11577, (516) 621-2195. This newsletter is edited by Jerry Mintz, a leading voice in the alternative school movement. He is also editor in chief of *The Almanac of Education Choices,* which lists private and public learning alternatives as well as homeschooling organizations and resources.

Cheapskate Monthly, P.O. Box 2135, Paramount, CA 90723-8135. A newsletter for families on a tight budget.

The Christian Conscience is a magazine edited and published by homeschoolers Lynn and Sarah Leslie. It addresses educational issues in depth. It is part of the growing alternative media which serves the growing alternative culture. For subscription information write: Iowa Research Group, Inc., P.O. Box 17346, Des Moines, IA 50317-0346 or fax: (515) 262-9854.

The Christian Family Guide to Movies & Videos by Ted Baehr, Vol. 1 (1988), Vol. 2 (1989). These 400-page books provide reviews and evaluations of hundreds of movies and videos from a Christian point of view. These well-indexed guides are excellent reference tools and timesavers for homeschooling parents who want to get decent videos for family viewing. Wolgemuth & Hyatt, Publishers, Inc., 1749 Mallory Ln., Brentwood, TN 37207. Ted Baehr's bi-weekly magazine, *Movieguide,* is also available. Write: Good News Communications, P.O. Box 190010, Atlanta, GA 31119, or call: (800) 899-6684.

Conservative Book Club, 33 Oakland Ave., Harrison, NY 10528. Frequently offers books of particular interest to homeschoolers.

Constitutional Coalition, P.O. Box 37054, St. Louis, MO 63141, (314) 434-7028. Donna Hearne is executive director of this organization, which holds a yearly conference on educational issues and also publishes books and pamphlets on important educational issues before Congress.

Education Reporter, 7800 Bonhomme Ave., St. Louis, MO 63105, (314) 721-1213. This monthly newsletter monitors the education reform movement closely and will keep you up to date on what is happening in Congress.

Foundation for Economic Education, 30 S. Broadway, Irvington-on-Hudson, NY 10533. Publishes *The Freeman,* an excellent monthly magazine available on request without charge.

4:20 Communications, P.O. Box 421027, Minneapolis, MN 55442-0027, (612) 323-8257. This software company has put Samuel Blumenfeld's Alpha-Phonics reading instruction program, titled PhonicsTutor, on CD-ROM. Available in Mac and Windows 95 versions.

Home Educator's Family Times, issued five times a year, available free of charge by calling (207) 657-2800. This organization puts on several very popular homeschool conferences a year with excellent speakers, workshops, and vendors. Address: Home Educator's Family Times, P.O. Box 708, Gray, ME 04039.

Homemade Money: How to Select, Manage, Market and Multiply the Profits of a Business at Home, by Barbara Brabec, Betterway Productions, P.O. Box 2137, Naperville, IL 60567-2137. A comprehensive book for those who want to start a business at home.

Homeschooler's Save-a-Penny Press, (909) 872-1128. Publishes classified ads mostly from homeschoolers selling used curriculum materials.

Homeschooling Book Club, 1000 E. Huron, Milford, MI 48381, (810) 685-8773. Offers great discounts on books for homeschoolers.

Imprimis is the monthly publication of Hillsdale College which invites distinguished personalities to speak at its monthly seminars. The texts of the speeches are published in *Imprimis*, which is available free of charge. To get on the mailing list write: Imprimis, Hillsdale College, Hillsdale, MI 49242 or call: (800) 437-2268.

The Independent Scholar's Handbook: The Indispensable Guide for the Stubborn Intelligence, by Ronald Gross, 1994, Ten Speed, P.O. Box 7123, Berkeley, CA 94707. This book tells you how to become an expert in any field or in any subject independently, without having to become attached to any institution.

Microchipped, How the Education Establishment Took Us Beyond Big Brother, by B. K. Eakman, 1994, 285 pages, Halcyon House, P.O. Box 8795, Portland, OR 97207-8795, (800) 827-2499. This chilling book is about how computer technology is being used to keep tabs on the American people, especially in the field of education, where students are a captive audience and are subjected to psychological tests that have nothing to do with academics. The documentation is thorough.

Minding Your Own Business, A Common Sense Guide to Home Management and Industry, by Raymond and Dorothy Moore, 1990, 261 pages, Wolgemuth & Hyatt, Publishers, Inc., 1749 Mallory Ln., Brentwood, TN 37027. If you're a homeschooling family thinking of starting a family-run business at home, this is the book that will help you get started, written by the two most renowned pioneers of the homeschool movement.

Miserly Moms: Living on One Income in a Two-Income Economy, by Jonni McCoy, GCB Publishing, 229 South Bridge St., Elkton, MD 21921, (410) 392-3590. For the mom who wants to leave her job and stay home to homeschool her kids.

Moore Report International, The Moore Foundation, Box 1, Camas, WA 98607, (360) 835-5500. This bimonthly report is published by Raymond and Dorothy Moore, pioneers in the homeschool movement who have been watching it grow from day one.

National Center for Constitutional Studies, HC 61 Box 1056, Malta, ID 83342, (208) 645-2625. Publishes and distributes study materials on constitutional government, and sponsors seminars developed by W. Cleon Skousen on constitutional history.

National Monitor of Education, P.O. Box 402, Alamo, CA 94507, (510) 945-6745. This newsletter will keep you up to date on all of the strange things going on in the public schools.

National Right to Read Foundation, P.O. Box 490, The Plains, VA 20198, (540) 349-1614. Provides information on phonics programs and general news about the phonics versus whole language controversy.

National Vaccine Information Center, organized by Dissatisfied Parents Together (DPT), distributes information and collects data on cases of children harmed by the DPT vaccine. The NVIC also publishes the *Vaccine Reaction Newsletter.* Address: 512 W. Maple Ave., Ste. 206, Vienna, VA 22180. Phone: (703) 938-DPT3 and (800) 909-SHOT.

New Attitude, The Christian Magazine for Home-School Teens, was edited and published by Joshua Harris. It was great while it lasted. Joshua maintains a web site at http://www.newattitude.com/~joshuah/ For back issues write: Christian Life Workshops, P.O. Box 2250, Gresham, OR 97030 or call: (503) 667-3942.

1,001 Bright Ideas to Stretch Your Dollars by Cynthia Yates, Servant Publications, P.O. Box 8617, Ann Arbor, MI 48107. The perfect book for those raising a family on a limited budget.

Orton Dyslexia Society, Chester Bldg., Ste. 382, 8600 LaSalle Rd., Baltimore, MD 21286-2044, (410) 296-0232. This is the nation's foremost association dealing with dyslexia and related learning disabilities. Their yearly conferences bring together the nation's leading experts on learning disabilities.

Preston/Speed Publications is engaged in an ambitious long-range project to reprint all of G. A. Henty's popular historical novels, by which young readers can learn history through enjoyable literature. Henty lived during the reign of Queen Victoria (1837–1901) and began his storytelling career with his own children. His young fictional heroes fight wars, sail the seas, discover land, conquer evil empires, and prospect for gold. Already available: *For the Temple, A Tale of the Fall of Jerusalem; Beric the Briton, A Story of the Roman Invasion; In Freedom's Cause, A Story of Wallace and Bruce; The Dragon and the Raven, Or the Days of King Alfred; By Pike and Dyke, The Rise of the Dutch Republic; St. Bartholemew's Eve, A Tale of the Huguenot Wars;* and *With Lee in Virginia, A Story of the American Civil War.* For a catalog, write: RR #4, P.O. Box 705, Mill Hall, PA 17751, or call: (717) 726-7844.

The Rewriting of America's History by Catherine Millard, 1991, 462 pages, Horizon House Publishers, 3825 Hartzdale Dr., Camp Hill, PA 17011. This beautifully researched book demonstrates to what extent America's history has been rewritten by those with an agenda to change our form of government. Millard writes in her Introduction, "Rewriting a nation's history is frequently one of the first strategies taken by a conquering nation. Why? Because a people who do not know from where they came also do not know where they are going." Catherine Millard is the founder and director of Christian Heritage Tours in Washington, D.C., whose sole purpose is to help people rediscover the rich Judeo-Christian heritage of our nation by conducting tours of our national monuments, landmarks, and memorials. For information about these tours for your family or homeschool group contact Christian Heritage Tours, 6597 Forest Dew Ct., Springfield, VA 22152, or call (703) 455-0333.

The Separation of School and State Alliance, 4578 N. First, #310, Fresno, CA 93726, (209) 292-1776. The ebullient Marshall Fritz is the director of this movement to get the government out of the education business. He expects to get 25 million Americans to sign a proclamation for separation. Their yearly conferences are drawing the crème de la crème of the education freedom movement. To get their monthly publication, *The Education Liberator,* call the number above. If you're chafing at the bit for a real live libertarian revolution, join up.

A Shot in the Dark by Harris L. Coulter and Barbara Loe Fisher, 1991, 246 pages, Avery Publishing Group, Garden City Park, Garden City, NY 11530. Extensive bibliography and index. This book is a chilling account of how dangerous the pertussis vaccine has proven to be. It provides a history of the vaccine's development and usage, and exposes the roles played by the FDA and the drug companies. It also tells the tragic stories of the children victimized by this vaccine. Anyone with young children should read this book and be prepared for the immunization onslaught.

The Spelling Newsletter, P.O. Box 1326 Camden, ME 04843. Published by Raymond E. Laurita, this unique publication provides fascinating information about English orthography.

The Successful Homeschool Family Handbook by Raymond and Dorothy Moore. Moore Foundation, Box 1, Camas, WA 98606, (360) 835-5500. This book has helped many new homeschoolers adjust to their new way of life. Written by two outstanding homeschool pioneers.

The Teenage Liberation Handbook: How to Quit School and Get a Real Life and Education, by Grace Llewellyn, 1991, Lowry House, P.O. Box 1014, Eugene, OR 97440, (541) 686-2315. This is an excellent guide to self-directed learning for teenagers. Tells you how to become a productive unschooler.

U.S. Congress Handbook, Box 566, McLean, VA 22101, (800) 229-3572. If you intend to "get involved," you're going to need this comprehensive directory of the U.S. Congress, Executive Branch, and Supreme Court. It lists all of the members of Congress with their photos, bios, phone and fax numbers, committee assignments, as well as the names of their aides. It lists the committees and subcommittees, the White House staff, cabinet members, and it even has a glossary of legislative terms. To order call: (703) 356-3572.

Index